# CONCENTRATE Q&A
## EMPLOYMENT LAW

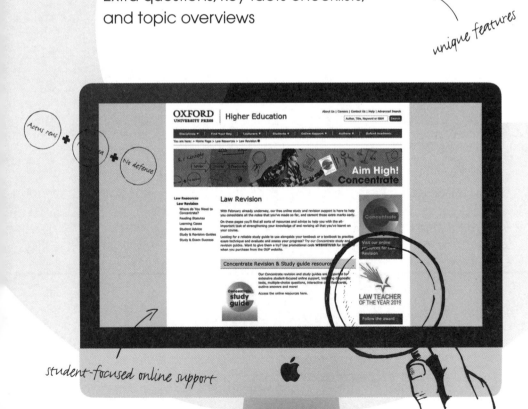

# CONCENTRATE Q&A EMPLOYMENT LAW

**Roseanne Russell**
Senior Lecturer in Law
University of Bristol

SECOND EDITION

Great Clarendon Street, Oxford, OX2 6DP,
United Kingdom

Oxford University Press is a department of the University of Oxford. It furthers the University's objective of excellence in research, scholarship, and education by publishing worldwide. Oxford is a registered trade mark of Oxford University Press in the UK and in certain other countries



First edition 2017

Impression: 1



Published in the United States of America by Oxford University Press
198 Madison Avenue, New York, NY 10016, United States of America

British Library Cataloguing in Publication Data
Data available

Library of Congress Control Number: 2021947771

ISBN 978–0–19–885675–7

Printed in Great Britain by
Ashford Colour Press Ltd, Gosport, Hampshire

# Contents

# Guide to the book

Every book in the Concentrate Q&A series contains the following features:

**ARE YOU READY?**

Are you ready to face the exam? This box at the start of each chapter identifies the key topics that you need to have learned, revised and understood before tackling the questions in each chapter.

Not sure where to begin? Clear diagram answer plans at the start of each question help you see how to structure your answer at a glance, and take you through each point step-by-step.

Demonstrating your knowledge of the crucial debates is a sure-fire way to impress examiners. These at-a-glance boxes help remind you of the key debates relevant to each topic, which you should discuss in your answers to get the highest marks.

What makes a great answer great? Our authors show you the thought process behind their own answers, and how you can do the same in your exam. Key sentences are highlighted and advice is given on how to structure your answer well and develop your arguments.

Each question represents a typical essay or problem question so that you know exactly what to expect in your exam.

Don't settle for a good answer—make it great! This feature gives you points to include in the exam if you want to gain more marks and make your answer stand out.

Don't fall into any traps! This feature points out common mistakes that students make, and which you need to avoid when answering each question.

Really push yourself and impress your examiner by going beyond what is expected. Focused further reading suggestions allow you to develop in-depth knowledge of the subject for when you are looking for the highest marks.

# Table of cases

# Table of legislation

## Statutes

# Table of secondary legislation

# Table of European and international legislation

## European Legislation



## Directives



## International Legislation

# Exam skills for success in employment law

1

This book is designed to be used by students who are preparing for an examination in employment law. It offers an insight into what examiners might expect to see in a well-written answer on a range of employment law topics and provides a range of useful, practical tips to help guide your revision. The book is not a substitute for a textbook or for reading the relevant statutes and key cases. It is assumed that you will be familiar with the substantive areas of the law that are discussed. Instead the book is intended to be used as an additional support either during your studies to consolidate what you have learned on specific topics or at the end of your course as you prepare for assessment. It is not an exhaustive revision guide full of 'model answers' but it is hoped that by showing you how to approach employment law exams through practical demonstrations, you will feel more confident about what the assessment process expects of you.

The chapters cover the main areas likely to be included in your employment law module and consist of a mixture of problem questions and essays. There is also a separate chapter showing you how to tackle coursework. Each chapter is structured so that you will be introduced to some of the topical issues in the area, provided with a range of example answers with useful annotations showing common mistakes and helpful insights, and pointers for further reading should you wish to explore topics in more depth.

## Answering problem questions

Problem questions test your ability to apply the law to a set of facts in order to resolve a legal problem. The two most common areas where students lose marks are poor structure and lack of relevance. This book uses the *IRAC* approach to problem questions. First, *identify* the legal issue raised by the question. Initially this may be relatively broad, such as whether there has been an unfair dismissal, but may also include more detailed legal issues, such as whether a person has the requisite length of service to claim unfair dismissal or whether there is a potentially fair reason to dismiss. The question may focus on one area of your module or may draw different topics together. Second, state the *relevant law*. For example, in relation to unfair dismissal you will need to state the relevant statutory protection in the Employment Rights Act 1996. Statements of law must be supported by reference to authority in case law or statute. Third, *apply* the law to the facts. It may be that different interpretations apply so make sure that you show this in your answer. Finally, reach a *conclusion* on the issue.

For every issue raised in the question, repeat the *IRAC* approach. This will help you ensure that you are providing the examiner with relevant material and reaching a conclusion on each issue raised.

Relevance is highly important so take care not to stray from the issues raised or to ponder what might happen with issues that are not raised by the facts. For example, if you are told that your client has been employed for five years, it would be wrong to spend lots of time on debating whether your client has the requisite length of service to bring a claim for unfair dismissal.

Using the *IRAC* method will also help structure your answer logically. You can similarly use the structure of the question itself to help organise your answer. You will see in the worked examples in the book how authority is used to provide support for a relevant legal rule. Full citations are given so that you know where to find the material but you would not need to give the full citation in an exam.

## Answering essay questions

Essay questions are designed to test your ability to argue and analyse. Begin by reading the question carefully to look at the subject area under examination and what the examiner is asking you to do. This book uses the *PEA* approach. For each issue raised, make a *P*oint, support it with *E*vidence (relevant statutory or case law or the opinions of academics), and provide *A*nalysis. As with *IRAC*, you can use the *PEA* approach for each issue raised.

Essays are often used in coursework. Unlike examinations which are limited to a few hours in length, it is usual to have several weeks to complete a piece of coursework. Therefore, the markers' assumptions will be that you have access to sufficient materials, in both hard-copy and electronic form, to complete the work. It is up to you to consult these materials, sift them, and organise your answer. You should also ensure that you express yourself clearly and succinctly and submit a polished piece of writing.

## General guidance

Unless a question tells you how marks will be allocated, you should assume that each question and each part of a question will count for equal marks. A common fault relates to mistiming the paper. If you have a three-hour exam requiring four questions to be answered, be strict and spend forty-five minutes per question. It is always better to write something for each question than miss out an answer by spending too long on the other questions. The best way to hone your exam technique is to practise. Attempt the questions in near-examination conditions by setting yourself forty-five minutes without access to materials.

It is also advisable to spend a few minutes at the start of each question writing a brief plan so that your answer has some structure to it, and it can prove useful to set down key thoughts initially in case you forget these whilst in the throes of answering the question! This is particularly the case in an essay question where it is helpful to know at the outset what you want to argue rather than risk a rambling answer where your argument is unclear.

Much of the worry about examinations is because you typically will not know what will be asked of you. There is a fear of the unknown if you have no idea exactly what questions you will encounter and you may be worried about not being prepared to answer what may be asked of you. By ensuring that you have a solid understanding of the area of law and have practised a range of questions in that area, you should feel confident in handling the exam. This book should assist you in finding out how to answer the question but you should always read the examination and question rubrics very carefully: make sure that you know what the examiner wants you to do, and then do it. If you approach this book in the way indicated above, and put in the work needed to grasp the subject, you should find that the examination is not an insurmountable barrier but rather an opportunity to display your knowledge. Good luck!

# Employment status

# 2

## ARE YOU READY?

In order to attempt this chapter, you must have covered the following areas in your revision:

- The definitions of 'employee' and 'worker' contained in employment legislation with particular reference to the differences in definitions across various legislation
- Which rights attach to different categories of 'employee' and 'worker'
- The importance of policy considerations behind the different definitions and associated rights
- The common law tests to determine whether a contract is a contract of service or a contract for services (such as control, integration, economic reality, and mutuality of obligation)
- The changing nature of the labour market and the difficulties in determining employment status for certain groups (e.g. agency workers, zero hours contractors)

## KEY DEBATES

Shifting patterns of work in today's flexible labour market mean that it can be difficult to determine a person's employment status. This has given rise to renewed debates on whether the current tests remain appropriate.

**Debate: Changing labour market**

Does the rise of the 'gig economy' mean that we have to reconsider the common law tests of whether a contract is a contract of employment? Do the common law tests remain relevant when applied to today's labour market?

**Debate: Unscrupulous behaviour**

How does the law allow or inhibit unscrupulous behaviour regarding employment status? Is it too easy for workers to claim self-employment for advantageous tax reasons? Does the law adequately prevent 'sham' self-employment practices by employers?

**Debate: Zero hours contracts**

What are the advantages and disadvantages of zero hours contracts? Are they used disproportionately amongst certain groups (such as care workers) and what are the implications of this?

## QUESTION 1

**The courts have resolved questions of employment status over the years by the application of various tests. Critically examine, by reference to case law, the tests used and briefly indicate the advantages and disadvantages of each test.**

## CAUTION!

- As with any question, take time to read precisely what the examiner is asking of you. Here you are being asked to 'critically examine'. This requires doing more than describing the various common law tests or 'telling all you know' about the topic. Critically examining a concept means that you have to discuss it in detail and give your view (supported by evidence) of the pros and cons of each test.
- There is no right way or wrong way to structure an essay answer but it is always worth spending a few minutes planning how best to present your material. Jot down the key points (including cases) that you want to mention and then think about what structure will allow you to present your argument in the most clear and convincing way.
- This area is dominated by case law, which the question asks you to discuss. Remember that it is usually the ratio that is most important so show the examiner that you understand the ratio, any relevant obiter comments, and the importance of any dissenting judgments. Lengthy descriptive accounts of the facts of a case should be avoided.
- To demonstrate your knowledge of the wider labour market context, a 'critical examination' could also highlight the continued relevance (or otherwise) of these tests.

## DIAGRAM ANSWER PLAN

Why is it necessary to consider case law (employee–worker distinction and limited statutory definitions)?

Various tests—control, integration, economic reality, mutuality of obligation, personal service

Development of each test as a response to problems with previous tests

Problem areas in a changing labour market

## SUGGESTED ANSWER

[1] Your opening sentence reassures the examiner that you understand the question and introduces the subject area of your answer.

The question of who is an employee is central in employment law but determination of employment status has sometimes proved difficult.[1] **Section 230(1) of the Employment Rights Act 1996 ('ERA')** defines an employee as 'an individual who has entered into or works under (or, where the employment has ceased, worked under) a contract of employment'. **Section 230(2) ERA** defines a 'contract of employment' as 'a contract of service or apprenticeship, whether express or implied, and (if it is express) whether oral or in writing'. While some protections in the employment field extend to workers (such as the **Working Time Regulations 1998** and the **National Minimum Wage Act 1998**), employees have certain important rights that other categories of workers do not have, such as the right in **s94(1) ERA** not to be unfairly dismissed. For that reason, being an 'employee' is important. As the statutory definitions are of limited assistance[2] to help distinguish the nature of the relationship, the courts have developed a range of tests to help identify whether a contract is one of employment.

[2] This opening paragraph shows succinctly that you understand the relevant statutory law and its limitations.

The first test was the 'control test'. This asked what was the degree of control the alleged employer ('the master') exercised over the alleged employee ('the servant'). The classic statement[3] concerning this test was given by MacKenna J in ***Ready Mixed Concrete (South East) Ltd* v *Minister of Pensions and National Insurance* [1968] 2 QB 497**, where he said that a contract of service exists if three conditions are fulfilled: (1) the servant agrees that, in consideration of a wage or other remuneration, he will provide his own work and skill in the performance of some service for his master; (2) he agrees, expressly or impliedly, that in the performance of that service he will be subject to the other's control in a sufficient degree to make that other master; and (3) the other provisions of the contract are consistent with its being a contract of service. Subsequent cases have taken this statement as a guide when determining employment status. Although this test appears simple, as work has become more complex and technology has increased, the test has proven to be inadequate as the sole determinant of employment in today's labour market. Although an essential component in a contract of service, it is a crude measure and,

[3] An explanation of a 'classic statement' is given here to show the depth of your knowledge.

as Kahn-Freund argued, 'based upon the social conditions of an earlier age' (O. Kahn-Freund, 'Servants and independent contractors' (1951) 14 *Modern Law Review* 504).[4] Highly skilled or senior employees or those with a significant degree of flexibility in their working conditions cannot be said to be 'controlled' by their employer in any real sense while carrying out their work. Although important, 'control' is no longer seen as conclusive.[5]

[4] Authority to support a particular point can be found in articles. This shows your wider reading and lends weight to your argument.

[5] This paragraph is a good example of the PEA method: the point is identified (control test), it is explained in detail by reference to a key case, and it is analysed with support from academic authority.

The second test that developed was the integration test. It was first identified in ***Cassidy* v *Ministry of Health* [1951] 2 KB 343, CA**, where it was applied to establish that a doctor working within the NHS was an employee of the health authority. Denning LJ referred again to this test in ***Stevenson, Jordan and Harrison Ltd* v *MacDonald and Evans* [1952] 1 TLR 101**. It asks whether a person is employed as part of the business, whether their work is done as 'an integral part of the business', or whether it is merely accessory to it. The test appears straightforward although it proved to be of limited use since, in asking whether a person was an integral part of the organisation, it was unclear precisely what constituted 'integration' into an 'organisation'.

The courts gradually moved away from seeing one factor as determinative of the issue of employment status.[6] A more flexible approach was taken by adopting what is known as the multiple test, i.e. no single factor will be conclusive—all factors are considered and weighed to decide the question (this is sometimes called 'the multi-factorial approach'). The question asked is, looking at all the factors, some of which may point to self-employment status and others to a finding of employment, does the evidence overall point to the person being an employee? This multi-factorial test was applied by Cooke J in ***Market Investigations* v *Minister of Social Security* [1969] 2 QB 173**. Cooke J stated that the fundamental question was: 'Is the person who has engaged himself to perform these services performing them as a person in business on his own account?' In other words, looking at the economic reality of the situation, does the individual bear the economic risk as a self-employed person? Factors to consider include whether the worker hires their own helpers; what degree of financial risk they take; what degree of financial responsibility they have for investment; and any management responsibility undertaken.

[6] This sentence helps structure the answer by showing the development of tests over time.

One distinct advantage[7] of the multiple test is that it allows the court or tribunal great flexibility: all relevant factors are considered, with no single factor being decisive. This approach is particularly useful when some factors may go towards self-employment, such as the contractual right given to the worker to substitute another worker for themselves, while other factors may point towards employment status, such as the unrestrained power to control the time and manner in which the work is performed. By looking at all the circumstances of the case, and giving appropriate weight to these (possibly opposing)

[7] Here the use of 'advantage' and 'disadvantage' allows you to analyse the test critically rather than just explain what the test involves.

factors, the court may reach a sound conclusion, without placing undue reliance on one factor as determinative. The disadvantage is that in cases involving complex factors it may be difficult for the parties to know whether the relationship is one of employment or not. To that extent, the 'multiple factor' test does not take us much further in determining employment status.

What is apparent from the cases is that the court will require, at the very least, an irreducible minimum of obligation for the contract to be one of service, i.e. an obligation on the employer to offer work and on the worker to accept it commonly known as the 'mutuality of obligation' test (see ***Nethermere (St Neots) Ltd*** v ***Taverna & Gardiner*** **[1984] ICR 612, CA**). Questions concerning the status of casual or temporary workers can be particularly difficult to resolve.[8] In such cases, whether there is mutuality of obligations is an important factor. In ***Clark*** v ***Oxfordshire Health Authority*** **[1998] IRLR 125, CA**, a 'bank nurse' retained by the health authority on a casual basis to fill temporary vacancies as and when they arose, was held not to be an employee. There was no mutuality of obligation during the periods when she was not engaged on a contract. Similarly, a finding of self-employment was made in a case concerning wine butlers, described as 'regular casuals', where there was no mutuality of obligations (see ***O'Kelly*** v ***Trusthouse Forte plc*** **[1983] ICR 728, CA**). Furthermore, in the House of Lords' decision in ***Carmichael*** v ***National Power plc*** **[2000] IRLR 43**, two 'casual as required' guides at a nuclear power station were held not to be employees. Their Lordships approved the tribunal's finding that the applicants' case 'founders upon the rock of absence of mutuality'. The guides were not obliged to take work, if offered, and the company was under no obligation to offer it. For Underhill LJ, the lack of mutuality does not just affect the period between engagements but also sheds light on the status of the relationship when working. As he opined in ***Secretary of State for Justice*** v ***Windle and Arada*** **[2016] EWCA Civ 459**, 'the ultimate question must be the nature of the relationship during the period that the work is being done. But it does not follow that the absence of mutuality of obligation outside that period may not influence, or shed light on, the character of the relationship within it'.

Finally, where the contract contains a term that the worker may substitute another person to carry out their work, this factor may weigh against finding an employment relationship. The requirement of 'personal service' would appear to be another irreducible minimum in establishing a contract of employment. In ***Express and Echo Publications Ltd*** v ***Tanton*** **[1999] IRLR 367**, the contract between the parties contained a term that Tanton could substitute another worker to carry out his duties if he was unable or unwilling to perform them and he had done so on occasion. The Court of Appeal held that the right of the worker to provide a substitute is inherently inconsistent

[8] This demonstrates a good understanding of a particular problem with casual workers.

with a contract of employment. The irreducible minimum of obligation in a contract of employment involved the obligation by the employee to provide their services personally. However, according to the EAT in ***MacFarlane* v *Glasgow City Council* [2001] IRLR 7**, the principle in ***Tanton*** does not necessarily preclude a finding of employment where there is a contractual provision allowing a limited power of substitution. The case involved gym instructors working for the council under contracts that allowed them, when they were unable to work, to find a replacement worker from a register kept by the council. The EAT stated that such a *limited* power of substitution or delegation was not inconsistent with a contract of employment. The clause in ***Tanton*** allowed substitution by the worker at any time and for any reason, whereas that in ***MacFarlane*** was a limited or occasional power invoked when the workers were unable to work and the council maintained a register of those who were able to be substituted.[9] In ***Pimlico Plumbers Ltd* v *Smith* [2017] EWCA Civ 51**, Sir Terence Etherton MR distinguished between an unfettered and conditional right to substitute. The former was, he held, 'inconsistent with an undertaking to [work or perform the services] personally' whereas 'a conditional right to substitute another person may or may not be inconsistent with personal performance depending upon the conditionality'.

[9] This is a good example of distinguishing between two cases.

In conclusion,[10] it is clear that the cases provide only guidance and do not identify rigid rules. The common law tests appear to suggest that three minimum factors are required for a contract of employment to exist: control, mutuality of obligation, and personal service. It is also clear that the courts will consider all the factors in a case and how the relationship is conducted in practice rather than what the parties have themselves stated to be the nature of the relationship (***Autoclenz Ltd* v *Belcher and Ors* [2011] UKSC 41**). The shifting nature of the labour market with the rise of the gig economy has arguably made it even more difficult to judge a person's employment status (***Pimlico Plumbers Ltd* v *Smith* [2018] UKSC 29**). It would appear that the law in this area is in need of greater clarification, particularly in a changing labour market where considerations of control and mutuality of obligation may seem a little outmoded.

[10] The conclusion provides a summary of your argument in answer to the question.

## LOOKING FOR EXTRA MARKS?

- This question calls for an excellent understanding of the various tests that have developed over time. The labels given to various tests can be a helpful way of structuring your answer but can be confusing. It is important that you show the examiner that you understand the minimum requirements for employment and that you appreciate the multi-factorial nature of deciding whether a contract is one of employment.

- It can be tempting in an essay question to write all you know about a topic particularly as, unlike problem questions, there is no inherent structure for you to follow. Be discerning about what you will exclude as much as what you will include in your answer! This question focuses on the test of employment so it would not be appropriate to give a lengthy description of the definition of worker or the various rights attaching to employees and workers.
- Distinguish yourself by drawing on academic authority where appropriate. Reading articles is an excellent way of seeing how essays are structured and helps to inform your own views.

## QUESTION 2

Lizzie has worked for Fit & Healthy Ltd as a fitness instructor for the past six years. Fit & Healthy manage a range of fitness centres on behalf of the local council. Her written contract states that her normal working period is Monday to Friday from 9 a.m. to 5 p.m. and her wages are paid net of tax and national insurance, which is deducted by Fit & Healthy. Her contract states that, with the agreement of Fit & Healthy, she may engage substitutes to work in her place when she is unavailable for work. Only those individuals whose names appear on a list kept by Fit & Healthy and who have been approved by the council may be used as substitutes. Lizzie may also only substitute for no more than a total of fourteen days per annum. She has used this provision on two occasions in the past year when she was on holiday for periods of three days and six days. Due to a drop in numbers of those attending the fitness classes, Fit & Healthy announced that a number of roles would be redundant and told Lizzie that her contract would be terminated. Lizzie is upset to learn that Fit & Healthy will not be paying her any redundancy pay as they insist that she is not an employee.

Bob has worked as a cleaner at Clean Cars Ltd for three years. He is one of a team of cleaners who signed contracts with Clean Cars to provide valeting and car cleaning services to the company. The contracts expressly refer to Bob as a 'Sub-contractor' and state: 'The Sub-contractor hereby confirms that he is a self-employed independent contractor'. The contract also states that Bob will be paid on submission of weekly invoices (prepared by Clean Cars on the basis of records submitted by Bob), that he is responsible for paying his own tax and national insurance contributions, purchasing his own liability insurance and uniforms, and providing his own cleaning materials. The contracts also state that there is no duty to accept work and that Clean Cars will be under no obligation to provide work and that 'as an independent contractor, you are entitled to engage one or more individuals to carry out the valeting on your behalf'. In practice, Clean Cars organises insurance cover for all cleaners and provides all necessary cleaning materials and equipment including uniforms. Bob has never used the substitution clause (he is clear that all valeters must carry out the cleaning themselves) and has to inform Clean Cars in advance if he is unable to attend work. Bob is concerned that his rate of pay is significantly less than the national minimum wage.

**Advise Lizzie and Bob.**

## CAUTION!

- Do not be put off by the length of the question. The question provides a lot of factors to consider but essentially is asking you to determine one question: what is the employment status of Lizzie and Bob?

- With questions involving two parties with two sets of circumstances, it can be tempting to deal with each in turn. However, that risks becoming a little repetitive if similar considerations apply to both. In this case, it makes more sense to discuss the relevant law applying to both parties first then briefly state how that will be applied to each.
- The facts of a question may be unclear. Here there are factors in both scenarios that could point towards or against an employment relationship. This is a deliberate strategy so that you can demonstrate your ability to reason carefully and provide a nuanced answer.

## DIAGRAM ANSWER PLAN

| | |
|---|---|
| Identify the issues | What is Lizzie and Bob's employment status?<br>Is Lizzie an employee and able to claim a redundancy payment?<br>Is Bob a worker and able to claim the national minimum wage? |
| Relevant law | Section 135(1)(a) ERA re right to redundancy payment; s155 ERA re qualifying period; s230(1) and (2) ERA re definition of employee<br>Section 54(3) National Minimum Wage Act 1998 ('NMW') re definition of worker<br>Common law tests of employment (NB: *MacFarlane*, *Pimlico*, and *Autoclenz* are highly relevant here) |
| Apply the law | Lizzie: does she fit the definition of employee under ERA? What is the effect of the substitution clause in her contract?<br>Bob: what factors point towards self-employment? Does it matter that the practice does not appear to match what is stated in his contract? |
| Conclude | Lizzie: facts are similar to *MacFarlane*; the limited right of substitution may not be fatal to employment status although it does point against her being an employee<br>Bob: facts are similar to *Autoclenz*; courts may consider this to be a 'sham' contract if it does not reflect reality of situation |

## SUGGESTED ANSWER

In advising Lizzie and Bob, the key issue to determine[1] is whether they are employees, workers, or self-employed independent contractors. Lizzie will only be able to claim a redundancy payment if she can show that she is an employee with over two years' service (**s135(1)(a)**

[1] The opening sentence gets to the heart of the matter and shows you have understood what the question is about.

**and s155 Employment Rights Act 1996 ('ERA')).** She has worked for Fit & Healthy for six years so the question turns on whether she is an employee.[2] **Section 230(1) ERA** defines an employee as 'an individual who has entered into or works under (or, where the employment has ceased, worked under) a contract of employment'. A contract of employment is defined in **s230(2) ERA** as 'a contract of service …'. She has an express written contract; the question is whether it is one 'of service'. Bob must show that he is an employee or worker to qualify for the national minimum wage. The definition of employee in **s54(1) and (2) of the National Minimum Wage Act 1998 ('NMW')** is the same as that in ERA. The definition of worker in the **NMW (s54(3))** extends to 'any other contract … whereby the individual undertakes to do or perform personally any work or services for another party to the contract whose status is not by virtue of the contract that of a client or customer of any profession or business undertaking carried on by the individual'.

[2] This point isolates the main issue that Lizzie needs to show. There is no need for a detailed explanation of length of service as that is clear from the question.

There are three irreducible minimum requirements for a contract of employment: control; mutuality of obligation; and personal service.[3] This is clear from the statement of MacKenna J in ***Ready Mixed Concrete (South East) Ltd* v *Minister of Pensions and National Insurance* [1968] 2 QB 497**. A contract of service exists if: (1) the servant agrees that, in consideration of a wage or other remuneration, he will provide his own work and skill in the performance of some service for his master; (2) he agrees that in the performance of that service he will be subject to the other's control in a sufficient degree to make that other master; and (3) the other provisions of the contract are consistent with its being a contract of service. For both Lizzie and Bob, the test of control appears to have limited relevance.[4] Both appear to have a great deal of freedom in their work (Lizzie in her fitness classes and Bob when valeting cars) and control on its own is not determinative of employment.

[3] This provides some structure for the following discussion.

[4] Here the control test is applied to the facts of the case and its limitations are discussed briefly.

Turning to mutuality of obligation, there must be an obligation on the employer to offer work and on the worker to accept it (***Nethermere (St Neots) Ltd* v *Taverna & Gardiner* [1984] ICR 612, CA**). Lizzie's contract states that her hours of work are 9 a.m. to 5 p.m. Monday to Friday suggesting that she is not engaged on a 'casual as required' basis and that there is an obligation on Fit & Healthy to provide her with work and for her to attend during those hours. Bob's case is less clear. While his contract states that there is no duty to accept work and that Clean Cars will be under no obligation to provide work, in practice he has to tell Clean Cars in advance if he is unable to attend. This suggests some obligation on him to attend unless other arrangements have been made.[5] This was similar to the conclusion in ***Autoclenz Ltd* v *Belcher and Ors* [2011] UKSC 41** that, despite the contract stating that there was no obligation to accept work, this was wholly inconsistent with the valeters calling in

[5] This is a good example of picking up on an apparently minor but important detail in the facts.

advance to inform the company if they could not attend. If the court is convinced that in practice Bob was obliged to accept the work given and that Clean Cars were obliged to provide work, it may overlook what is stated in the contract. Otherwise the absence of mutuality of obligation will be fatal as this is a necessary requirement to show employment (***Carmichael* v *National Power plc* [2000] IRLR 43; *Windle* v *Secretary of State for Justice* [2016] ICR 721**).

The third requirement of personal service is potentially problematic.[6] Both Lizzie's and Bob's contracts contain a power of substitution. In ***Express and Echo Publications Ltd* v *Tanton* [1999] IRLR 367**, Tanton had worked as an employee but he was made redundant. He was re-engaged as a driver on what the company intended to be a self-employed basis. He was sent a document for signature containing a clause that in the event that he is unable or unwilling to perform the services personally, he will arrange for another person to perform the work at his own expense. Although he refused to sign this document, he continued working in accordance with its terms and, occasionally, used the substitution power.[7] The Court of Appeal held that the right of substitution was inherently inconsistent with a contract of employment, which must necessarily contain an obligation of personal service. Peter Gibson LJ called such a provision 'a remarkable clause to find in a contract of service'. Furthermore, the Court of Appeal held that the implied term of mutual trust and confidence was consistent with a requirement of personal service. The court also referred to MacKenna J's comments in ***Ready Mixed Concrete*** (itself a case involving substitution by the owner/driver of a vehicle, which strongly pointed towards a finding of self-employment), where he said that one condition for a contract of service was that the servant agrees to provide their own work and skill.

However, the idea of a limited power of substitution not necessarily contradicting employment status was considered by the EAT in ***MacFarlane* v *Glasgow City Council* [2001] IRLR 7**. The facts of this case are similar to Lizzie's situation. There, a number of gym instructors worked under a contract that allowed them to provide a replacement from a register kept by the council when they were unable to work. The replacements were paid directly by the council. Lindsay P stated that the decision in ***Tanton*** 'does not oblige the tribunal to conclude that under a contract of service the individual has, always and in every event, however exceptional, personally to provide his services'. He said the clause in ***Tanton*** was 'extreme' as it permitted the worker to use any substitute *at any time*, whether the worker was unable or unwilling to work, and at their own expense. There were, however, a number of reasons to distinguish ***MacFarlane*** from ***Tanton***:[8] the workers in ***MacFarlane*** could only invoke the substitution clause if they were unable to work; the right was limited to a replacement from the council's register (which the council could veto); the council sometimes arranged a replacement without the workers objecting;

[6] Identifies the next major issue to be analysed.

[7] A brief explanation of the facts in the case is helpful to understand the context in which the judgment was reached. Lengthy descriptive re-tellings of the facts will, however, detract from a good answer.

[8] Discussion of the distinguishing factors of two key cases is given here.

and the council paid the substitute direct. Therefore, the substitution power did not overwhelm the factors pointing towards employment.

Lizzie may invoke the substitution clause when she is 'unavailable' for work. This would seem to include circumstances in which she is unwilling to work as well as when she is unable (see ***James v Redcats (Brands) Ltd* [2007] IRLR 296, EAT**). This provision is nearer the wide power of substitution present in ***Tanton***. Furthermore, it is clear that this substitution provision is not a mere sham: it has been used by Lizzie (see ***Autoclenz***). On balance, however, the stronger argument seems to be that Lizzie's case is closer to the ***MacFarlane*** decision, in that she has a limited power of substitution.[9] She must secure the agreement of Fit & Healthy, the replacements must be selected from those pre-approved, and she may only use the power for a maximum of fourteen days per annum. In conclusion, these constraints do not prevent a finding of employment status in Lizzie's case. Moreover, the fact that Lizzie's wages are paid net of tax and national insurance contributions also points towards employment status. Employees are paid the net amount after such deductions have been made whereas self-employed workers are usually paid gross.

[9] A conclusion is reached on an important issue in the case following careful reasoning. There then follows a clear explanation as to why that conclusion was reached.

In Bob's case there is a wide substitution clause but it has never been invoked and he is clear that it does not accurately reflect reality. Bob's situation is similar to that in ***Autoclenz*** where the Supreme Court held that although there was a substitution clause in the written contract, it had never been invoked and the valeters were expected to undertake any work allocated to them and did so. Using the multi-factorial test applied by Cooke J in ***Market Investigations v Minister of Social Security* [1969] 2 QB 173**, does the evidence overall point to Bob being an employee? Although he is required to organise his own tax affairs, Clean Cars prepares his invoices and provides all material and equipment. He works as part of a team and the rate of pay is determined by Clean Cars (about which he is unhappy). He has to wear the company uniform and there appears to be an element of personal service and mutuality of obligation in that he is under an obligation to attend work (or inform Clean Cars if unable to do so) and cannot substitute despite what his contract says. The Supreme Court in ***Autoclenz*** has been clear that employment contracts differ from other commercial contracts due to the inequality of bargaining power between the parties and has held that any written agreement may be disregarded where it does not correspond with the parties' true legal obligations. It is the substance or reality of the relationship that must be determined, which involves considering all the evidence including the parties' conduct. Applying that analysis, the claimants in ***Autoclenz*** were held to be employees. Despite what his contract says, Bob may also be able to argue that he is an employee or worker for the purposes of the **NMW**.[10]

[10] Clear conclusion to the problem set.

## LOOKING FOR EXTRA MARKS?

- Strong students will be able to identify the major and minor points of any question. If you are told certain information, consider why the examiner has included it. Here Lizzie's right to substitute for a limited period each year and Bob's requirement to call in advance if he cannot work are good examples of where students could gain extra marks for spotting why these facts might be relevant.
- Never assume in an employment status question that the issue will be clear-cut as it rarely will be! Instead show the examiner that you appreciate that this is a difficult area where a number of factors need to be weighed in the balance.
- While the area is not clear-cut, this does not mean that you should avoid giving a clear answer to the question. Show where there might be alternative outcomes but remember that you have been asked to advise a hypothetical client so be sure to give a clear conclusion to the question that the client has asked.

## QUESTION 3

**Today's complex labour market has made it even more difficult to determine employment status, particularly in the case of agency workers. Discuss.**

## CAUTION!

- When you are directed simply to 'Discuss' a statement, this is asking you to look at the evidence in support and against the proposition and to arrive at a conclusion based on careful reasoning and evidence.
- This is a potentially very wide question but break it down carefully and you will see that there are certain points that the examiner is inviting you to discuss, which should help you structure your answer: the nature of today's labour market, how we determine employment status, and the particular difficulties associated with agency workers.
- The reference to today's labour market allows you to bring in evidence from outside case law and statute. Material from your course reading, such as articles that make reference to this issue, would be appropriate sources.

## DIAGRAM ANSWER PLAN

The evolution of the labour market

Tests for determining employment status

Problem with applying tests to today's labour market especially re agency workers

Influence of policy in this area

## SUGGESTED ANSWER

Today's labour market is characterised by flexibility. As Fredman[1] has argued, a range of working patterns (such as part-time, temporary, or casual engagements) can help provide for an employer's changing needs (S. Fredman, 'Labour law in flux: The changing composition of the workforce' (1997) 26 *Industrial Law Journal* 337) but it has been suggested[2] that an increasingly flexible labour market has given rise to a more precarious category of atypical workers (G. Standing, *The Precariat: The New Dangerous Class* (Bloomsbury: London, 2011)) who may not benefit from the protections of employment status. One example of such an alternative working relationship is that of agency workers where an agency will place a worker on a particular assignment with an end-user/hirer. The hirer pays the agency a fee and the agency pays the worker. In determining employment status, the courts have typically imposed a range of requirements. First, there is a requirement that the employee must perform their services personally (***Express and Echo Publications Ltd*** **v** ***Tanton*** **[1999] IRLR 367;** ***MacFarlane*** **v** ***Glasgow City Council*** **[2001] IRLR 7**). Second, there must exist mutuality of obligation (the employer must be obliged to offer work and the worker to accept it (***Nethermere (St Neots) Ltd*** **v** ***Taverna & Gardiner*** **[1984] ICR 612**)). Agencies will typically only offer engagements to the worker as and when they become available with no obligation on the worker to accept and so workers will be unlikely to show the requisite mutuality of obligation to claim employee status. The third and final irreducible minimum requirement for employment, and the one on which I will focus in this essay,[3] is the need to show employer control. As will be discussed, particular difficulties arise when applying the control test in an agency context leaving agency workers, at common law, with little employment protection. Moreover, in attempting to stretch the tests to provide agency workers with employment protection, the courts arguably created further uncertainty in this area.[4]

MacKenna J in ***Ready Mixed Concrete (South East) Ltd*** **v** ***Minister of Pensions and National Insurance*** **[1968] 2 QB 497** stated that a crucial factor in the employment relationship is that the 'servant' agrees that in the performance of that service they will be subject to the other's control in a sufficient degree to make that other master. In an

[1] Academic authority is used to support the statement on flexibility. There is no need to give the full citation in an exam.

[2] Give details of where any suggestion/claim is made. Where there are opposing views (as there may be here), present both positions.

[3] This is a good example of where it is made clear to the examiner that the student is aware of all relevant law but, due to the inevitable limits of time in the exam, will focus on that which is most relevant.

[4] The introduction shows understanding of the question and sets out what will be argued.

agency relationship, control is divided between the hirer who supervises the agency worker on a day-to-day basis and the agency who pays the worker.[5] This complex tripartite arrangement has given rise to a number of cases regarding whether an employment relationship exists and, if so, who is the employer. Employment agencies may themselves be the employer (***McMeechan* v *Secretary of State for Employment* [1997] ICR 549, CA**). However the fact that the employment agency has control over the selection and payment of the worker does not necessarily result in an employment relationship. In ***Motorola Ltd* v *Davidson and Melville Craig Group Ltd* [2001] IRLR 4, EAT**, Motorola, the client company, which had *indirect* control of a worker, was held to be the employer.

The confusion over the status of agency workers and the desire on the part of agency workers to attempt to show an employment relationship with the end-user/hirer led to a series of decisions,[6] which arguably can only be understood by considering the policy reasons in favour of extending employee status to those engaged on agency contracts (***Franks* v *Reuters* [2003] ICR 1166, CA; *Dacas* v *Brook Street Bureau* [2004] IRLR 358; *Cable & Wireless* v *Muscat* [2006] IRLR 354, CA**). **Section 230(2) of the Employment Rights Act 1996** provides that a 'contract of employment' means a contract of service or apprenticeship, whether express or *implied*, and (if it is express) whether oral or in writing. The key question motivating the claimants in these cases was whether a contract of employment could be implied between the agency worker and the end-user/hirer. In ***Dacas***, the Court of Appeal stated, obiter, that it might be necessary to imply a contract of employment. Sedley LJ stated that it was 'simply not credible' that Dacas would be employed by no one. In ***Cable & Wireless* v *Muscat* [2006] IRLR 354, CA**, another triangular relationship case involving an agency, an agency worker, and an end-user/hirer, the court found a contract of employment should be implied between the end-user/hirer and the agency worker.

These cases are difficult to understand as they appear to circumvent the strict requirements of control and mutuality of obligation required in an employment relationship and so go against the orthodox doctrine in this area. In the case of ***James* v *Greenwich* LBC [2007] IRLR 168**, the EAT (Elias J, presiding) took a rather more restrictive interpretation. The EAT held that: (1) such a contract would be implied between the agency worker and the end-user/hirer only where a *necessary* inference could be drawn to that effect; and (2) the way in which the contract is performed is consistent *only* with such an implied contract and where it would be inconsistent with there being no such contract. The Court of Appeal reached the same conclusion, reasoning along similar lines, when ***James*** was appealed to that court (see **[2008] IRLR 302** and **[2008] ICR 545**). As there will typically be two express contracts already in existence (one between the end-user/hirer and the agency, and a second between the agency and the agency worker), it would be unusual for another contract to be implied on grounds of necessity.

[5] This discussion follows the PEA formula.

[6] A new point is introduced here and then analysed later in the paragraph.

Moreover, as Mummery LJ explained in his judgment, courts are 'builders in the law' and 'not architects of economic and social policy'. While he acknowledged the tensions between the need for a flexible labour market on the one hand and the growth of a 'two-tier workforce' without employment protection on the other, he was clear that it was not for the courts to initiate any changes to social policy.[7]

[7] Shows intimate understanding of the judgment and supports the earlier claim that policy factors influenced the development of the law in this area.

The decision in ***James*** would therefore seem to limit severely the scope of courts and tribunals to imply a contract of employment between the agency worker and end-user/hirer and represented a significant shift in emphasis and/or approach by the courts to this issue. Support for this view[8] can be found in ***Tilson* v *Alstom Transport* [2011] IRLR 169, CA**, where the Court of Appeal held that there was no basis upon which a contract of employment could be implied. In reaching this decision, weight was given to the fact that there was no common intention between the parties concerning such a contract. Therefore, it would appear that, in agency cases, a contract of employment will be implied only where it is a *necessary* inference: the court in ***Tilson*** made it clear that courts and tribunals may not make such an implication simply because they disapprove of the putative employer's attempts to avoid the obligations of an employer by using agency arrangements. In other words, the circumstances in which such a contract will be implied will be rare. This reasoning also seems consistent with the law on express and implied terms.[9] In ***Consistent Group* v *Kalwak* [2008] IRLR 505, CA**, the express terms of the contract excluded mutuality of obligation from arising between the parties. The Court of Appeal, overruling the EAT (see the EAT decision at **[2007] IRLR 560**), held that where express terms excluded these obligations, a contract of employment could not be implied since an implied term cannot flatly contradict an express term unless the agreement was a sham. In ***Kalwak***, the court held that there was no sham (and for there to be one, *both* parties must have the intention to give a false impression of their true obligations). In relation to express, written terms excluding mutuality of obligations from arising, the Court of Appeal in ***Protectacoat Firthglow Ltd* v *Szilagyi* [2009] IRLR 365** held that if these did not accurately reflect the substance of the relationship, they could be disregarded, i.e. if it was a sham (***Autoclenz Ltd* v *Belcher and Ors* [2011] UKSC 41**).

[8] Case law is used to support the earlier claim made.

[9] Although it is not necessary to discuss this point in answer to the question, showing that you can draw from various aspects of the course where it is relevant to do so is a good thing to do as it shows you can spot connections with different areas.

The example of agency workers shows the difficulties that exist in attempting to apply the common law tests to determine whether a contract of employment exists to the complexities of today's labour market. In attempting to fit these tests to the tripartite agency relationship, the courts appeared to be driven by policy considerations to protect agency workers but this arguably came at the expense of clarity of legal doctrine. Some of the concerns about the treatment of agency workers have been addressed by the introduction of the **Agency Workers Regulations 2010**. Moreover, from April 2020 temping agencies are required to provide those seeking work with certain key information such as the type of contract on which they will be engaged and who will be responsible for payment (**Conduct of Employment Agencies and Employment Businesses (Amendment) Regulations 2019**). However the broader question of whether these tests remain fit for purpose remains.[10]

[10] The conclusion attempts to draw the different themes of the answer together.

## LOOKING FOR EXTRA MARKS?

- This answer began with a brief point on the flexibility of the labour market before making clear that its focus would be on agency workers. It would also be acceptable in an answer to discuss other forms of atypical work particularly where there are topical debates that you can reference.
- The tension between policy and legal considerations should be made clear in your answer.
- Strong students often excel by showing some originality in their answers. Distinguish yourself by reading and referring to material beyond your reading list or suggesting what reforms might be appropriate in this area.

## QUESTION 4

Joe works as a private hire driver providing taxi services. To hire Joe, his customers download an app from the company 'Hireco' to their smartphones. The terms between Hireco and the customer state that Hireco is accepting bookings as agent for the driver (the 'principal'). The terms state that Hireco is not a party to the hire contract, which is between the driver and the customer.

Joe's original contract with Hireco described him as a Partner, which is further defined as the person with sole responsibility for providing the driving services requested by the customer. The terms state that Joe accepts that a direct legal relationship is created between him and the customer, with Hireco acting as an intermediary. Moreover, there is a clause which states 'Hireco does not have, and does not intend to have, any control over the Partner. Nothing in this contract is deemed to constitute an employment relationship between the Partner and Hireco.' Further important terms of the contract include the obligation by a Partner not to speak of Hireco in derogatory terms, that a Partner must comply with all quality standards set by Hireco, that the terms can be amended unilaterally by Hireco, and that the Partner agrees to constant monitoring by Hireco. The contract would be terminated automatically if the Partner was no longer qualified to drive or might be terminated by Hireco in a range of circumstances including if a significant number of customer complaints were received about a Partner. Fares could be recovered by Hireco from a customer on behalf of a Partner.

A few months ago, Hireco issued revised terms to all Partners, which had to be accepted by all Partners via an app before they could continue to receive further work. These described the contract as a 'service agreement' and included a new provision regarding service ratings: if customers' ratings of a Partner drop below an acceptable standard, Hireco may terminate the agreement.

Joe must provide his own car, although Hireco states that it must be in good condition and only certain makes and models will be accepted by it. Joe is responsible for all costs of running the car. When he signed up with Hireco, he received a welcome booklet explaining that Hireco would continuously look at his approval ratings. Joe is not obliged to turn on the app and take bookings but if he does not turn on the app and declines three trips in a row while on duty, Hireco will log him off the booking app for a period of time. Joe treats himself as self-employed for tax purposes.

**Advise Joe, who believes that he is entitled to be paid the national minimum wage and receive paid holiday, on his employment status.**

## CAUTION!

- You will no doubt have spotted that the facts of the case mirror the much-publicised ***Uber*** litigation. The question is, however, a fairly straightforward one looking at the tests of employment status but in the context of the trend for persons to work in the 'gig economy'.
- Discussions about the gig economy are highly topical but take care not to stray too far into exploring ideas of the changing labour market. This is a problem question and the examiner will expect you to apply the law closely to the facts of the case rather than provide a more reflective, contextual discussion as you would in an essay answer.

## DIAGRAM ANSWER PLAN

| | |
|---|---|
| Identify the issues | ■ Is Joe a worker for the purposes of the Working Time Regulations ('WTR') and NMW? |
| Relevant law | ■ Section 54 NMW; reg. 2 WTR<br>■ Relevant case law including *Byrne Brothers*, *Cotswold Developments*, *Autoclenz*, *Mingeley*, *Westwood*, and *Uber* |
| Apply the law | ■ Is there a contract between Joe and Hireco?<br>■ Is there an obligation on Joe to perform the services personally?<br>■ Is Hireco a client or customer of Joe?<br>■ Do the express terms of the written agreement between Joe and Hireco reflect reality? |
| Conclude | ■ Joe may struggle to show mutuality of obligation although the existence of a penalty for declining hires may help him; Hireco appears to exercise a wide degree of control over Joe<br>■ If he can show mutuality of obligation, likely that he would fall into category of worker and be eligible to claim<br>■ Court may be prepared to look beyond express terms of agreement if these do not reflect reality |

## SUGGESTED ANSWER

[1] An obvious point but the definitions of worker vary depending on the statute so ensure that you use the definition for the relevant statute.

Joe is concerned that he is not receiving paid holiday leave or the national minimum wage.[1] **Section 1(2) National Minimum Wage Act 1998 ('NMW')** provides that a person qualifies for the national minimum wage if they are an individual who is a worker, is working or ordinarily works in the UK under their contract, and has ceased to be of compulsory school age. A worker is then defined in **s54(3) NMW** as either an individual who works or has worked under a contract of employment or 'any other contract, whether express or implied ... whereby the individual undertakes to do or perform personally any work or services for another party to the contract whose status is not by virtue of the contract that of a client or customer of any profession or business undertaking carried on by the individual'.

For the purposes of Joe's query about paid holiday, this is governed by the **Working Time Regulations 1998 ('WTR')**. The protections of the **WTR** also apply to workers. The definition of worker under **reg. 2 WTR** is the same as that in the **NMW**.

Both the **NMW** and **WTR** also contain definitions of agency workers. In **s34(1) NMW**, an agency worker is defined as where an individual is supplied by a person to do the work for another under a contract or other arrangements made between the agent and principal. A similar provision is found in **reg. 36 WTR**.

[2] Framing the key issue as a question helps you keep your focus.

The question then is this: is Joe a worker? If the answer is yes, he will be eligible to bring claims under the **NMW** and **WTR**.[2]

In ***Byrne Brothers (Formwork) Ltd* v *Baird and Ors* [2002] ICR 667**, the notion of 'carrying on a business undertaking' was given a wide interpretation by the EAT. As Underhill J noted, this could potentially be construed as capturing genuinely self-employed persons who will be carrying on business undertakings on their own behalf. As he noted, however, this could not have been the intention of the legislature. Instead he opined that the intention behind the definition of worker 'is plainly to create an intermediate class of protected worker, who is on the one hand not an employee but on the other hand cannot in some narrower sense be regarded as carrying on a business'. Underhill J focused on the policy goals behind the legislation, which he argued were to extend protections to those who may be 'required to work excessive hours' or 'suffer unlawful deductions from their earnings or to be paid too little'. A distinction must therefore be drawn between those who have a degree of dependence on the alleged employer in contrast to those who are sufficiently independent and capable of being 'treated as being able to look after themselves'.[3]

[3] This is a key case in this area.

In attempting to draw that distinction and consider the degree of dependence of the worker, relevant considerations could include 'the degree of control exercised by the putative employer, the exclusivity of the engagement and its typical duration, the method of payment, what equipment the putative worker supplies, the level of risk undertaken etc'. Further guidance[4] may be found in another EAT case of ***Cotswold Developments Construction Ltd* v *Williams* [2006] IRLR 181** where Langstaff J commented that whether a person markets their services as an independent person to the world or whether they are recruited by a principal to work in the principal's business 'will in most cases demonstrate on which side of the line a given person falls'. The role of the courts in cases such as these is to determine the true nature of the contract (***James* v *Redcats (Brands) Ltd* [2007] ICR 1006**). In short, 'what was the true agreement between the parties' even if this does not fit with the express terms of the contract (per Lord Clarke in ***Autoclenz Ltd* v *Belcher and Ors* [2011] ICR 1157**). Tribunals should therefore be mindful of the risk that 'armies of lawyers' will draft into contracts clauses such as the right to substitute another person to provide services as a matter of course in an attempt to minimise the risk of an employment relationship being created 'even where such terms do not begin to reflect the real relationship' (per Elias J in ***Consistent Group Ltd* v *Kalwak* [2007] IRLR 560**).

[4] Demonstrates strong understanding of the relevant case law and the factors to take into account.

There are a number of factors in this case that point against Joe being a worker.[5] Hireco acts as an intermediary to allow Joe to pair up with customers seeking a taxi service. He is under no obligation to log on to the app and accept hires and even if he is not dormant and logged on, he can decline bookings (albeit that he will suffer a small penalty in that Hireco will log him off the service for a short period). This appears inconsistent with the requirement of mutuality of obligation in an employment relationship (***Carmichael* v *National Power plc* [2000] IRLR 43**). He enjoys the tax benefits of being a self-employed person and provides his own equipment. The fact that Joe is in effect running his own business may not, however, necessarily be fatal to a finding that he is a worker. In ***Hospital Medical Group* v *Westwood* [2012] EWCA Civ 1005**, the group entered into an arrangement with Dr Westwood for him to provide hair loss treatment. Although Dr Westwood was running his own business and was not paid by the group unless a patient wished to obtain treatment from him, he was sufficiently integrated into the group's business and held out by them as one of its doctors such that he qualified as a worker.[6] Considering the extent to which Joe is integrated into Hireco's business may be of assistance here although as Lady Hale pointed out in ***Bates van Winkelhof* v *Clyde & Co. LLP* [2014] 1 WLR 2047**, 'there can be no substitute for applying the words of the statute to the facts of the individual case'. Each case is fact-sensitive.

[5] You need to show that you have weighed up both sides of the argument. This helps you demonstrate to the examiner that you are taking a considered, thoughtful approach.

[6] Here the ratio of another case is applied to the facts of the current one to help form a view as to how the courts will interpret Joe's situation.

[7] This helps you maintain relevance and provides a good link with the earlier discussion.

Turning again to the wording of the statute, there are three aspects to this.[7] There must be a contract with the individual claiming to be a worker, that individual must provide some personal service, and the person to whom that service is provided must not be the individual's client or customer. It would appear difficult for Joe to argue that a contract of service exists when his app is turned off and he is unavailable for work unless he is able to show that there is an umbrella contract covering all engagements. However, when his app is turned on and he is able to accept hires, this may be a different matter. This was the view of the Employment Tribunal in ***Aslam and Ors* v *Uber* [2017] IRLR 4**, which concerned Uber drivers in a case which is very factually similar to Joe's. The tribunal found that drivers in ***Uber*** were workers for the purposes of the **NMW** and **WTR**, a decision subsequently upheld by the EAT, the Court of Appeal, and the Supreme Court (**[2021] UKSC 5**).

Joe may struggle to show the requisite degree of mutuality of obligation as was required in ***Byrne Brothers***. In ***Mingeley* v *Pennock (t/a Amber Cars)* [2004] EWCA Civ 328**, the Court of Appeal considered a claim of race discrimination brought by Mingeley. Amber Cars ran a taxi business. Mingeley paid a sum of money to Amber Cars each week and in return he was given a radio and access to the company's computer system which allocated customer calls. Mingeley kept all fare money and could work any hours he pleased. He was under no obligation to work at all. The Court of Appeal found that there was no mutuality of obligation. In Joe's case, however, the penalty imposed on Joe in logging him off for a period if he declines hires suggests that some degree of mutuality of obligation may exist.[8] Moreover, there appears a significant degree of control over Joe by Hireco. Customer feedback is monitored closely, the terms of the service agreement are presented on a 'take it or leave it' basis, and Hireco has a right of veto on the type of car Joe wishes to use. If Joe can show that a contract with Hireco exists, he must show that he is engaged to perform the work personally. We are not told of any substitution clause in the contract with Hireco. Finally, is Hireco a customer or client of a business operated by Joe? It would not seem accurate to portray Joe's relationship with Hireco in this light.

[8] There are some similarities with this case but the penalty issue appears an important distinguishing feature as does the degree of control exercised by Hireco.

The key difficulty that Joe appears to have will be showing that the requisite mutuality of obligation exists, albeit in ***Uber*** the courts were prepared to find mutuality of obligation in similar circumstances. If he can demonstrate this, it is likely that he would qualify as a worker. This then leaves the question of the express written agreement between him and Hireco, which makes clear that no employment relationship exists between the parties. In recent years, the courts appear alive to the fact that contracts in an employment relationship may not always reflect reality. The Court of Appeal in ***Uber*** **([2018] EWCA Civ 2748)** was clear that the contract can be disregarded if it does not reflect the reality of the situation. In ***Snook*** **v** ***London and West Riding Investments Ltd*** **[1967] 2 QB 786**, the Court of Appeal described 'sham' contracts as where parties have the common intention that the contract will not create the obligations it has the appearance of creating. This was widened in ***Autoclenz*** where the Supreme Court took into account the relative bargaining power of the parties. It may therefore be possible for Joe to argue that the terms of his service agreement do not reflect the contractual reality although Joe should not assume that the courts will readily disregard express written terms unless there is clear evidence that these terms do not reflect the real position between the parties.[9]

[9] Solid conclusion that also shows discernment.

## LOOKING FOR EXTRA MARKS?

- Strong students often distinguish themselves by presenting measured answers rather than ill-considered, emotional responses (Not 'he will definitely win. This is the same as ***Uber***!'). It can be tempting to rush to a conclusion that Joe will clearly be a worker as the facts are largely based on the ***Uber*** case. While it is certainly arguable that the courts appear more sceptical of express terms that seek to deny an employment relationship and are alive to shifting ways of working that can be to the detriment of workers, be discerning in your approach.
- Reading judgments is one of the best ways of learning how to answer a problem question. Look at how the judges present the submissions for one side then the other, set out the law, and apply it to the facts before reaching a conclusion.

## TAKING THINGS FURTHER

- A. Bogg, 'Sham self-employment in the Supreme Court' (2012) 41(3) *Industrial Law Journal* 328
  *Analyses the Supreme Court decision of* **Autoclenz Ltd *v* Belcher and Ors *[2011] UKSC 41***
- A. Bogg, 'Taken for a Ride: Workers in the Gig Economy' (2019) 135 *Law Quarterly Review* 219
  *Comment on the case of* **R *v* Central Arbitration Committee** *and whether delivery drivers are workers*
- P. Elias, 'Changes and Challenges to the Contract of Employment' (2018) 38(4) *Oxford Journal of Legal Studies* 869
  *Book review with interesting discussion of treatment by courts of atypical workers and those on zero hours contracts*

- M. Ford and A. Bogg, 'Between Statute and Contract: Who is a Worker' (2019) 135 *Law Quarterly Review* 347

  *Analyses the Court of Appeal decision of* **Uber BV *v* Aslam *[2018] EWCA Civ 2748***

- M. Freedland, 'From the contract of employment to the personal work nexus' (2006) 35(1) *Industrial Law Journal* 1

  *Analyses ideas of a 'family of personal work contracts' and the 'personal work nexus'*

## Online resources

www.oup.com/uk/qanda/

For extra essay and problem questions on this topic, as well as advice on revision and exam technique, please visit the online resources.

# Express and implied terms

# 3

## ARE YOU READY?

In order to attempt the questions in this chapter, you must have covered the following areas in your revision:

- The different sources of contractual terms
- When terms of collective agreements will be incorporated into an individual contract of employment
- When custom and practice may give rise to a contractual term
- The distinction between terms implied in fact and in law
- Implied terms on employers
- Implied terms on employees
- The basics of the law on wrongful dismissal

## KEY DEBATES

Although the area of contractual terms is relatively settled, cases such as *Consistent Group* **v** *Kalwak* **[2008] IRLR 505**, *Protectacoat Firthglow Ltd* **v** *Szilagyi* **[2009] IRLR 365**, and *Autoclenz Ltd* **v** *Belcher and Ors* **[2011] UKSC 41** have revealed how the courts are prepared to take a more liberal view about the parties' intentions when it comes to contracts of employment, particularly when a party is attempting to argue that the terms of the written agreement are a 'sham'.

**Debate: The distinctiveness of employment contracts**

Employment contracts differ from other commercial contracts due to the fact that they are incomplete, usually of indefinite duration, and typically the parties have unequal bargaining power. How helpful is it to continue relying on ordinary contractual principles when considering contracts of employment?

**Debate: The importance of implied terms**

Why do implied terms feature so significantly in the contract of employment?

## QUESTION 1

Ash, Bijal, and Carla work for a manufacturing company that is in the process of making redundancies. Ash has been selected for redundancy and, having worked for the company for five years, has been told that he will receive a statutory redundancy payment based on his length of service. He is unhappy about this as he has heard that when the company last made redundancies a few years ago, colleagues were given a much more generous package. Due to an administrative error, he has never received a written contract of employment but he has checked the staff handbook on the company intranet and it says: 'In the event of redundancies, staff may be entitled to an enhanced payment. This will be discussed during the consultation.'

Bijal, a highly skilled expert who heads the company's technical development division and has regular contact with customers, has recently resigned. Her line manager has instructed Bijal to remain at home during her notice period as he wants to limit Bijal's contact with clients. Bijal has checked her contract, which is silent on the matter. She would like to work during the six months of her notice period as she is leaving to join a newly created applied research centre at a local university where she will teach students and help develop new technologies. She is concerned that her skills will become rusty if she cannot work.

Carla's contract contains a term that the company, in its discretion, may award her a bonus but that the decision on whether to award a bonus and in what amount rests with the company. In recent years, she has received bonuses on an annual basis. Her bonuses have ranged from £5,000 to £20,000. She has recently been told that in light of the company's financial situation, her bonus payment will be £350. Carla is furious and wants to challenge this decision.

**Advise Ash, Bijal, and Carla.**

## CAUTION!

- This question raises issues about whether Ash, Bijal, and Carla can rely on contractual terms to achieve their intended outcomes. Work logically through the various sources of contractual terms beginning with express written terms before looking at other sources.
- Consider whether the question has an internal structure that you can follow. Here the examiner has helped you by dividing the question into three clear parts.
- The question is relatively brief but that does not mean that you should avoid giving a detailed answer. Show your detailed knowledge by discussing each scenario fully.

## DIAGRAM ANSWER PLAN

**Identify the issues**

- Ash: he has no written contract—does he have a section 1 statement? Can he argue that an entitlement exists due to custom and practice? What is the status of the term in the handbook?
- Bijal: can her employer oblige her to go on 'garden leave'? Is there a duty on her employer to provide her with work?
- Carla: is the company entitled to exercise its discretion in a way that gives Carla a significantly smaller bonus than usual?

**Relevant law**

- Ash: s1 Employment Rights Act 1996; *Keeley v Fosroc International*, *Park Cakes*
- Bijal: *Turner*, *William Hill Organisation Ltd*, *Standard Life Health Care Ltd*
- Carla: implied term of mutual trust and confidence; requirement that decisions on discretionary benefits are not irrational, perverse, or contrary to good faith; *Clark*, *Keen*, *Horkulak*

**Apply the law**

- Ash: need for section 1 statement; little evidence of custom and practice; distinguish term from that in *Keeley*
- Bijal: is there an implied duty to provide work as she is highly skilled?; no express garden leave clause
- Carla: express term is subject to implied term of mutual trust and confidence and must be exercised rationally. Given financial circumstances, is there any evidence that company has acted in bad faith?

**Conclude**

- Ash: should have received section 1 statement; unlikely that he can insist on enhanced payment
- Bijal: if she can show that she is highly skilled, breach to put her on garden leave
- Carla: has company acted within limits placed on its discretion?

## SUGGESTED ANSWER

This question concerns the terms of the employment contract. In order for Ash, Bijal, and Carla to succeed, it is necessary for them to show contractual entitlements to enhanced redundancy pay, work, and bonus respectively.

[1] Using sub-headings can be a useful way of structuring or 'signposting' your answer.

[2] This shows a logical approach. It may be tempting to jump straight to discussion of the handbook/custom and practice but 'show your working' by working through each step.

[3] Framing issues as questions can be a useful way of moving between issues, showing that you are clear on what questions are raised by the topic, and leading you to provide a clear answer.

[4] Shows strong analysis and that you understand the factors that led to the decision.

### Ash[1]

The starting point[2] is to consider whether there is an express term entitling Ash to receive enhanced redundancy pay. Express terms may be in writing, agreed orally, or developed through the parties' conduct. Turning to the question of written terms, since April 2020 employers must provide an extended 'section 1 statement' (**s1 Employment Rights Act 1996 ('ERA')**) of 'initial employment particulars' to workers and employees either before or on the first day of employment/engagement. It must contain certain information including details of dates of employment/engagement, hours of work, pay, and other benefits including non-contractual benefits. It does not appear that a **section 1** statement has been provided. Ash may therefore complain to the Employment Tribunal for a determination of what terms should have been included (**s11 ERA**).

Can Ash argue that the statement in the employee handbook that staff 'may be entitled to an enhanced redundancy payment' is legally enforceable and gives rise to a contractual right to the payment?[3] There is no rule that terms in an employee handbook will be given contractual force; however, like collective agreements between an employer and trade union, they may be legally enforceable if their terms are incorporated into individual contracts either expressly or impliedly, and it is 'apt' to do so (***Alexander* v *Standard Telephones Ltd (No. 2)* [1991] IRLR 286**). In the Court of Appeal case of ***Keeley* v *Fosroc International* [2006] IRLR 961**, the contract of employment expressly incorporated the terms of the staff handbook, which contained a statement that employees with the requisite length of service 'are entitled to receive an enhanced redundancy payment'. The employee was able to rely on this term. There are, however, two features that distinguish ***Keeley*** from the present case.[4] The first is that the terms were expressly incorporated into the contract of employment, which is not the case here. Second, even if it could be shown that the term is legally enforceable, its content is different from that given here where the statement is only that staff 'may' be entitled to an enhanced payment. In other words, even if Ash could show a contractual right to the term (which appears unlikely), his only right is a discretionary one. The employer 'may' consider making an enhanced payment. While the exercise of discretion in relation to discretionary payments must not be exercised irrationally or perversely, Ash needs to show that 'no reasonable employer would have exercised his discretion in this way' (per Burton J in ***Clark* v *Nomura International Plc* [2000] IRLR 766**). This is a high hurdle to overcome.

There has, however, been a previous example of the company exercising its discretion and making an enhanced payment some years before and so Ash might argue that a contractual term has arisen by virtue of custom and practice. The courts have typically been cautious in their approach to custom and practice cases. On the one hand, employees like Ash may reasonably expect a particular benefit or outcome based on what has gone before; on the other hand,[5] it would appear unfair to bind an employer contractually to a particular practice simply because the employer has behaved that way in the past. The test for whether a term has been incorporated by virtue of custom and practice in a particular industry is whether it is reasonable, notorious, and certain (***Devonald* v *Rosser & Sons* [1906] 2 KB 728**). There is no suggestion that Ash is arguing that the manufacturing industry generally makes enhanced redundancy payments; his claim is that a practice has arisen with his employer. In this case, the courts will also consider what has been communicated to the employee. As has been discussed, the only express communication on this matter in the handbook has been that an enhanced payment 'may' be made. Can it be shown that there has been a regular application of the practice such that it has 'crystallised' into a contractual right (per Elias J in ***Solectron Scotland Ltd* v *Roper* [2004] IRLR 4**)? In a relatively recent Court of Appeal case (***Park Cakes Ltd* v *Shumba* [2013] EWCA Civ 974**) Underhill LJ appeared to move beyond the 'reasonable, notorious and certain' criteria and set out a range of factors that should be considered. These included on how many occasions and over how long the benefits have been paid (here this appears to have been once a few years ago), whether the benefits are always the same (we do not know but there is nothing to compare if it has only happened once), the extent to which the benefits are publicised (the staff handbook only says than an enhanced payment 'may' be made), and what is said in the express contract (there is none).[6] On balance, it appears unlikely that Ash will be able to show that he is contractually entitled to an enhanced redundancy payment.

[5] This is a good demonstration that you are aware of the underlying policy factors. Using the device of 'on the one hand ... on the other' is also a good way of discussing competing arguments succinctly.

[6] Applying the facts to the case in this way (with application in brackets) can make your answer read more clearly than a long-winded explanation.

**Bijal**

Can Bijal insist on her employer providing her with work during her notice period?[7] There is no provision regarding continued work in Bijal's written contract of employment or the express ability to deny her work via what is known as a 'garden leave' clause. The courts have, historically, been reluctant to imply a duty on the employer to provide work. In ***Turner* v *Sawdon & Co.* [1901] 2 KB 653**, it was held that it was within the province of the master (employer) to continue paying wages but it is under no obligation to provide work. While it may seem odd that an employee would object to being compelled not to work, the open-ended nature of the employment contract may mean that it is not always possible to guarantee continued work. The courts have, however, taken a more relaxed approach in the

[7] A new issue is introduced using the same questioning technique highlighted earlier.

case of highly skilled employees who want to maintain specific skills which may go 'rusty' if not used regularly. In these circumstances, the courts have held that where there is work available, the employee has a right to perform it (***William Hill Organisation Ltd* v *Tucker* [1999] ICR 291**). As a highly skilled technician, the courts are likely to conclude that Bijal falls within the category of employees who have the right to be provided with work. Moreover, there is no evidence of a 'garden leave' clause in Bijal's contract, which would provide the employer with the ability to deny her work during her notice period. In the absence of such a clause, the employer is obliged to provide Bijal with work. In any event, it is difficult to see what legitimate interest the employer is trying to protect by putting Bijal on garden leave. She is departing for a new role in education and will not compete with the company (contrast the situation[8] in ***Standard Life Health Care Ltd* v *Gorman* [2009] EWCA Civ 1292** where although Gorman had an implied right to work and despite the absence of a garden leave clause, the employer was not in breach of contract to insist on Gorman taking garden leave where the employee was in prior breach of the duty of good faith).

[8] Here there is no suggestion that there has been a breach of contract by Bijal. Resist the urge to hypothesise about what might have happened had there been as this could be construed as irrelevance. This example shows the examiner you are aware of the issue that is contained.

### Carla

As stated by Lord Steyn in ***Malik* v *BCCI* [1998] AC 20**, the implied term of mutual trust and confidence obliges the employer not to act, without reasonable and proper cause, in a manner calculated and likely to destroy or seriously damage the relationship of confidence between it and the employee. When it comes to the payment of discretionary benefits such as bonuses, there is also a more nuanced term limiting how that discretion can be exercised. As discussed in relation to Ash above,[9] ***Clark*** is authority for the proposition that such discretion must not be exercised irrationally, perversely, or contrary to good faith. Decisions on discretionary payments must also not be arbitrary (***Horkulak* v *Cantor Fitzgerald International* [2005] ICR 402**). In Carla's case, her express contractual entitlement is only to be considered for the award of bonus; there is no guarantee as to amount or even that she will be paid a bonus. The company therefore has a very wide contractual discretion which Carla will need to show was exercised irrationally. In ***Keen* v *Commerzbank AG* [2007] ICR 623**, Mummery LJ was clear that this was a high hurdle to surmount. He stated that when so much depends on the company's discretion in fluctuating conditions, it would require an 'overwhelming case' to persuade a court that the level of bonus was perverse or irrational. Given the context of the company making redundancies, its claim that it cannot afford a higher award of bonus is a rational and credible one.

[9] Where similar issues arise in relation to different parts of the question, refer back to previous discussions rather than repeating yourself.

Moreover, attempting to show that a custom and practice of paying bonuses in a certain amount has developed would appear difficult (***Park Cakes Ltd***). While Carla has received bonuses each year, the amount has varied considerably and Underhill LJ made clear in ***Park Cakes Ltd*** that as a matter of ordinary contractual principles, no term should be implied (by virtue of custom or otherwise) which is inconsistent with the express terms of the contract 'at least until an intention to vary can be understood'. The express term is clear and it would seem difficult to show that the parties intended to vary this.

Carla is advised[10] that any claim for breach of contract in relation to her bonus is unlikely to succeed.

[10] A clear conclusion is reached in relation to the advice sought.

## LOOKING FOR EXTRA MARKS?

- Be careful not to overlook any facts. If the examiner has included certain facts, ask why they might be relevant. In this question, why might the examiner tell you that Bijal is leaving to work in an alternative industry?
- Do not make assumptions. For example, if there has been a history of enhanced payments do not assume that there must now be a contractual entitlement by virtue of custom and practice. Explain the law and how it might apply to the facts of the problem.
- Where relevant information is missing, say so and how this might affect your answer. For example, had the question been silent on whether there was a garden leave clause in Bijal's contract, explore whether this would make a difference to your conclusion.

## QUESTION 2

**It is difficult to underestimate the influence of the implied term of mutual trust and confidence on the contract of employment. Discuss.**

## CAUTION!

- This question tests your ability to argue. It does not matter whether your examiner shares your views—what matters is that you present your case convincingly and support it with evidence.
- 'Implied terms' is a large area. This question focuses on one. While you may want to show that you understand that other implied terms exist, a long description of these terms will not allow you to analyse the question in depth (or even to answer it!). You are being asked to weigh up the influence of one particular term.
- Keep in mind the exam question as you write and ask yourself 'how is what I am writing helping me answer the question?'

## DIAGRAM ANSWER PLAN

Definition of implied terms

Purpose of implied terms especially implied term of trust and confidence

Influence of implied term of trust and confidence on employment relationship

## SUGGESTED ANSWER

Contracts of employment have become much more formal over the past half-century or so. This has developed partly in connection with the shift to individualised contracts and a lessening of collective bargaining, and with the requirement for a written statement of particulars of employment (**s1 Employment Rights Act 1996 ('ERA')**). These changes have led to the diminution in significance of, for example, custom and practice as a source of implied obligations. Nevertheless, there is still room for implied terms, as can most easily be seen by reference to the rise of the implied term of mutual trust and confidence in recent years.[1]

As Collins observes,[2] implied terms can fill gaps in incomplete express contracts, help interpret express terms, and provide principles limiting the exercise of express powers and governing how the parties should behave (H. Collins, 'Legal responses to the standard form contract of employment' (2007) 36(1) *Industrial Law Journal* 2). The implied term of trust and confidence is a clear example of where the common law has attempted to provide some parameters on the behaviour of the parties and to limit how express powers may be exercised. Lord Steyn said in ***Malik* v *BCCI SA* [1998] AC 20, HL** that the duty of trust and confidence was defined[3] thus: 'the employer shall not, without reasonable and proper cause, conduct itself in a manner calculated or likely to damage the relationship of trust and confidence between employer and employee'. This implied term has the potential to swallow up much of the law of terms implied in law (such as the duty of fidelity) and this is why Lord Nicholls in ***BCCI*** described the term as a 'portmanteau' one; big enough to swallow the other implied terms. It is now a central feature of the contract of employment and, as Brodie has argued,[4] highlights the fact that the employment relationship is not just about the economic exchange of labour for

[1] This is a clear, succinct introduction leading into discussion of the main theme of the question.

[2] Good example of wider reading.

[3] The definition of trust and confidence is given by reference to a key case.

[4] Another good example of wider reading. Note how just a brief comment on the author's argument is required to support your view.

pay; it is also about personal relations (D. Brodie, 'Mutual trust and the values of the employment contract' (2001) 30(1) *Industrial Law Journal* 84).

[5] The question asks about the influence of the term. This phrase introduces how the term has developed.

The influence of the implied term of trust and confidence arguably developed[5] with the concept of constructive dismissal after ***Western Excavating (ECC) Ltd*** **v** ***Sharp*** **[1978] QB 761, CA**. In ***Sharp***, the court held that according to what is now **s95(1)(c) ERA**, the definition of constructive dismissal is satisfied only when the employer had acted in breach of a fundamental term in the contract; it was insufficient that it had acted unreasonably. The effect, it was thought, was that fewer employees would succeed in claiming unfair dismissal (and redundancy payments) than before because they would have to prove a breach of a fundamental term, not merely that the employer had acted unreasonably. Breach of the implied term of mutual trust and confidence is, however, always a breach of a fundamental term. This means that it is a breach of condition in contract parlance and therefore such a breach gives rise to a claim whether at common law (wrongful dismissal) or under statute (redundancy payments, unfair dismissal). When one adds that 'last straws' (meaning conduct by the employer that is the last straw before an employee resigns) are a breach of this fundamental implied term *and* that the last straw need not in itself be a breach of contract (see ***Omilaju*** **v** ***Waltham Forest LBC*** **[2005] ICR 481, CA**), one can see how wide the term is.

[6] This summarises the previous discussion and links to the next idea.

The result of this development[6] of the implied term of trust and confidence is that when the employer acts unreasonably, it could be argued that it acts in breach of an implied term (see e.g. ***United Bank*** **v** ***Akhtar*** **[1989] IRLR 507, EAT**, where the express mobility clause was qualified by an implied term that the employer would not move the employee without giving him reasonable notice). A more modern authority is ***Horkulak*** **v** ***Cantor Fitzgerald International*** **[2005] ICR 402, CA**, where the express term that the employer could bestow or withhold a bonus at its discretion was construed as being subject to the implied term of trust and confidence that the employer would exercise its discretion in good faith and not irrationally. This application of the implied term is *not far* from a duty on the employer to act reasonably, although it would be wrong to say that the implied term is concerned with the reasonableness of the employer's behaviour. What matters is whether there has been behaviour which is calculated or likely to damage the relationship of trust and confidence between employer and employee.

[7] Repeating the question helps show the examiner that you are providing a clear answer in response to the precise question set.

[8] This is a good example of critical analysis. Here the statement is not being accepted at face-value but is being critiqued in light of more recent case law developments.

The implied term of trust and confidence has, undeniably, been influential on the contract of employment as noted above.[7] However, has its influence begun to diminish?[8] To answer this, it is helpful to consider the House of Lords' decision in ***Johnson*** **v** ***Unisys Ltd*** **[2003] 1 AC 518**. In this case, as a result of the manner of his dismissal,

Johnson suffered a breakdown. He was a long-serving employee and his employer was aware of his history of work-related stress. On the day he was dismissed, he was asked to attend a meeting where no specific allegations of misconduct were put to him. Later that day he was summarily dismissed. As a result of the circumstances of his dismissal, he suffered a major psychiatric illness involving in-patient treatment. Johnson was successful in claiming unfair dismissal but also argued that he was entitled to damages in wrongful dismissal.[9] The basis of his claim was that the employer had breached the implied term of trust and confidence in the way in which it had dismissed him. The House of Lords held that the implied term of mutual trust and confidence does not apply to a dismissal. In other words, Johnson could not rely on the implied term to constrain the employer's power of dismissal. One reason for this is that the implied term of trust and confidence is concerned with preserving the employment relationship; it does not make sense to apply it to the termination of that relationship. Moreover, dismissals are regulated by the statutory scheme in the **ERA** and it would be unconstitutional to extend the common law to cover the act of dismissal in this way. This has led to the development of the concept of the 'Johnson exclusion zone'. The implied term of trust and confidence does not apply to the dismissal but conduct preceding the 'Johnson exclusion zone' (such as during a period of suspension to investigate misconduct leading to dismissal) could be governed by the implied term and give rise to a cause of action preceding, and independent of, the act of dismissal (***Eastwood* v *Magnox Electric plc* [2005] 1 AC 503**).

[9] A brief summary of the facts of this case help to show why the term was being relied upon. The following paragraph shows clear understanding of the ratio.

In an era where employers retain the upper hand over express terms, one might have expected that the courts and tribunals would seek to restrain managerial prerogatives by extending employment protection through the use of implied terms. There is a strong indication of this approach when one looks at how express terms have been circumscribed by the implied term of mutual trust and confidence. To this extent, it is clear that the term has had a significant impact on how the contract of employment has developed. However, ***Johnson*** suggests that we might be witnessing a 'rolling back' of this development as the House of Lords sought to contain the term. The fact that the term does not apply to the act of dismissal itself but may still be applicable in the stages leading up to that dismissal (depending on how broadly the Johnson exclusion zone is drawn) means that there is every incentive on employers to dismiss the employee with haste rather than using a longer period of suspension to consider matters.[10] If this practice develops, it would seem that unlike the earlier development of the term largely in favour of employees, we might witness a rather more negative influence of the term on contracts of employment.

[10] A clear conclusion, which also sets out possible developments in the future influence of the term.

## LOOKING FOR EXTRA MARKS?

- Avoid giving a superficial answer to the statement. While it may be easy to point towards evidence of the influence of the implied term of mutual trust and confidence, a more thoughtful answer reflects more carefully on both the positive and negative implications of that influence.
- Be sure to support your contentions with evidence. What is the best evidence you can provide to make your argument convincing?

## QUESTION 3

**The Supreme Court's judgment in *Tillman* v *Egon Zehnder Ltd* [2019] UKSC 32 has provided welcome clarity about when the doctrine of severability will be used in an examination of restrictive covenants. Discuss.**

## CAUTION!

- This statement is a good example of where the examiner is asking you to 'question the question'. You are being asked for your view on whether the position really is clearer. However you choose to respond, remember to support your answer with evidence.
- 'Restrictive covenants' is a large area. This question focuses on one aspect. While you will want to show that you understand what restrictive covenants are, a long description of the general law in this area will not allow you to analyse the question in depth (or even to answer it!).
- Questions asking you to engage fully with a particular case are not uncommon especially when the judgment is a very important one. Clearly, you should not attempt to answer such a question unless you have intimate knowledge of the case.

## DIAGRAM ANSWER PLAN

What are restrictive covenants?

What is the doctrine of severability?

Brief overview of issues in *Tillman*

Has this provided clarity?

## SUGGESTED ANSWER

Restrictive covenants are an agreement between employer and employee that act to restrain the behaviour of the employee due to the employer's legitimate business interests. They are typically engaged when an employee leaves their employment. The legitimate business interests of the employer could include, for example, protecting the employer's workforce (by prohibiting the employee from poaching colleagues), protecting its suppliers (by prohibiting the employee from dealing with those same suppliers), and protecting its customers (by prohibiting the employee from dealing with those customers and/or from practising in the same geographical location as the employer). The starting point is that such covenants must be no more than is reasonably necessary to protect the employer's legitimate commercial/ proprietary interests or the public generally (***Herbert Morris Ltd* v *Saxelby* [1916] 1 AC 688, HL**).[1] The question of reasonableness is judged at the time the contract was entered into (***Bartholomews Agri Food Ltd* v *Thornton* [2016] EWHC 648 (QB)**) although an earlier judgment in the ***Tillman*** litigation warned against taking too narrow an approach to what the employee's responsibilities were at the time of the appointment. Tillman was in a far more senior, promoted role at the time of her departure than when she was first appointed but, even in her more junior status, the High Court held that it was also important to consider what the parties contemplated, such as the employer's view that Tillman would progress rapidly (***Egon Zehnder Ltd* v *Tillman* [2017] EWHC 1278 (Ch)**).[2]

[1] Legitimate business interests could also include the protection of confidential information. The point of this introduction is not to describe in detail the background to restrictive covenants but to reassure the examiner that you understand what the question is about and that you appreciate the fundamental tension between protecting business interests while not being unreasonably restrictive on the employee.

[2] Shows good knowledge of the whole *Tillman* litigation rather than merely the Supreme Court case.

The doctrine of severability is a method by which a covenant that is too wide may nevertheless be made reasonable by removing or 'severing' parts of it. In what circumstances will the rule be engaged?[3] The Supreme Court considered the question of restrictive covenants for the first time in ***Tillman* v *Egon Zehnder Ltd* [2019] UKSC 32** and, particularly, the question of severability.

[3] Using questions can be a concise way of focussing on the precise issue to be examined.

In ***Tillman***, the employee entered into a contract of employment dated 10 December 2003 containing five restraints on her activities for a period of six months following the termination of her employment. Despite Tillman being promoted to senior roles during her employment with the company, the agreement of December 2003 was never updated. The particular covenant at the heart of the Supreme Court litigation was one stating that for a period of six months following the end of her appointment she would not 'directly or indirectly engage or be concerned or interested in any business carried on in competition with any of the businesses of the Company or any Group Company which were carried on at the Termination Date or during the period of 12 months prior to that date and with which you were materially concerned during such period'.[4]

[4] In an exam, you would not be expected to recite the precise contents of a clause.

The prohibition on 'being interested in' any business in competition with her former employer was, argued Tillman, unnecessarily broad. This would, in effect, prevent her from holding a minor shareholding in a rival company.[5] The company conceded that if the restriction were to apply to owning a small shareholding (it argued that it did not), then it would be an unreasonable restraint. However, it argued that it was open to the court to sever the phrase 'or be interested in' so that the remainder of the clause would be valid. Removing a phrase in this way is often known as the 'blue pencil' rule, meaning that the courts can take a pencil to the offending phrase and score through it. The Court of Appeal refused to sever the offending words. First, it held that the clause would still be too wide even if the words 'or interested' were to be removed. Second, it was 'well settled' that parts of a single covenant cannot be severed; only distinct covenants can be severed. This was the finding in the much earlier case of ***Attwood* v *Lamont* [1920] 3 KB 571**, which was followed more recently in ***Beckett Investment Management Group Ltd* v *Hall* [2007] EWCA Civ 613**. In ***Beckett***, the court reminded us of the three tests for determining when wording could be severed: (1) the unenforceable provision can be removed without it being necessary to add or change the remaining wording; (2) the remaining terms continue to be supported by adequate consideration; and (3) removing the unenforceable provision does not so change the contract that it becomes an agreement that the parties had not entered into.[6]

The Supreme Court declined to follow the Court of Appeal and held that the offending wording could be severed. Reviewing the three-stage test in ***Beckett*** on which the Court of Appeal relied, Lord Wilson (the remainder of the court agreed with him[7]) concluded that: (1) the blue pencil test remains good law and acts as an 'appropriate brake' on employers who could easily argue for words to be removed to make good a covenant it has itself drafted; and (2) adequate consideration must be given for the remaining terms. Turning to the third criterion, Lord Wilson considered that this would be better expressed as 'being whether removal of the provision would not generate any major change in the overall effect of all the post-employment restraints in the contract'. The burden falls to the employer to show that removing the wording would not result in a major change. Applying this reasoning to the facts of the present case, the Supreme Court held in favour of the company that the offending words could be severed because there would be no need to modify the remaining wording and it would not generate any major change in the overall effect of the covenant.

Has the Supreme Court provided greater clarity in this area?[8] The Supreme Court judgment has certainly provided a welcome review of the authorities in this area and Lord Wilson's recasting of the third criterion on severability to ask whether removal generates a major

[5] Here remembering the precise wording is important as it helps illustrate the central issue that the Supreme Court had to determine.

[6] This demonstrates that you understand why the Court of Appeal reached the decision it did. It also leads on to the discussion later on in your answer.

[7] Be sure to engage with any dissenting judgments or those that agree with the majority but for different reasons.

[8] Refers back to the wording of the question.

change in the overall effect of the restraint is arguably clearer than the previous ***Beckett*** formulation. However, there remain two areas where further questions remain. The first is what is meant by 'major change' and the threshold required. The second is a practical question. Although the Supreme Court found for the employer and the winning party will typically recover the majority of its costs, the court suggested that there might be a 'sting in the tail' when it came to recovering costs due to the 'legal litter' that the employer had left for others to clear up. This suggests that employers would be better taking care when drafting to ensure that a covenant goes no further than necessary. If the courts have to sever wording to make the covenant enforceable, it may well be that they will not be sympathetic to allowing a successful employer to recover most of its costs.

## LOOKING FOR EXTRA MARKS?

- Read case notes on leading judgments in any respected law journal. Not only will these provide you with excellent examples of how to write a case analysis, they also contain very helpful discussion of the tricky parts of judgments and of any remaining questions.

## TAKING THINGS FURTHER

- A. Bogg, 'Good faith in the contract of employment: A case of the English reserve? (2011) 32(3) *Comparative Labor Law and Policy Journal* 729

  *Analyses the role of the implied term of mutual trust and confidence in preventing the disappointment of an employee's reasonable expectations with reference to four main ways it achieves this aim*
- D. Brodie, 'Fair dealing and the world of work' (2014) 43(1) *Industrial Law Journal* 29

  *Discusses the concept of fair dealing and obligations of fidelity on employees*
- D. Ryan, 'Restating Restraint of Trade: The Implications of the Supreme Court's Judgment in *Tillman v Egon Zehnder Limited*' (2020) 49(4) *Industrial Law Journal* 595

  *Provides detailed analysis of the doctrine of restraint of trade and particularly the rules on severance discussed in* **Tillman**

## Online resources

www.oup.com/uk/qanda/

For extra essay and problem questions on this topic, as well as advice on revision and exam technique, please visit the online resources.

# Termination of the contract of employment

# 4

## ARE YOU READY?

In order to attempt the questions in this chapter, you must have covered the following areas in your revision:

- The different ways in which the employment contract may be terminated
- Which of the different modes of termination amount to a dismissal for common law or statutory purposes
- The requirement for a dismissal for the rights of wrongful dismissal, unfair dismissal, and a redundancy payment
- The rules regarding reasonable notice
- 'Elective' and 'automatic' theories of termination

## KEY DEBATES

**Debate: Relevance of general contract law doctrines**

Although much of the employment relationship is now governed by statute, in the area of termination of contract, general contract law doctrines (such as the law on frustration) are still relevant. How helpful is it to continue to apply general contract law principles to the contract of employment?

**Debate: Reasonable notice rule**

Is the common law rule that an employer may terminate the contract on giving a reasonable period of notice satisfactory? What advantages and disadvantages might this rule have for employers and employees?

**Debate: Elective v automatic theory of termination**

Two theories (elective and automatic) have been used to explain repudiatory breaches of contract. What are the pros and cons of each theory?

## QUESTION 1

**Two theories have typically been used to explain the effect of a repudiatory breach of contract: elective and automatic. Critically assess each concept. Which do you find more persuasive and why?**

## CAUTION!

- Although this question will require brief discussion of termination of the employment contract generally, it is necessary to have a deep and secure understanding of these two theories and the case of ***Société Générale (London Branch)* v *Geys*** **[2013] 1 AC 523**.
- You are asked explicitly to 'critically assess' each concept. This means that you have to go beyond describing the concepts but instead discuss the advantages and disadvantages of each one.
- The question directs you to explain which concept you prefer and to explain why. Engaging with the majority and dissenting judgments in ***Geys***, together with relevant academic commentary, will help you formulate your own views and also provide important authority to support any arguments you make.

## DIAGRAM ANSWER PLAN

Relevance of repudiatory breach in employment relationship

↓

Elective theory

↓

Automatic theory

↓

Did the majority in *Geys* reach the correct judgment?

## SUGGESTED ANSWER

When it comes to a repudiatory breach of the contract of employment, two theories have typically been deployed to explain its effect. As its name suggests, the 'automatic' theory explains that when confronted with the employer's repudiatory breach, the contract is automatically terminated. By contrast, the elective theory suggests that in these circumstances the employee can elect (or choose) whether to accept the breach and consider themselves wrongfully dismissed or, alternatively, to affirm the contract. In this essay, I will examine[1] both theories and argue[2] that while problems exist with the elective theory of termination, it is nevertheless the more persuasive of the two.

[1] Check with your module leader whether writing in the first person is allowed. In this question you are asked to give your view so using 'I' seems appropriate here.

[2] Tell the reader in the introduction what you will argue in your answer.

It is typically accepted that in cases of constructive wrongful dismissal an employee can elect whether or not to continue with the employment contract (***Gunton* v *Richmond upon Thames London Borough Council* [1981] 1 Ch 448; *Rigby* v *Ferodo Ltd* [1987] IRLR 516**). Even in the case of an employer's unilateral reduction in wages, the House of Lords held that the elective theory continued to apply and the employee could choose whether or not to affirm the contract (***Rigby***). While this theory accords with general principles of contract law regarding repudiatory breach and is attractive in permitting the innocent party to the contract to decide whether or not to continue with the contract, it is difficult to reconcile[3] with those cases of repudiatory breach where the employer's breach amounts to an outright wrongful dismissal. In such a case where an employee has been dismissed outright, it makes little sense to suggest that they have the choice as to whether to continue in the employment contract especially as, taken to its logical conclusion, this would mean that the employee could compel the employer to continue to provide them with work and wages. In short, as Cabrelli and Zahn[4] (D. Cabrelli and R. Zahn, 'The elective and automatic theories of termination at common law: resolving the conundrum' (2012) 41(3) *Industrial Law Journal* 346) have shown, the elective theory sits uncomfortably with the reality of the employment relationship in cases where the employer has dismissed the employee outright. One way around this situation was to presume, as suggested by the Court of Appeal in ***Gunton***, that the employee's acceptance of a wrongful dismissal in repudiatory breach should be 'easily inferred'. In this way, the elective theory would still apply as it would be inferred that the employee had elected or chosen to accept the breach rather than affirm the contract. The problem with this solution[5] is that in attempting to ensure doctrinal coherence, the Court of Appeal introduced a layer of artificiality. It cannot really be said that an employee is exercising genuine choice to accept the breach or affirm the contract in circumstances where acceptance is so easily inferred. Indeed, the Court of Appeal subsequently expressed its disquiet with this stance in a later case of ***Boyo* v *London Borough of Lambeth* [1994] ICR 727**, where they preferred the need for 'real acceptance' of the contract.

[3] This statement gets to the heart of why the debate is so contentious.

[4] This shows clear engagement with academic authority in the area.

[5] Here the answer goes beyond describing the principle to analysing it by reflecting on its weaknesses.

The difficulty in applying the elective theory under general contract principles to the particular situation of wrongful repudiation of the employment contract was again considered by the Supreme Court in ***Société Générale (London Branch)* v *Geys* [2013] 1 AC 523.** In this case,[6] Geys was told that he was to be dismissed with immediate effect but no reasons were given for the employer's decision. A couple of weeks later, the employer paid a sum on money into Geys's account but did not explain what it represented. A short while after that, Geys wrote to his employer and affirmed the contract. In response, his employer stated that his employment contract had been terminated with immediate effect and that Geys had received a payment in lieu of notice. The key question in this case was the effective date of termination and this required consideration of whether the automatic or elective theory of termination applied. If it was the former, the contract would have terminated automatically with the employer's repudiatory breach when it dismissed Geys outright. If, however, the elective theory was preferred, Geys had chosen to affirm the contract. The reason why this was so critical in this case was that the later termination date would have meant that Geys would have been eligible for a far higher bonus payment. In their *Modern Law Review* paper,[7] Cabrelli and Zahn have pointed to the advantages and disadvantages of both theories (D. Cabrelli and R. Zahn, 'The elective and automatic theories of termination in the common law of the contract of employment: conundrum resolved? (2013) 76(6) *Modern Law Review* 1106). The elective theory respects the autonomy of the individual and lends weight to the views of the innocent party but it is 'artificial' as the employment relationship is over. On the contrary, the automatic theory sits more comfortably with the reality of the situation and the fact that there is generally no duty on an employer to provide an employee with work.

The Supreme Court, on a majority of four to one, preferred the elective theory. As Lord Wilson explained, if the automatic theory were to be preferred, this would have the effect of rewarding the wrongdoer as they could decide when it would be most advantageous to bring the contract to an end. Moreover, it was clear that Lord Wilson did not want to depart too far from orthodox contract principles stating that 'we should keep the contract of employment firmly within the harbour which the common law has solidly constructed for the entire fleet of contracts in order to protect the innocent party'.

The Supreme Court, however, did not speak with one voice and Lord Sumption gave the dissenting judgment.[8] He was influenced by the nature of the employment relationship and found it 'difficult to see' why the law should recognise a right of election which simply did not fit with reality. Moreover, he argued that the earlier Court of Appeal case of ***Gunton*** had been wrongly decided and that it was not for the law to 'reflect moral indignation' about the way a party to the contract had behaved. In sum, Lord Sumption considered that 'it was always dangerous to allow the law to part company with reality'.

[6] A brief summary of the facts is relevant here to show the practical effect of preferring one theory over the other.

[7] You do not need to give the title for any academic paper you cite. Here two separate papers by the same authors are used as authority so the title of the journal is given to distinguish the paper.

[8] To do well, it is vital that you read the judgments in full. If you rely only on a brief summary from a textbook, you risk missing important information particularly in respect of dissenting judgments.

As Blackham notes, Lord Sumption was motivated by the general contractual rule that an innocent party to a repudiated contract could not insist on the contract continuing unless he could perform the contract without the other party or could compel the other party to perform his side of the bargain through specific performance (A. Blackham, 'Uncertain junctures between employment and contract law' (2013) 72(2) *Industrial Law Journal* 269). As it is generally impossible for specific performance to be ordered in the employment context, Lord Sumption was alive to the fact that the elective theory was rendered meaningless when applied to the contract of employment.

Following ***Geys***, it is now clear that the orthodox contractual principle that the innocent party in a repudiated contract may elect whether to accept the breach or affirm the contract also applies to the employment relationship and particularly cases where the employee has been dismissed outright. In my view, this is a welcome development.[9] Were the automatic theory to be preferred, this would have the effect of treating contracts of employment in a different manner from ordinary contracts. While the courts have acknowledged the special considerations that apply in the employment relationship compared to other commercial contracts (such as the inequality of bargaining power between the parties: ***Autoclenz Ltd* v *Belcher* [2011] UKSC 41**), these differences do not justify differential treatment in this area. If the automatic theory were to be preferred, this would arguably have the effect of giving an employer more power in terminating the contract at will. Moreover, as Lord Wilson noted, if the rationale behind the automatic theory is that no remedy of specific performance is available such that it is artificial to follow the elective theory, this might be extended to other contracts of service where performance is dependent on the other party. It remains to be seen,[10] however, how the courts will address the situation where an employee does elect to affirm the contract and seeks some form of equitable relief such as an injunction to continue the employment relationship.

[9] A clear opinion is given as to which theory is preferred.

[10] This shows an awareness of the complexity of the area and a question that remains unresolved by the courts.

## LOOKING FOR EXTRA MARKS?

- Distinguish yourself by looking beyond the reading list to read one or two extra articles. These will likely offer different perspectives which will help inform your views and make your work stand out from that of others who have concentrated largely on the same material.
- Where you are asked to give your opinion, it does not matter whether the examiner shares your view. What is important is that you argue persuasively. Here it would be entirely appropriate for you to argue that you preferred Lord Sumption's judgment in ***Geys*** so long as you can justify your position.

## QUESTION 2

Four months ago, Tina was appointed as head of department at a local college, having spent the previous five years as deputy head of a similar college. She has a contract which states that she may be dismissed with three months' notice. The contract also provides that she is subject to a disciplinary procedure. She found herself the subject of an investigation into her running of the department. The investigation panel found that she had mismanaged the budget of the department by overspending on hospitality. On one occasion, a significant number of expensive bottles of champagne were bought at the college's expense and Tina's expense claim simply noted 'after work drinks'. On another occasion, a double room for two adults in a London hotel was claimed. This was despite the work meeting against which it was claimed only requiring Tina's attendance and it lasted for two hours over a lunchtime. In the panel's view, Tina's overspending constituted gross misconduct. The college has since sent her a letter notifying her that she has been dismissed without notice.

Steve, the deputy head, has been told to 'act up' and take on Tina's management role with some increase in his salary until a permanent head of department can be found. He also has to continue with his own job as deputy head. Steve, who has always enjoyed good health, found that he could not cope with the strain of doing two jobs and has had to take time off work. His doctor has told him not to go back for at least two months and has issued him with a medical note to this effect. The two months have now passed and it is uncertain when Steve will return to work. He is beginning to feel better but he and his doctor think it will be about another two months before he is able to return. The college has written to him stating that the contract under which he has been employed has been frustrated.

**Advise Tina and Steve.**

## CAUTION!

- One of the key skills for succeeding with problem questions is being able to identify clearly the areas of law that require discussion. Here the examiner helps you by mentioning frustration and dismissal.
- Be careful not to discuss claims that are not supported by the facts. It would be tempting in relation to Tina to discuss unfair dismissal but the facts do not give rise to such a claim because Tina does not have sufficient length of service to be able to claim unfair dismissal. Instead the examiner is asking you to discuss wrongful dismissal.
- Some examiners may make clear whether or not they intend a student to discuss matters falling under the Equality Act 2010. There is no such direction in this question but discussion of whether or not Steve has a claim for disability discrimination would be irrelevant (or worth a sentence at most) because there are no facts suggesting that his condition is likely to be long term.
- Remember to include remedy at the end of your answer.

## DIAGRAM ANSWER PLAN

| | |
|---|---|
| Identify the issues | ■ Tina: does she have sufficient service to claim unfair dismissal? If not, can she claim wrongful dismissal? Was she given sufficient notice? Has she been dismissed for good cause?<br>■ Steve: do the facts suggest that the contract has been frustrated? If so, what would be the consequences? If not, has he been dismissed? Has he received sufficient notice? What procedure should the employer have followed? |
| Relevant law | ■ Tina: s86 Employment Rights Act 1996; *Williams*<br>■ Steve: *Marshall*, *Walker*, *Spencer* |
| Apply the law | ■ Tina: insufficient service for unfair dismissal claim; gross misconduct depends on the facts—unclear the severity of her actions so may be cause to dismiss; disciplinary procedure should have been followed<br>■ Steve: sickness for this period of time is unlikely to be a frustrating act; should the employer have been obliged to wait any longer before dismissing? |
| Conclude | ■ Tina: employer may have been entitled to dismiss without notice but should have followed disciplinary procedure<br>■ Steve: contract is unlikely to have been frustrated; he may have been unfairly dismissed |

## SUGGESTED ANSWER

The question states that Tina has been dismissed. She has only recently been appointed head therefore she does not have the two years' continuous employment[1] normally demanded before she qualifies to bring a claim for unfair dismissal (**s108(1) Employment Rights Act 1996 ('ERA')**). There is nevertheless the possibility of her bringing a claim for wrongful dismissal. She has been dismissed and the dismissal has been without notice. On the facts, she should have been given three months' notice as stated in her contract (the statutory period in **s86 ERA** would have been shorter and it is the longer period which applies), but she has been given none. Therefore, the dismissal is 'wrongful'; that is, she has been provided with no or insufficient notice.[2]

[1] This shows that you are aware that unfair dismissal could be relevant but you have discounted it because of Tina's lack of qualifying service.

[2] Clear conclusion reached on the first issue.

The issue then becomes one of enquiring whether or not the college has a 'cause' so that it is justified in dismissing Tina outright in an instant dismissal. Gross misconduct is such a cause, but has Tina behaved in such a way?[3] If there was an express term to the effect that inappropriate or excessive spending is considered by the college to be gross misconduct, there would be gross misconduct (see ***Uzoamaka*** **v** ***Conflict and Change Ltd*** **[1999] IRLR 624**). There is, however, no mention of such a term. Accordingly, implied terms should be investigated. Among examples of gross misconduct are theft, obtaining secret profits, disobeying lawful orders, violence, and, in the case of ***Williams*** **v** ***Leeds United Football Club*** **[2015] IRLR 383**, using the work email system to send obscene messages to friends. In ***Williams***, the court considered that a range of factors should be taken into account to determine whether there has been a repudiatory breach including the nature and degree of the breach, the consequences of the breach, the nature of the employer, and the employee's position.

[3] The issue of cause is introduced by framing the matter as a question. This is a helpful technique to ensure that you remain focused on what is relevant.

In Tina's case,[4] she is in a position of great trust and responsibility as a senior manager. Her employer is an educational establishment and likely to operate under strict budgets, and spending significant sums on champagne for no good reason apart from socialising with colleagues seems excessive. Moreover, although we are not told the location of the college (so it may have been necessary to stay overnight), booking a room for two persons seems highly inappropriate when only Tina needed to attend the relevant meeting. It is likely that such behaviour could amount to gross misconduct, in which case the college will be justified in sacking Tina with no contractual notice and the statutory period of notice also does not apply (**s86(6) ERA**). If, however, there was no cause, then the dismissal is wrongful and Tina could obtain damages for the notice period (three months' salary subject to the usual deductions such as mitigation). On balance,[5] however, her actions would appear to fall within the nature of behaviour that would be regarded as gross misconduct entitling the college to dismiss summarily.

[4] Here the principles that can be abstracted from the relevant cases are applied to the facts of the case in an attempt to determine whether Tina's behaviour might amount to gross misconduct.

[5] Where two different outcomes are available, it is good to show these competing views but you must still reach a view on what you will advise the client and why.

Tina's contract also provides for a disciplinary procedure. This procedure has not been invoked. Therefore, the college is in breach of contract and can be sued for damages in the normal way.[6] The aim of contractual damages is to put the parties into the position they would have been in had the contract been performed. Therefore, damages would be assessed on the basis of: 'How long would the procedure have taken?' ***Gunton*** **v** ***Richmond BC*** **[1990] ICR 755** illustrates the manner in which the courts reach the quantum. There is also the possibility of obtaining the equitable remedy of an injunction to prevent the dismissal taking place. The normal equitable rules apply, for example Tina must come with clean hands. An injunction will also not be ordered where damages are adequate. The type of

[6] A new issue is introduced and a confident and succinct answer given.

injunction that Tina will be seeking immediately is an interim one to preserve the position, the status quo, until trial. Under the law laid down by the House of Lords in ***American Cyanamid Co.* v *Ethicon Ltd* [1975] AC 396**, she has merely to show an arguable case that her employer is in breach of contract, which she is likely to be able to demonstrate on the facts.

Steve may well have been employed for more than two years continuously by the college. Therefore, there is the possibility of both a wrongful and an unfair dismissal claim. However, there is for both claims the requirement of a dismissal and there will be no dismissal if the contract has been frustrated.[7] Frustration bears its normal contract law definition. This means that the contract comes to an end by law and not by dismissal when: (1) performance is radically different from that envisaged; or (2) the contract becomes illegal; or (3) the contract cannot be performed—impossibility—in all cases without either party being at fault. Illness is a potentially frustrating event as sickness means that the contract cannot be performed as intended by the parties (cf. the *Coronation* cases—e.g. ***Krell* v *Henry* [1903] KB 740**, on which see R. G. McElroy and G. Williams, 'The Coronation Cases—I' (1941) 4(4) *Modern Law Review* 241 and R. G. McElroy and G. Williams, 'The Coronation Cases—II' (1941) 5(1) *Modern Law Review* 1). Whether it is so depends on the tests laid down in ***Marshall* v *Harland and Wolff Ltd* [1972] 1 WLR 899, NIRC** and ***Egg Stores (Stamford Hill) Ltd* v *Leibovici* [1977] ICR 260**. We do not know the terms of the contract, including any reference to sick pay. It is certainly likely that there would be some provision in the contract for the payment of sick pay if an employee is on sick leave for a period of time and, in any event, statutory sick pay is available for up to 28 weeks[8] (**s155 Social Security Contributions and Benefits Act 1992**). This suggests that it is not envisaged that any sickness would bring the employment to an end; the statutory system (and possibly the contract itself) allows for a period of ill health. Steve's employment was intended to be indefinite and the job looks like a key one. We know that Steve will return in the not too distant future. We do not, however, know how long he has worked at the college, but perhaps in the light of his job title and the fact that he was trusted to 'act up' it may have been some time. It looks as if no replacement has been found yet. Wages may well have continued to be paid. The employer does, however, want to treat the contract as frustrated and it may be that they can wait no longer before engaging a new person in Steve's post. Certainly, sickness is not the fault of either party.

On balance, it is suggested that the contract is not frustrated and that the letter from the employer could be seen as a breach of the duty of trust and confidence, in which case there is a constructive dismissal. There may be a fair dismissal for illness which is part of the

[7] This shows a clear understanding of what is at issue in Steve's case.

[8] This is a good example (as is the discussion on capability dismissals that follows) of drawing in knowledge from different parts of the course. This demonstrates a realistic appreciation that 'real life' problems do not fit easily into module topics and shows a level of sophistication in being able to make connections across these different topics.

'capability' reason for the purposes of unfair dismissal. All will turn on whether the reasonableness test in **s98(4) ERA** has been satisfied. There has been no consultation with Steve and the employer seems not to have used the doctor's report as a basis for deciding what to do. ***Spencer* v *Paragon Wallpapers Ltd* [1977] ICR 301** suggests that the employer should consider the nature of the illness, the possible length of the absence, the personal circumstances of the employee, the urgency of finding a replacement, and the size and nature of the firm. While there is no evidence as to all of these factors, as ***Spencer*** holds, the question is basically one of whether the employer can reasonably be expected to wait any longer. Certainly, the lack of consultation may be decisive in the mind of the tribunal: ***East Lindsey DC* v *Daubney* [1977] ICR 566**. If the dismissal was unfair, the usual remedies of reinstatement, re-engagement, and compensation (in that order) are available. Note too that Steve may also have an action for negligence against his employer for overloading him.[9] See especially ***Walker* v *Northumberland CC* [1995] IRLR 35** (Colman J) (on stress, also as here) and ***Johnstone* v *Bloomsbury HA* [1992] QB 333** (on overwork, also as here). The former case was a tort action for negligence; the latter a contract case on possible breach of the term of trust and confidence.

In conclusion,[10] it is suggested that Tina may lawfully be dismissed without notice but that the employer should have used the contractual discipline procedure, and that Steve's contract is not frustrated but that he may well have been dismissed unfairly.

[9] This shows that you are aware of the issues regarding a possible stress at work claim. As there is very little information upon which to advise, it is better to highlight that you are aware of the issue but not stray into irrelevancy by discussing the claim in detail.

[10] The conclusion neatly rounds off the question and leaves the examiner in no doubt that you have understood the issues raised and provided a clear answer in relation to them.

## LOOKING FOR EXTRA MARKS?

- Even in relatively simple factual scenarios such as those in this question, it is helpful to use the IRAC method. Many students can explain the relevant law but often find it difficult to apply it to the facts in the question and come to a conclusion. By keeping IRAC in mind, you are more likely to give a full answer and will not miss out steps.
- Although the legal principles regarding dismissal are relatively settled, examples of the types of behaviour that may constitute gross misconduct evolve over time (e.g. the rise of social media has given rise to new grounds for gross misconduct). You can keep up to date with general trends in employment by subscribing to Human Resources and Employment Law websites and newsletters.

## QUESTION 3

**Discuss the non-dismissal forms of termination of employment contracts at common law.**

## DIAGRAM ANSWER PLAN

Distinction between dismissal and termination of contract

Limitations of non-dismissals in respect of important statutory rights

Different types of termination and their associated difficulties

## CAUTION!

- This is a wide question and it would be tempting simply to list the different ways in which the contract of employment may be terminated. While this will show your basic knowledge, the question is asking you to discuss the different forms of termination. This means that you need to show that you understand the particular issues associated with each form.
- When you are planning your answer, give some thought to how you will structure your essay so that it reads well. If you were simply to write 'one way of terminating the contract', 'another way of terminating the contract', 'and another way ...' this would be very repetitive! Strong candidates often distinguish themselves by their elegant writing style so think about how you might make your essay engaging.

## SUGGESTED ANSWER

When considering the termination of contracts of employment, it is tempting to assume that this will only have been brought about in one of two key ways. First, an employee may resign. Second, the employee may be dismissed. The former involves no dismissal; the latter self-evidently does. However, there are many more ways in which a contract of employment may be terminated. This essay is concerned with non-dismissal forms of termination. Aside from the example of resignation, it may appear at first glance that such forms will be limited. As this essay will show, however, there remain a number of ways in which the contract may be terminated without an employer dismissing the employee. This has relevance because a number of important rights, including unfair dismissal, wrongful dismissal, and a redundancy payment, are all conditional on the employee having been dismissed.

The contract of employment is a contract of personal service, therefore if an employee or the employer (being a natural person) dies, the contract is terminated without dismissal. Similarly, if the employer is a company that is wound up by the court, the contract is terminated without dismissal. Dissolution of a partnership also terminates the contract without dismissal. These forms of termination are relatively clear to establish as one party is no longer able to perform its side of the bargain. Where the courts have been more troubled, however, is where it is less clear whether a party is able to continue performance, namely in cases of illness or imprisonment. For that reason, the doctrine of frustration has been engaged on a number of occasions in the employment context.

The contract is terminated automatically by frustration if performance becomes illegal, would produce a result radically different from that agreed, or if it becomes impossible to perform the contract, provided that neither party is at fault. This doctrine is the same as that in general contract law as laid down in cases such as ***Davis* v *Fareham UDC* [1956] AC 696**. If there is frustration, the contract is terminated by operation of law and there is no dismissal (except where the frustrating event is the death of the employer or the dissolution of a company, in which case the event is deemed to be a dismissal for the purposes of redundancy payments: **s136(5) Employment Rights Act 1996 ('ERA')**). Another example of frustration is ***Morgan* v *Manser* [1948] 1 KB 184**, where a wartime call-up frustrated the contract. Employment cases in which the doctrine has been invoked tend to involve either illness or imprisonment. Illness may frustrate the contract, as in ***Condor* v *Barron Knights* [1966] 1 WLR 87**, where the drummer in a comedy band fell mentally ill and could not drum seven nights per week. Where the contract is for a long term or is of indefinite duration, whether frustration occurs is determined by the guidelines in ***Marshall* v *Harland & Wolff Ltd* [1972] 1 WLR 899** (Donaldson P) and ***Egg Stores (Stamford Hill) Ltd* v *Leibovici* [1977] 1 WLR 260**: what were the terms of the contract, including any provision as to sick pay? How long was the job likely to last? (It is more likely that a short-term contract will be frustrated than a long-term one.) What is the nature of employment? (The holder of a key post is more likely to have their contract frustrated than another.) What is the nature of the illness and what are the prospects of recovery? How long has the employee worked for the employer? (The longer the length, the less likelihood there is of frustration.) Is there a risk of a redundancy payment, or a remedy for unfair dismissal, or both? Have wages continued to be paid? What has the employer done or said? Was it reasonable for the employer to wait any longer? The Court of Appeal in ***Notcutt* v *Universal Equipment Co. (London) Ltd* [1986] 1 WLR 641**, the leading authority, held that frustration could apply even when the contract was terminable by a short period of notice. The employee had a heart attack which frustrated the contract. The date of frustration was the day when his doctor told him that he would probably not work again. The fact that the employment was terminable by one week's notice was immaterial when the parties had the expectation that it would continue indefinitely.

A further problem arises in relation to imprisonment. It would seem axiomatic that if someone is imprisoned then that person is at fault and therefore the doctrine of frustration does not apply. However, Lord Denning MR said in ***Hare* v *Murphy Bros* [1974] ICR 603** that frustration was caused not by the accused's misconduct but by the sentence of the court. Sentencing was outwith the control of the parties and therefore the frustrating event was not self-induced. The time of frustration is the date when it is commercially necessary to replace the employee: ***Chakki* v *United Yeast Co. Ltd* [1982] ICR 140**. The main authority is ***F. C. Shepherd & Co. Ltd* v *Jerrom* [1985] ICR 552** where it was held that a contract of employment may be frustrated, but that principle does not apply when the parties have foreseen the alleged frustrating event. An apprentice's contract contained a clause that his employer could dismiss him for misconduct. He was imprisoned. Since the parties had foreseen the misconduct through using terms dealing with the situation in the contract, there was no frustration when the employer was seeking to rely on the misconduct. However, if it had been the apprentice (or employee) who had sought to rely on his own misconduct, there would have been frustration.

Another way of terminating the contract at common law without dismissal is the expiry of a fixed-term contract. The non-renewal of a limited-term contract is deemed to be a dismissal for the purposes of redundancy payments and unfair dismissal: **s136(1)(b)** and **s95(1)(b) ERA** respectively.

As mentioned above, many contracts end by the employee resigning. Again, there is no dismissal. This is also the case for contracts 'terminated by mutual agreement' (***S. W. Strange Ltd* v *Mann* [1965] 1 WLR 629**). Courts and tribunals must be aware that where there is a termination by agreement, there is no dismissal and thus no possibility of a wrongful dismissal, redundancy payment, or unfair dismissal claim, as ***Birch* v *University of Liverpool* [1985] ICR 470** demonstrates. Two members of staff applied for early retirement. The scheme gave them more money than did the statutory redundancy payment system, and compensation expressly covered a statutory redundancy payment. It was held that the contracts had been terminated by mutual consent. Therefore, there was no dismissal for the purposes of redundancy payments and the employee could not get a redundancy payment.

The leading authority, which shows that the courts are careful not to let employers have free rein when it comes to termination by agreement, is ***Igbo* v *Johnson Matthey Chemicals Ltd* [1986] ICR 505**. The employee requested leave to visit her children. She was granted it subject to a condition that if she did not return to England by a certain date, her contract would be terminated automatically. She was not back by the agreed date. The court held that the condition was a means of evading her employment rights and was for that reason void under what is now **s203 ERA**. The court opined that if the employer could insert such a clause, it would do so, thereby depriving employees of their rights.

It is suggested that in general the courts and tribunals show that they are keen not to let the employer determine the outcome of the question of whether or not an employee has been dismissed, for only if there is a dismissal can they deal with the merits of the case. Their jurisdiction depends on a finding of dismissal: where there is no dismissal, there is no claim for redundancy payment, unfair dismissal, or wrongful dismissal.

## LOOKING FOR EXTRA MARKS?

- The tension in the law between courts applying general contract principles to the contract of employment yet acknowledging the employer's upper hand should be clear in your answer. As the case of ***Igbo*** showed, it would be very easy for an employer to insert provisions regarding automatic termination into the contract and so the law has had to develop appropriate safeguards for employees.
- Being able to show the strengths and weaknesses of various forms of termination will allow an examiner to assess your skills of analysis, which in turn will be rewarded with higher marks.

## TAKING THINGS FURTHER

- A. Burrows, 'What is the effect of a repudiatory breach of a contract of employment?' (2013) 42(3) *Industrial Law Journal* 281

  *Provides a detailed analysis of the elective and automatic theories regarding a repudiatory breach of the contract of employment*
- K. D. Ewing, 'Remedies for breach of the contract of employment' (1993) 52(3) *Cambridge Law Journal* 405

  *Analyses the remedies available for a breach of the employment contract*
- A. Sanders, 'Fairness in the contract of employment' (2017) 46(4) *Industrial Law Journal* 508

  *Discusses recent judgments on the contract of employment and considers whether these reveal an emerging duty of fairness in employment contracts*

## Online resources

www.oup.com/uk/qanda/

For extra essay and problem questions on this topic, as well as advice on revision and exam technique, please visit the online resources.

# 5 Continuity of employment

## ARE YOU READY?

In order to attempt the questions in this chapter, you must have covered the following areas in your revision:

- The qualifying periods for important rights including the right not to be unfairly dismissed and the right to receive a redundancy payment
- Exceptions to the minimum qualifying period for certain types of dismissal
- Rights that do not need a qualifying period such as discrimination
- How to determine start date and the effective date of termination of employment
- The effect of certain absences on continuity of employment including the weeks that count in calculating the length of service
- The effect of changing employer particularly in the context of a TUPE transfer

## KEY DEBATES

Length of service is important because many employment rights are conditional on an employee having been employed for a particular period of time. Striking an appropriate balance between allowing the employer some flexibility to dismiss an employee quickly and protecting employees from unscrupulous behaviour underlies many of the debates in this area.

**Debate: Determining an appropriate qualifying period**

The law in this area tries to strike a balance between rewarding employee loyalty and protecting employers. Given the changing qualifying periods for certain rights, to what extent are the chosen periods arbitrary and motivated by political and/or policy considerations?

**Debate: Sharp practice**

Does the law provide sufficient safeguards for employees against employers engaging in sharp practice? Is it too easy for employers to use fixed-term contracts of less than two years' duration or to dismiss employees just before they accrue important employment rights?

**Debate: Incentive to claim other rights**

Does the law have the unintended consequence of encouraging employees to make claims based on rights that do not require that they have been employed for a minimum period of time? Is there a risk that straightforward unfair dismissal claims will be replaced by allegations of discriminatory dismissals or dismissals as a result of whistle-blowing?

## QUESTION 1

Fruit and Veg Ltd, which operates a grocery supply business, has decided to reduce its workforce. It plans to achieve this by operating a 'last in, first out' policy. It will begin by dismissing all those with less than two years' continuous service so that none of the individuals concerned can make a claim for unfair dismissal. The dismissals took effect last week. A number of those who were dismissed believe that they have cause for complaint and come to you for help.

Ambreena thinks that the requirement to have two years' continuous employment before an unfair dismissal claim discriminates against women workers.

Bob joined the company two years ago but has been absent from work for the last three months because of an injury sustained at work. It is not known at the present time whether this injury will permanently stop him from returning to work.

Carlos is a fruit packer who has worked for the company off and on for three years. His work tends to be seasonal and he is laid off when there is little or no fruit to pack.

Devi is an executive who has only been with the company for nine months. She joined because her previous employer, by whom she had been employed for six years, was taken over by Fruit and Veg Ltd.

**Provide legal advice to each individual with regard to their circumstances in relation to having sufficient continuity of employment in order to make a claim.**

## CAUTION!

- The examiner has given you a structure to follow as you are asked to consider each person in turn. Given the limited time that you will have in an exam, take care to be focused so that you deal with all four in sufficient depth. Unless otherwise stated, it is likely that the examiner will award equal marks to each part so it is better to write something for each individual rather than answer two in depth and run out of time for the others.

- Pay careful attention to the instructions. The examiner is asking you to focus on continuity of employment.
- Remember that this is a problem question where you have to give advice to each person. This may seem an obvious point but it could be tempting to discuss the issues in an abstract way, which would mean that your answer reads more like an essay and you may forget to give advice.

## DIAGRAM ANSWER PLAN

| | |
|---|---|
| Identify the issues | ■ Ambreena: does the requirement for two years' service amount to indirect sex discrimination?<br>■ Bob: does absence due to a work-related illness break continuity of employment?<br>■ Carlos: what effect does a temporary cessation of work have upon continuity of employment?<br>■ Devi: is it possible to count service with a previous employer for the purposes of continuity of employment? |
| Relevant law | ■ Ambreena: s19(1) Equality Act 2010; *Seymour-Smith and Perez*<br>■ Bob: s212 Employment Rights Act 1996; *Pearson*<br>■ Carlos: s212 Employment Rights Act 1996: *Flack*, *Sillars*<br>■ Devi: reg. 4 Transfer of Undertakings (Protection of Employment) Regulations 2006: *Spijkers* |
| Apply the law | ■ Ambreena: following *Seymour-Smith*, likely that qualifying period can be justified as a proportionate means of achieving a legitimate aim<br>■ Bob: sickness absence should count towards continuous service (s212 ERA)<br>■ Carlos: likely that breaks may be regarded as 'temporary cessations'<br>■ Devi: if transfer was caught by the TUPE Regulations, she will have sufficient service |
| Conclude | ■ Ambreena: unlikely that she will be able to show indirect sex discrimination<br>■ Bob: likely to have sufficient service to claim unfair dismissal; may have claim regarding disability discrimination<br>■ Carlos: overall require more information regarding how 'temporary' the breaks are in overall context of employment<br>■ Devi: although some factors point to a TUPE transfer, need more information on nature of undertaking and what transferred |

## SUGGESTED ANSWER

[1] Sub-headings can help structure your answer.

[2] This opening sentence and use of the phrase 'raises the question' gets straight to the heart of the issue and shows the examiner that you understand precisely what is under consideration.

### Ambreena[1]

Ambreena's concern that the two-year qualifying period puts women at a particular disadvantage raises the question[2] of whether this policy could amount to indirect discrimination under **s19(1) of the Equality Act 2010**. To succeed in a complaint of indirect sex discrimination, she would need to show that the continuous service requirement is a provision, criterion, or practice that applies equally to male workers but that would put women at a particular disadvantage when compared to men. If that is the case, there is a rebuttable presumption of indirect sex discrimination but the employer has a defence if it could be shown that the provision, criterion, or practice was a proportionate means of achieving a legitimate aim.

This issue of indirect sex discrimination in relation to qualifying service was considered in ***R* v *Secretary of State for Employment, ex parte Seymour-Smith and Perez*** **[2000] IRLR 263**. The complainants were individuals who were stopped from bringing a complaint for unfair dismissal because they did not have the necessary two years' continuous service. They complained that the proportion of women who could comply with the two-year qualifying period was considerably smaller than the proportion of men. The House of Lords referred a number of questions to the ECJ (**[1997] IRLR 315**). The ECJ held (**[1999] IRLR 253**) that the entitlement to compensation and redress for unfair dismissal came within the scope of **Art. 141 of the EC Treaty (now Art. 157 TFEU)** and the **Equal Treatment Directive**, but that it was for the national courts to verify whether the statistics showed that the measure in question had a disparate impact on men or women. The Court accepted that the qualification period could have a disparately adverse effect on women and that the onus was on the Member State to show that the alleged discriminatory rule reflected a legitimate aim of its social policy, and that this aim was unrelated to any discrimination based on sex. The UK government argued that the extension of the qualifying period should help reduce the reluctance of employers to take on more people. The Court was sympathetic to the government's case and accepted objective justification.

[3] A clear answer is given to Ambreena's question.

It would seem unlikely, therefore, that Ambreena's complaint would be successful, as the period of continuous service required is two years.[3] In order to arrive at a different conclusion, it would need to be shown that the government's justification no longer applied.

[4] A fresh issue is raised here. The use of the phrase 'the issue is' is another way to highlight to the examiner that you understand the problem raised by distilling it succinctly. This shows a clear and confident approach.

### Bob

Bob appears to have the necessary two years' continuous employment to make a claim for unfair dismissal but the issue is[4] whether his contract of employment was still in effect during his illness. If so, continuity is not broken as **s212(1) of the Employment Rights Act 1996 ('ERA')** applies. This would mean that Bob would have the relevant period of continuous employment. However, if no contract of employment covered this period, the question arising is whether the period of absence due to a work-related illness is to be counted as part of that two years' service. If it is not, then he will have less than the period required. However, in these circumstances, **s212(3)(b) ERA**[5] provides that any week during the whole or part of which an employee is incapable of work in consequence of sickness or injury counts in calculating the individual's period of employment. There needs to be a causal relationship between the absence and the incapacity for work in consequence of sickness or injury. The absence from work also needs to be related to the work on offer (see ***Pearson* v *Kent County Council* [1993] IRLR 165**). If Bob had been offered different work, for which he was suitable, from that which he normally did, the tribunal would have to decide whether the employee was absent from that newly offered work as a result of the sickness or injury.

Although it is likely that Bob will be successful in his claim that he does have sufficient continuity of service to make a claim for unfair dismissal, there also appears to be an issue related to disability. If he were able to show unfavourable treatment as a result of a disability—**s15(1) Equality Act 2010**—then he might have a substantial claim under that Act.[6] The employer's knowledge of the employee's disability is relevant when considering whether an individual has been treated less favourably for reasons of disability (**s15(2) Equality Act 2010**).

### Carlos

Carlos has three years' service but as a seasonal worker. This means that there are periods when he will not be working. The issue is what effect these temporary cessations of work have on his continuity of employment. According to **s212(3)(b) ERA**, absence from work on account of a temporary cessation of work will not break continuity of employment. The word 'temporary'[7] indicates a period of time that is of relatively short duration when compared to the periods of work. Although it is possible to look back over the whole period of an individual's employment in order to come to a judgment, 'temporary' is still likely to mean a short time in comparison with the period in work (see ***Berwick Salmon Fisheries* v *Rutherford* [1991] IRLR 203**). Thus, seasonal workers who were out of work each year for longer than they actually worked could not be considered to have continuity of employment (see the Court of Appeal case of ***Flack* v *Kodak Ltd* [1986] IRLR 255** where a

[5] This level of precision is required.

[6] This paragraph strikes an appropriate balance between showing the examiner that you understand that there is a relevant issue regarding disability but does not stray too far from what you have been asked to discuss; namely, whether the client has sufficient continuity of employment.

[7] This close analysis of the wording shows excellent attention to detail and the ability to analyse critically.

group of seasonal employees in a photo-finishing department tried to establish their continuity of employment).

Other seasonal workers who were regularly out of work for long periods were in the same position even though, at the beginning of the next season, it was the intention of both parties that they should resume employment (see ***Sillars* v *Charrington Fuels Ltd* [1989] IRLR 152**). However, in ***University of Aston in Birmingham* v *Malik* [1984] ICR 492** breaks in July and August, during which an academic prepared future teaching, were held to be a temporary cessation when judged against the overall periods of work and therefore did not break the individual's continuity of employment. In Carlos's case, one would need more information about the overall period of employment and the periods of absence to come to any conclusion, although the precedents would suggest that he is unlikely to succeed in a claim.[8]

[8] It is never usually a good idea to simply state that more information is required as this can suggest a lack of knowledge or confidence. If it is the case that more information really would be required, say so but spell out the necessary information that is missing.

## Devi

For Devi to have more than two years' service, she will need to show[9] that the time spent with her previous employer will have transferred so that all the previous six years' service can be added to her time spent at Fruit and Veg Ltd. This may have been achieved by the operation of the **Transfer of Undertakings (Protection of Employment) Regulations 2006 ('TUPE Regulations')**. If her work was part of an entity that retained its identity on transfer (see ***Spijkers* v *Gebroeders Benedik Abattoir* [1986] ECR 1119**) then her continuity of service may have transferred also. Where the trade, business, or undertaking is transferred to a new employer, then continuity is also preserved by **s218(2) ERA** and the employee's length of service moves to the new employer. There have been difficulties in defining when a business has transferred rather than a disposal of assets taking place. ***Melon* v *Hector Powe Ltd* [1980] IRLR 447** concerned the disposal by the employer of one of two factories to another company. The disposal included the transfer of the work in progress and all the employees in the factory. The court held that there was a distinction between a transfer of a going concern, which amounted to a transfer of a business that remains the same business but in different hands, and the disposal of part of the assets of a business. Further information is therefore required, in Devi's case, with respect to whether a transfer took place. If the transfer is caught by the **TUPE Regulations,** she should have sufficient continuity of service to make a claim for unfair dismissal as the effect of the **TUPE Regulations** is that the contract of employment has effect as though originally made between Devi and Fruit and Veg (**reg. 4(1) TUPE**).[10]

[9] This sentence introduces a new topic by highlighting what the client will need to prove.

[10] This is a good example of how you can be succinct without being superficial. Here a clear answer is given, the law is applied to the facts of the case, and the full statutory reference is given.

## LOOKING FOR EXTRA MARKS?

- Having to advise four clients means that you will probably have only around ten minutes on each scenario. The key to doing well in this style of question is to ensure that you do not waste time discussing irrelevant points or giving long introductions to the relevant law. Instead, get straight to the heart of the matter.
- When citing statute, be very precise. **Section 212 ERA** is a good example of where **subsection (3)** deals with a number of different scenarios so be very clear about which sections or subsections you consider relevant. As many courses allow you to take your statute books into the exam (check with your module leader), examiners are unlikely to be sympathetic to sloppy referencing (although remember that citing dates of cases and full journal titles is not necessary in an exam)!

## QUESTION 2

**Critically consider the approach of statute and the courts to the concept of 'continuity of employment' in relation to employment protection.**

## CAUTION!

- This is a very broad question so take time to interrogate it carefully and think about how you will structure your answer. The examiner is asking you to consider statute, case law, and the wider question of the purpose of continuity of employment.
- Perhaps the biggest challenge of this question is that there is a lot of material for you to address so it may be difficult to remain focused. For example, when discussing qualifying periods for unfair dismissal, it is tempting to stray into discussing unfair dismissal itself. Instead, remain focused and refer back to the question. As you write, ask yourself 'how is what I am writing helping me answer this question?'

## DIAGRAM ANSWER PLAN

What is meant by continuity of employment?

What are the policy factors behind the approach of the law in this area?

What factors suggest that the law promotes employment protection?

What factors point against the law promoting employment protection?

## SUGGESTED ANSWER

Continuity of employment is important as a number of statutory rights, such as the right to be protected from unfair dismissal, the right to request flexible working, and the right to a statutory redundancy payment, depend upon the employee having a period of continuous employment with an employer. This essay argues that[1] statute and case law attempt to promote a balance between important policy goals of promoting employee loyalty while allowing employers a degree of flexibility to manage recent appointments.

[1] A clear line of argument is introduced to show that you understand the topic.

What is 'continuous employment'? An employee's period of continuous employment begins, as stated in **s211 Employment Rights Act 1996 ('ERA')**, on the day on which the employee starts work. In ***Welton* v *DeLuxe Retail Ltd* [2013] IRLR 166**, the EAT held that the day on which an employee starts work is intended to refer to the beginning of the employee's employment under the relevant contract of employment. This may be different from the actual date on which work commences. In this case,[2] an employee resigned when the store in which he was working closed down. More than one week later he started work again for the same employer in a different store. When he resigned from this second post, did he have sufficient continuity of service to claim unfair dismissal? The EAT held that continuity of employment had been maintained even though more than a week had passed between resigning from one store and starting at another. As soon as the employee had accepted the offer of the new post, a contract of employment had come into existence so there had not been a week when such a contract did not exist, even though he was not due to start work immediately.

[2] A brief summary of the facts of the case gives a clear example to support the point that you are making.

There is a presumption[3] that an individual's period of employment is continuous unless otherwise shown: **s210(5) ERA**. The onus is on those who wish to challenge the presumption to show that there was not continuous service. **Section 212(1) ERA** states that any week during the whole or part of which an employee's relations with their employer are governed by a contract of employment counts in computing the employee's period of employment. A week is defined in **s235(1) ERA** as a week ending with Saturday or, for a weekly paid employee, a week ending with the day used in calculating the week's remuneration. Thus, if a contract of employment exists in any one week, then that week counts for continuity purposes (see ***Sweeney* v *J. & S. Henderson* [1999] IRLR 306** where an employee worked under a contract of employment with the employer during each of the two weeks in question and thus fulfilled the requirements of **s212(1) ERA** despite the fact that the employee worked for another employer during the same period). The employment concerned must relate to employment with one employer (**s218(1) ERA**), although this can include associated employers.

[3] A new idea is introduced in this paragraph.

[4] This demonstrates your understanding of the broader context in which the law is situated; namely, the composition of the labour market.

Given the fact that women are more likely than men to take time out of the labour market for caring reasons,[4] concern has been raised that the rules regarding continuous service may amount to indirect sex discrimination. This was considered in ***R* v *Secretary of State for Employment, ex parte Seymour-Smith and Perez*** **[2000] IRLR 263**. The case was brought when the qualifying period to claim unfair dismissal was two years (this was subsequently reduced but has now been restored to two years: **s108(1) ERA**). The claimants complained that the proportion of women who could comply with the two-year qualifying period was considerably smaller than the proportion of men. The House of Lords referred a number of questions to the ECJ, which ruled (**[1999] IRLR 253**) that the entitlement to compensation and redress for unfair dismissal came within the scope of **Art. 119 of the EC Treaty** (which became **Art. 141, now Art. 157 TFEU**) and the **Equal Treatment Directive (76/207/EEC)**. The UK government argued that the extension of the qualifying period should help reduce the reluctance of employers to take on more people. The Court was sympathetic to the government's case. Although it acknowledged that the qualification period did have a disparately adverse effect on women, it also accepted objective justification.

[5] Here the competing policy considerations underlying the question of continuity of service are discussed.

The rationale underlying this ruling is a somewhat contentious one.[5] Some employers may be reluctant for employees to accrue important employment protections on 'day one' as this would mean that when it is apparent that a new recruit is not capable of performing the role, the employer would be compelled to follow its performance management procedure or risk facing a claim for unfair dismissal. For employees, however, two years may seem like a long time to work for an employer before gaining important protections. This is a point that has been made forcefully by the trade union movement. This is particularly the case for those who may already be in a more vulnerable position in the labour market such as women who have more breaks due to childcare or those on zero hours contracts who may not accrue qualifying service due to the nature of their work.

[6] This provides a clear link to the previous discussion of competing goals while linking to a new idea to be discussed.

A further tension[6] emerges regarding how the law should treat absences from work, i.e. not performing in substance the contract that previously existed between the parties. Such a definition applied to a coach driver whose work was greatly reduced by the miners' strike in 1984. A substantial part of the individual's work was removed but the employee was able to claim a temporary cessation of work (see ***G. W. Stephens & Son* v *Fish*** **[1989] ICR 324**). There are a number of reasons for which a person can be absent from work without breaking their statutory continuity of employment. However, it should be noted that, under **s212(1) ERA**, any week 'during the whole or part of which an employee's relations with his employer are governed by a contract of employment counts in computing the employee's period of employment'. It is only in situations where the circumstances fall outside this subsection that the provisions in **s212(3)** and **(4)** apply. These are, first, if the employee is incapable of work as a result of sickness or injury: **s212(3)(a) ERA**. Absences of no more than twenty-six weeks under this category will not be held to break continuity. The second situation is if there is a temporary cessation of work. According to **s212(3)(b) ERA**, absence from work on account of a temporary cessation of work will not break continuity of employment. The word 'temporary' is likely to mean a short time in comparison with the period in work.[7] Thus, seasonal workers who were out of work each year for longer than they actually worked could not be considered to have continuity of employment (see ***Berwick Salmon Fisheries Co. Ltd*** **v** ***Rutherford*** **[1991] IRLR 203**). In ***University of Aston in Birmingham*** **v** ***Malik*** **[1984] ICR 492**, an individual who was employed on regular fixed-term contracts to teach was held to have continuity. During the summer, the employee prepared for the coming year's teaching and the EAT decided that this amounted to a temporary cessation of work. A similar decision was reached in ***Cornwall County Council*** **v** ***Prater*** **[2006] IRLR 362**, where an individual who worked on a number of assignments as a home tutor over a period of ten years was held to be an employee. The breaks between assignments were to be treated as temporary cessations of work. The third situation that may not break the statutory concept of continuity is absence from work in circumstances under which, by custom or arrangement, the employee is regarded as having continuity of employment. In ***Booth*** **v** ***United States of America*** **[1999] IRLR 16**, the employees were employed on a series of fixed-term contracts with a gap of about two weeks between contracts. On each return to work, they were given the same employee number, the same tools and equipment, and the same lockers. Despite the employees arguing that this arrangement was designed to defeat the underlying purpose of the legislation, the EAT could not find an arrangement that would require, in advance of the break, some discussion and agreement that continuity could be preserved. It was clear that the employer did not want such an arrangement.

[7] This is a good example of PEA analysis being used to illustrate one point. The point is made that temporary cessations will not break continuity and is evidenced by reference to statute. This is then analysed using relevant case law to illustrate how it can be difficult to judge whether a cessation is 'temporary'.

A week does not count for the purposes of calculating continuity of service if during that week, or any part of it, the employee takes part in a strike: **s216 ERA**. Periods when the employee is subject to a lockout do count for continuity purposes. However, in neither case is continuity itself broken.

Although the continuity provisions normally apply to employment by one employer, there are situations where a transfer from one employer to another can preserve continuity of employment. One such situation is when there is a relevant transfer under the **Transfer of Undertakings (Protection of Employment) Regulations 2006**. These Regulations create a situation where it is as if the original contract of employment was agreed with the new employer. Thus an employee's period of service will transfer to the new employer (**reg. 4(1)**). Where the trade, business, or undertaking is transferred to a new employer, then continuity is also preserved by **s218(2) ERA** and the employee's length of service moves to the new employer (see ***Nokes* v *Doncaster Amalgamated Collieries Ltd* [1940] AC 1014**).

In conclusion,[8] it is evident that the law acknowledges that continuity of employment is not always a straightforward matter. Breaks in employment can occur for a number of reasons. However, it is also clear that this area is influenced by important policy considerations regarding who is—and who is not—in scope for certain employment rights.

[8] A clear and coherent conclusion is reached in which the different elements of the question are condensed into an overall summary.

## LOOKING FOR EXTRA MARKS?

- Take a step back from your detailed consideration of the rules regarding the calculation of continuous service to reflect on the policy goals behind them. This will help you reflect on why the rules are framed as they are and will help you analyse rather than describe the relevant material.
- If there are any current proposals for reform in this area or ongoing discussions by relevant parties such as the TUC, CBI, or ACAS, be sure to mention them. The underlying tensions in this area mean that different representative groups may have different views and it would be perfectly appropriate to mention any current debates in your answer.

## QUESTION 3

Mel had been employed by Contract Cleaners Ltd (CCL) for three years. CCL had won a tender to provide cleaning services to Middlesex Airport and Mel had been employed on a contract for the cleaning of the airport during the whole three years of his employment. The cleaning contract was put out for re-tendering. CCL were unsuccessful in obtaining the new contract for work. Instead, the tender was won by New Cleaners Ltd (NCL).

NCL did not take over any of the assets of CCL and refused to employ any of their employees. It preferred to move its own employees and equipment to the airport to carry out the cleaning work.

Mel and his colleagues have come to you for advice. They state that CCL claimed that there had been a transfer of an undertaking in accordance with the **Transfer of Undertakings (Protection of Employment) Regulations 2006**. Mel has been told by CCL that this means that he and his colleagues are now employed by NCL and so are not due any redundancy payment from CCL. NCL deny that there has been a TUPE transfer and have told Mel that he needs to sort this matter out with CCL.

**Advise Mel and his colleagues as to whether the Transfer of Undertakings (Protection of Employment) Regulations 2006 apply in their situation.**

## CAUTION!

- This question is asking you to focus on whether the **TUPE Regulations** apply. This is because the purpose of this chapter is to explore the law on continuity of employment. It may be that in an exam a question on TUPE will be more expansive than this and ask you to consider what rights and remedies the affected employees might have.
- As this question is limited to discussion of whether there has been a relevant transfer in the first place, focus your attention on that rather than on the substantive rights that flow from a TUPE transfer.

## DIAGRAM ANSWER PLAN

| | |
|---|---|
| Identify the issues | ■ What is the purpose and effect of the TUPE Regulations?<br>■ When does a relevant transfer take place?<br>■ What is meant by a service provision change?<br>■ Has there been a TUPE transfer here? If so, what is the effect for Mel and his colleagues? |
| Relevant law | ■ TUPE Regulations especially reg. 3 (relevant transfer), reg. 4 (effect of transfer on employment contracts), reg. 7 (dismissal)<br>■ Relevant case law including *Spijkers* and *Metropolitan Resources* |
| Apply the law | ■ Facts of case suggest that there has been a second-generation outsourcing which will amount to a service provision change<br>■ Mel appears to have belonged to an organised grouping of employees which had as its principal purpose the cleaning of the airport<br>■ The transfer is likely to be protected by TUPE Regulations and Mel should have transferred |
| Conclude | ■ Likely that transfer is a service provision change and therefore a relevant transfer under reg. 3<br>■ Mel is likely to have a claim for unfair dismissal (reg. 7(1)) |

## SUGGESTED ANSWER

The **Transfer of Undertakings (Protection of Employment) Regulations 2006 ('TUPE Regulations')** (which replaced the 1981 Regulations of the same name) were introduced to give effect to the **Acquired Rights Directive (77/187/EEC)** consolidated into **Directive 2001/23/EC**. The purpose of the Directive and the **TUPE Regulations** is to safeguard the employment relationship and contracts of employment of employees in the event of there being a change in employer as a result of a transfer of an undertaking. In this case, if the regulations apply it will be as if Mel's contract of employment had been entered into with NCL Ltd. **Regulation 4(1)** provides that a transfer does not operate to terminate a contract of employment and **reg. 7(1)** provides that any dismissal for reasons connected to the transfer will be unfair. The key issue to be examined[1] therefore is whether there has been a TUPE transfer, such that the regulations will apply.

In ***Spijkers* v *Gebroeders Bendik Abattoir CV* [1986] ECR 1119**, it was held that the key question is whether there has been a transfer of an economic entity that has retained its identity. If the answer is yes, then there is likely to have been a relevant transfer of an undertaking for the purposes of the **Acquired Rights Directive**. The ECJ[2] defined an economic entity as 'an organised grouping of resources which has the objective of pursuing an economic activity' (see also ***Seawell Ltd* v *Ceva Freight Ltd* [2012] IRLR 802**). ***Spijkers*** concerned an abattoir that was sold by a company which then became insolvent. The abattoir was closed for a period and Mr Spijkers was not employed by the new owners. The ECJ looked at the purpose of the **Acquired Rights Directive** and concluded that it was to ensure the continuity of existing employment relationships. The Court listed a variety of factors that might indicate whether the entity had retained its identity and stated that each of these factors was only part of the assessment. One had to examine what existed before the transfer and then examine the entity after the change in order to decide whether the operation was continued. The protective nature of the Directive was further emphasised by the case of ***Schmidt* v *Spar und Leihkasse der Früheren Ämter Bordersholm* [1994] IRLR 302**, which concerned a part-time cleaner[3] in a bank branch office. Here the ECJ concluded that the Directive could be applied to a situation such as the outsourcing of work carried out by a single person. It also concluded that the absence of the transfer of tangible assets was not conclusive. Three important conclusions[4] can be taken from the case of ***Schmidt***. First, the size of the operation was not an issue. Second, the test is whether the activity continued or resumed after

[1] Stating clearly the key issue to be examined helps you retain your focus as you write.

[2] The **TUPE Regulations** implement the EU **Acquired Rights Directive** so you must be familiar with the relevant European judgments in this area to do well in a question concerning TUPE.

[3] Where a case is factually similar to the one in the question, it is helpful to draw attention to this to show why you consider it to be relevant authority.

[4] This is a 'running conclusion' where you conclude or summarise your views on a relevant point before going on to consider how subsequent judgments arguably confused matters.

the transfer. Third, that there need not be a transfer of tangible assets, even in a labour-intensive activity such as the cleaning of a bank branch office. This view was confirmed in ***Merckx* v *Ford Motor Co. Belgium SA* [1996] IRLR 467**, where a company that held a Ford dealership had gone into liquidation. Ford awarded the dealership to another business and the Court held that there had been a relevant transfer, even though no tangible assets had passed to the new dealership from the old. The activity of the dealership continued in the same sector and subject to similar conditions. This approach was followed in the UK in, for example, ***Kenny* v *South Manchester College* [1993] IRLR 265** and ***Wren* v *Eastbourne DC* [1993] IRLR 245**. Both of these cases concerned outsourcing.

Confusion as to the meaning of what is a transfer of an undertaking was then caused by the ECJ in ***Süzen* v *Zehnacker Gebaudereinigung GmbH Krankenhausservice* [1997] IRLR 255**. This case also concerned a cleaning activity but of a secondary school. The Court held that an entity cannot be reduced to the activity that it carries out. The transfer of an activity only, such as cleaning, could not be a relevant transfer. This seemed to weaken the application of the Directive. It could be possible[5] for a transferee employer, in a labour-intensive business such as cleaning, to deny the applicability of the regulations by not transferring any assets and not transferring any of the current employees working on a contract. Following the introduction of the **TUPE Regulations 2006**, however, the concept of 'service provision change' (**reg. 3(1)(b)**) is expressly included as a form of transfer, which is especially relevant to Mel's case. A service provision change[6] takes place when a person (client) first contracts out some part of its activities to a contractor; when such a contract is taken over by another contractor (so-called second-generation transfers); and when the client takes back the activity in-house from a contractor. The change in contractor would therefore appear to be caught here. However, in addition to showing that the activities of the previous contractor are now being carried out by a new contractor, Mel also needs to satisfy the conditions in **reg. 3(3)(a)(i)**; namely, that there is 'an organised grouping of employees,[7] situated in Great Britain, which has, as its principal purpose, the carrying out of activities concerned'. An example of a service provision change can be found in ***Metropolitan Resources Ltd* v *Churchill Dulwich Ltd* [2009] IRLR 700**, where there was a change of contractor providing accommodation for asylum seekers. This met one of the criteria for a service provision change, namely a transfer from one contractor to another of an organised group of employees carrying out the service. The 'organised grouping' must exist pre-transfer and means a team deliberately organised to carry out the relevant work (***Ceva Freight (UK) Ltd* v *Seawell Ltd* [2013] CSIH 59**).

[5] This shows that you understand the consequences of the judgment in a scenario such as the one given in the question.

[6] Here the three different types of service provision change are summarised.

[7] Unlike the summary of **reg. 3** discussed in note 6 above, here the precise wording is quoted from the regulations as this is important. If you were to summarise/paraphrase here, it would appear sloppy.

For Mel who has only ever worked on this particular cleaning contract, it is probable[8] that an Employment Tribunal will hold that a service provision change has taken place. His case highlights, however, one of the problems[9] in second-generation transfers of contracts in that the new contractor is not always aware of all the liabilities owed to employees who transfer across. As a result, NCL denies any responsibility for Mel yet the operation of **reg. 4(1)** means that Mel's contract will be treated as though originally made with NCL. Moreover, **reg. 7(1)** provides that an employee will be treated as having been unfairly dismissed where, as appears to be the case here, the sole or principal reason for the dismissal is the transfer. In this situation, Mel will have a claim[10] for unfair dismissal against the transferee NCL. He has the necessary minimum of two years' continuous service and was employed at the time of the transfer (see ***Litster* v *Forth Dry Dock Engineering*** **[1989] IRLR 161**). Alternatively, in the unlikely event that no transfer has taken place, then his claim will rest against CCL for unfair dismissal and possibly a redundancy payment.

[8] This is a sensible conclusion that shows that while there is some doubt on the matter due to the state of the EU case law, it is probable following the **TUPE Regulations** that a service provision change will have taken place.

[9] This shows a good understanding of the wider commercial context.

[10] Although you are not asked specifically to discuss claims, a brief line or two is appropriate and rounds off your answer nicely.

## LOOKING FOR EXTRA MARKS?

- Your answer could be enhanced by discussing the effect of **reg. 11** and the requirement that the transferor must notify the new employer of certain 'employee liability information'. A brief sentence or two about the remedy that NCL might seek from the old employer if it has not informed it about the transferring employees shows excellent commercial awareness.
- It can sometimes be difficult to understand why, when TUPE appears relatively protective of employees, business transfers ever occur. The reason why transfers take place despite the law providing that a new employer will inherit the old employer's liabilities is that the contractual documentation governing the transaction will be carefully drafted to include indemnities from the old employer. Reading some articles from practitioner journals on TUPE can help you appreciate how TUPE works 'in practice', which might help you understand better the underlying regulatory framework.

## TAKING THINGS FURTHER

- A. C. L. Davies, 'Casual workers and continuity of employment' (2006) 35(2) *Industrial Law Journal* 196

  *Analyses the Court of Appeal decision in* **Cornwall County Council *v* Prater** ***[2006] IRLR 362*** *and considers* ***s212 ERA*** *in detail*
- J. McMullen, 'Transfer of Undertakings: The Purposive Approach' (2019) 48(2) *Industrial Law Journal* 317

  *Examines a CJEU case concerning the implementation of the* ***Acquired Rights Directive*** *in Spain in the context of a service provision change*

- C. Wynn-Evans, 'In defence of service provision changes?' (2013) 42(2) *Industrial Law Journal* 152

  *While the government is no longer considering repealing the provisions on service provision changes (which prompted the writing of this article), this paper provides a detailed analysis of the law on service provision changes and the clarification provided by the* ***TUPE Regulations****.*

## Online resources

www.oup.com/uk/qanda/

For extra essay and problem questions on this topic, as well as advice on revision and exam technique, please visit the online resources.

# Statutory employment protection and related contractual issues

# 6

## ARE YOU READY?

In order to attempt the questions in this chapter, you must have covered the following areas in your revision:

- Preliminary requirements for statutory protection of unfair dismissal such as length of service and status as an employee
- Right to request written reasons for dismissal
- Statutory minimum periods of notice
- The right to be accompanied to a disciplinary or grievance hearing
- The ACAS Code of Practice on Disciplinary and Grievance Procedures
- The basics of the law on unfair dismissal

## KEY DEBATES

The statutory protections discussed in this chapter will often not be examined separately in an exam but instead may form part of a broader question on unfair dismissal. For that reason, the key debates in this area will also be relevant to the law of dismissal generally.

**Debate: Form over substance?**

Much of the law regarding dismissal is concerned with ensuring that a fair process is followed. Is it right that a dismissal can be deemed unfair by virtue of the procedure followed or lack of it? What would be the consequences of not following a fair process?

**Debate: Reasons for dismissal**

Does it matter why you are dismissed? On one view, what matters is the fact that you have lost your job and the consequences that flow from it. On another view, the reason is vitally important when it comes to matters such as redundancy payments or entitlements under deferred compensation schemes, which are often forfeited if an employee is dismissed for misconduct.

## QUESTION 1

Tim has worked as an accountant for Digit & Numbacrunch, a firm of accountants, for a continuous period of 103 weeks. Although he has a three-month contractual notice period, he is dismissed without notice and without any explanation being given as to the reason for his dismissal, although he believes it is because he had an argument with David, the managing director, last week. Sonali has worked for the firm for three months as a receptionist. Sonali has recently discovered that she is pregnant and she informed the firm of this fact yesterday. She was immediately dismissed by the firm, without notice (her contractual notice period is one week) and without being given a reason.

**Advise Tim and Sonali as to their rights to obtain reasons for their dismissal and any remedies available to them under these rights.**

## CAUTION!

- Focus carefully on what the examiner is asking you to do. While it may be unusual in an exam for a question to focus so narrowly on the right to obtain reasons for dismissal (it may be more likely that this topic will form part of a question on dismissal generally), get into the habit of looking carefully at precisely what is being asked.
- This question requires a consideration of the provisions relating to the right to request written reasons for dismissal, including the qualifying period normally required in order to exercise such a right. When you see that someone has less than two years' service, be sure to consider whether their circumstances might give rise to claims other than unfair dismissal or whether they fall within the exceptions to the rule on qualifying periods.

## DIAGRAM ANSWER PLAN

| | |
|---|---|
| Identify the issues | ■ Tim: does he have sufficient qualifying service to claim unfair dismissal? Is he entitled to be given a reason for his dismissal? What notice is he entitled to?<br>■ Sonali: does she have sufficient qualifying service to claim unfair dismissal? Is she entitled to reasons for her dismissal? |
| Relevant law | ■ Tim and Sonali: s92 Employment Rights Act 1996 ('ERA') re right to written statement of reasons for dismissal; s86 ERA on minimum notice; s108(1) ERA re qualifying period to claim unfair dismissal |
| Apply the law | ■ Tim: statutory notice of one week should be added to his service (s86(1)(a)); can request written reasons for dismissal, which employer must provide within fourteen days of request (s92(7))<br>■ Sonali: as she was dismissed while pregnant, she is entitled to written reasons for her dismissal without having to request them (s92(4)) |
| Conclude | ■ Tim: would have sufficient qualifying service to claim unfair dismissal; may request written reasons for dismissal<br>■ Sonali: automatically entitled to written reasons for dismissal without having to request them; possible claims of unfair dismissal and sex discrimination |

## SUGGESTED ANSWER

Under **s92 of the Employment Rights Act 1996 ('ERA')** employees have a right to be provided by their employer with a written statement giving particulars of the reasons for their dismissal, where termination is with or without notice, or the expiry of a fixed-term contract (the provision does not apply to a constructive dismissal: **s92(1)**). This is a valuable right for employees[1] who wish to bring a claim of unfair dismissal, since, to resist such a claim, an employer will want to bring the reason for dismissal under one of the potentially fair categories for dismissal under the **ERA** and employees will be seeking to challenge the reason identified or the procedure adopted by the employer in relation to the reason given. Further, the written statement of the reason for dismissal is admissible in evidence in any proceedings: **s92(5)**. The qualifying period for this entitlement is two

[1] This brief discussion of the right shows not just knowledge but also understanding of why the right exists.

years' continuous employment by the effective date of termination (**s92(3)** as amended), although this is subject to the exceptions set out in **s92(4)** and **(4A)** relating to pregnancy and childbirth, maternity leave, and adoption leave.

Tim has accrued only 103 weeks of continuous employment, so it would seem that he does not qualify[2] for the entitlement as his effective date of termination is the date of termination of his contract (**s97(1)(b)**). However, since he has been continuously employed for more than one month, he is entitled to the statutory minimum notice period of one week (**s86(1)(a)**) which is added on to his period of continuous employment for the purposes of calculating his length of service in accordance with **s92(7)**. By adding the statutory one-week period to his 103 weeks of accrued service, this would give Tim the necessary 104 weeks of continuous employment.[3]

The only difficulty may be if the employer argues successfully that Tim's dismissal was for gross misconduct, in which case the Employment Tribunal may not extend the effective date of termination in this way (**s86(6)**). However, an employer may not categorise conduct as 'gross misconduct' simply in order to prevent the extension of the effective date of termination under the section (see ***Lanton Leisure Ltd* v *White & Gibson*** **[1987] IRLR 119**, in which the EAT held that, before such an argument is allowed, an enquiry on the merits is necessary to determine whether there was conduct to justify termination without notice[4]). This stands to reason as it would be too easy for an employer to simply claim that any misconduct amounted to gross misconduct in order to get round the notice requirements.

Therefore, Tim may request from his employer written reasons for dismissal under **s92**, which the employer must provide within fourteen days of the request: **s92(2)**. If the employer unreasonably fails to provide such a statement, or if he believes that the reasons given are inadequate or untrue, Tim may complain to the Employment Tribunal[5] under **s93** within three months of the effective date of termination. If the tribunal finds that the complaint is well founded, it 'may make a declaration as to what it finds the employer's reasons were for dismissing the employee' and it may award two weeks' pay to Tim (**s93(2)(a)** and **(b)**), which is not subject to the statutory maximum (**s227(1)**).

Sonali clearly does not have two years' continuous employment, having worked for only three months, and adding on the one week of minimum statutory notice would not assist her. However, because she was dismissed while she was pregnant,[6] she is entitled to a statement of written reasons for dismissal, irrespective of her length of continuous employment *and* without having to request it: **s92(4)**. As in Tim's case, if written reasons are not supplied to her, or if she believes that they are inaccurate or untrue, Sonali may

[2] A logical discussion showing how the student is not taking the information given at face value but instead is interrogating the information further.

[3] Clear and confident summary of the issue.

[4] Case law is used to add weight to the earlier discussion.

[5] Mentioning the appropriate remedy always rounds off discussion of a particular point nicely!

[6] This demonstrates a clear understanding of how the law treats the circumstances of pregnancy differently.

apply to the Employment Tribunal under **s93**, within three months of her effective date of termination, for the remedies available under that section, already discussed. She may also claim automatic unfair dismissal if she can show that the reason for her dismissal was pregnancy (**s99(3)**) and would also not need the qualifying period of two years (**s108(3)(b)**). Sonali may also have a claim for sex discrimination under the **Equality Act 2010** since it appears that the dismissal is because she is pregnant (but that topic is beyond the scope of the question[7]).

Finally, the employer would have to follow any contractual procedures applicable in the cases of both Sonali and Tim, otherwise both would have claims for breach of contract.

[7] This is a nice strategy to use to highlight to the examiner that you understand the broader issues but that you are sticking to the rubric of the question by only answering the question set.

## LOOKING FOR EXTRA MARKS?

- Although the instructions in this question asked you to focus only on the right to request written reasons, had the question asked you to comment more generally this would be an excellent opportunity to show how you can advise across a range of topics including unfair dismissal and sex discrimination.

## QUESTION 2

Before proceeding to claim unfair dismissal, employees need to overcome a number of procedural hurdles that exclude a vast number of workers from this important statutory protection. Showing that you are an employee with two years' service is too high a hurdle to jump.

**Discuss. Confine your answer only to discussion of the requirement to be an employee with two years' service.**

## CAUTION!

- Although the rubric may appear a little narrow here (unfair dismissal is covered more fully in Chapter 7), examiners do sometimes ask students to exclude certain matters from discussion. Do not be thrown by this but instead focus on how much you can say about the topic.
- This question touches on other areas of employment including employee status. It can be easy in an exam to get carried away discussing a topic on which there is much to write so keep an eye on the clock and always remember to keep referring back to the question to maintain relevance.

## DIAGRAM ANSWER PLAN

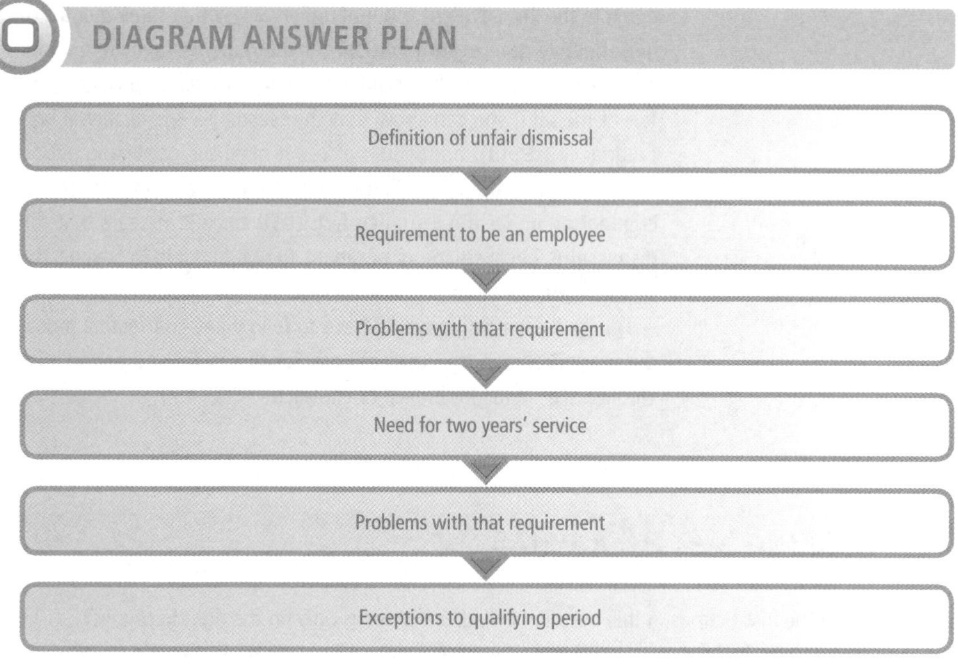

## SUGGESTED ANSWER

**Section 94 of the Employment Rights Act 1996 ('ERA')** provides that an employee has the right not to be unfairly dismissed by their employer. That right relates to 'employees', defined in **s230(1) ERA** as an individual who has entered into or works (or worked) under a contract of employment. While the statute is silent on the meaning of contract of employment, the common law has developed a series of tests designed to help determine the status of a worker. While detailed discussion of this case law is beyond the scope of this question,[1] it is important to note that the matter will be determined on the basis of the facts and through the application of a number of tests. These include whether the employer asserts sufficient control over the person such that it may resemble a master–servant relationship (***Ready Mixed Concrete (South East) Ltd* v *Minister of Pensions and National Insurance* [1968] 2 QB 497**) and whether the individual bears the economic risk in the relationship (***Market Investigations Ltd* v *Minister of Social Security* [1969] 2 QB 173**). In other words, if the individual assumes the financial risk (such as would be the case for a tradesperson who carries out work for a customer who does not pay an invoice),[2] then it is more likely that the individual is not an employee. The terms of the contract must not be inconsistent with employment status (***Express & Echo Publications* v *Tanton* [1999] ICR 693**) and, importantly, there must exist mutuality of obligation

[1] An elegant way of showing that you appreciate the influence of the common law here but that you will contain your discussion of it.

[2] A clear example to show your understanding of the nature of economic risk.

in that the employer agrees to provide the employee with work and the employee undertakes to do it (***O'Kelly* v *Trusthouse Forte plc* [1984] QB 90**). As the relatively recent case[3] of ***Pimlico Plumbers Ltd* v *Smith* [2018] UKSC 29** highlighted, however, the growth in the 'gig economy' has meant that the traditional distinction between employed and self-employed persons has become harder to draw. Many workers may have portfolio careers either through choice or necessity, and the use of zero hours contracts where workers and employers have no obligation to accept or offer work appears common in certain industries such as the care and hospitality sectors. While these workers may be able to show that they are statutory workers[4] for the purposes of **s230(3) ERA** as they may well work under a contract that, while not a contract of employment, is a contract whereby the individual undertakes to perform personally any work or services for the other party to the contract, this will not help them in claiming unfair dismissal. The right not to be unfairly dismissed is only available to the more restricted category of employees.

The second hurdle to jump is that not all employees are entitled to claim unfair dismissal. That right is limited to the even more restricted category of those who have the requisite qualifying period of service.[5] This period has changed throughout the years as successive governments have sought to either expand or restrict the numbers able to claim unfair dismissal. Currently, the right not to be unfairly dismissed does not apply to the dismissal of an employee unless they have been continuously employed for a period of not less than two years ending with the effective date of termination (**s108(1)**). It is not difficult to see how this requirement can impact on certain groups of workers.[6] For example, younger employees who have only recently graduated and are starting out in their careers may have shorter lengths of service as might those with caring responsibilities who may need to move to alternative jobs in order to balance their caring commitments. Furthermore, in some sectors such as construction it may be that the employee is only engaged for a short period to complete a particular project and so it may be unlikely that the two-year qualifying period would be reached.

There is, however, one important exception to these two procedural hurdles. This is where the employee can show that the reason for the dismissal falls within one of the examples of automatically unfair reasons for dismissal. The list of reasons reflects the influence of policy in this area where the legislature has sought fit to declare that certain reasons for dismissal are inexcusable[7] and therefore automatically unfair. These include where the employee has been dismissed due to pregnancy, for being a member of a trade union, or for having blown the whistle by making a protected disclosure (**s108(3)**). While these exceptions are important, they may be of little assistance to many employees who find themselves dismissed with less than two years' service and who have no opportunity to seek redress for what may have been an unfair dismissal.

[3] Employment law is a fast-moving area. In the weeks between teaching ending and the exams beginning, you may find that an important case has been published that is relevant. Speak with your module leader about their expectations here, but keeping abreast of any developments so that you can use that knowledge in the exam will impress an examiner.

[4] This gets to the heart of the issue. Think of employment status as a little like a series of concentric circles with employees with two years' service at the heart in the smallest circle. Then comes employees without two years' service, then workers, and at the outer edges furthest removed from employment protection are those who are self-employed.

[5] Not all employees are equal. Unfair dismissal rights are usually restricted to those who satisfy the qualifying period requirements.

[6] This echoes the wording of the question and helps keep your answer relevant.

[7] Demonstrates your understanding of why there are exceptions to the default rule.

## LOOKING FOR EXTRA MARKS?

- As was mentioned earlier, it is usually more likely that questions about the preliminary requirements for unfair dismissal will form part of a broader question on the subject. However, in a broader question bear in mind that discussion of these preliminary requirements can often be relevant.

## QUESTION 3

### (a) Chris and Fred

Fred has worked for Soopa Doopa Cleaners Ltd for two months. Last week, Chris, his friend and work colleague who has worked for the company for two years, was informed that a disciplinary hearing was to be held in three days' time concerning an incident of fighting at work involving Chris. Chris has been informed of the charges against him and he has been given all the evidence in the company's possession, including witness statements. He has requested that Fred be allowed to accompany him to the hearing, speak on his behalf, and advise him during the hearing. Chris also informs the company that Fred will not be available in three days' time since he does not return from holiday for another four days. He asks for the hearing to be postponed until Fred's first day back at work. Soopa Doopa's manager, Charles, tells Chris that the hearing cannot be postponed and that Fred will not be given time off to accompany him. When Chris informs Fred of this by telephone, Fred telephones Charles and insists that he be given time off to accompany Chris and that the hearing date be postponed until his return to work. Charles refuses these requests and tells Fred, 'Since you're being so stroppy, you can consider yourself dismissed with immediate effect.'

**Advise Chris and Fred as to any rights they may have as regards the disciplinary hearing matter, and indicate the remedies available to them.**

### (b) Tina

Tina has worked as a bar-person for Plinkers Wine Bar Ltd for two years. Over the past two months, she has been thirty minutes late for work on eighteen occasions, with the same excuse, i.e. that she had been partying the night before and could not get up in time for work. Plinkers has a disciplinary code incorporated into all its contracts of employment which states that for misconduct (including lateness) employees will receive an oral warning (after investigation of the matter) followed, in the case of repetition of the offences, by a first written warning followed, in the case of further repetition of the offences, by a second written warning. If the offences are repeated, a final written warning will be given and, if no improvement occurs, dismissal will be the penalty imposed. Appeals may be made to the managing director within seven working days of the disciplinary decision.

After giving her excuse concerning partying on each occasion she was late for work, Tina received an oral warning from Tom, Plinkers' bar supervisor, after her first three late arrivals for work together with a warning that if her timekeeping did not improve over the following two weeks she would receive her first written warning. After further late arrivals, she was given her first and second written warnings with an indication that if her timekeeping did not improve over the next two weeks she would be given a final written warning. As her timekeeping did not improve, Tina was given her final written warning last week. She was told that if her timekeeping did not improve over the next week she could be dismissed. Over the last week, her late arrival on several occasions led Paul, the managing director, to suspend Tina on full pay for three weeks to allow her to sort herself out. Paul warned Tina that any further lateness would lead to summary dismissal.

**Advise Tina of her rights, if any, as regards the disciplinary action taken by Plinkers.**

**(c) Djimon**

Djimon works as a computer software adviser and servicing specialist for SupaFast Internet Technology Systems Ltd. The trade union to which he belongs is in dispute with the company over terms of employment. It has instructed its members to refuse to carry out some of their duties, namely servicing computers, and Djimon has informed his line manager, Terry, that he will not be servicing computers until further notice, only giving advice to customers on software enquiries. Terry informs Djimon that SupaFast will not accept anything less than the carrying out by employees of all their duties, and sends Djimon home, telling him that he will not be paid at all unless he agrees to work normally. Terry also points out to him that his contract contains a clause stating, 'The Company may refuse anything less than the carrying out of all your contractual duties, or your willingness to carry out all such duties where no work is available.'

**Advise Djimon as to any rights he may have against the company.**

**PLEASE NOTE: Candidates must answer all parts of the question. Equal marks are available for each section.**

## CAUTION!

- This multi-part question covers a limited range of topics engaging rights of various kinds. It is possible that one or more of these areas may comprise part of a wider question. Familiarity with these areas may assist in providing a full answer to all the issues arising in that wider context.
- Although the length of the question may be off-putting, do not let it phase you. Break the question down into each part and tackle each one as though it was its own mini-problem question. Also bear in mind that if you are answering three mini-problem questions in the time allocated for a larger question, realistically you will probably have only around fifteen to twenty minutes in a standard three-hour exam to answer each part.

## DIAGRAM ANSWER PLAN

**Identify the issues**
- Does Chris have a right to be accompanied to the disciplinary hearing? What are the remedies for infringement of that right?
- What rights does Fred have in respect of his dismissal?
- Has Tina's employer complied with its contractual disciplinary procedure?
- Has Djimon refused to carry out contractual duties? What terms (express and implied) might he have breached?

**Relevant law**
- Chris and Fred: s10 Employment Relations Act 1999 ('ERelsA') re right to be accompanied; s12 ERelsA re Fred's dismissal
- Tina: ACAS Code of Practice on Disciplinary and Grievance Procedures
- Djimon: *Western Excavating, ASLEF (No. 2), Ticehurst, Wiluszynski*

**Apply the law**
- Chris has the statutory right to be accompanied and meeting should have been postponed as he suggested an alternative date within five working days
- Fred: employer is in breach of s12 ERelsA
- Tina: arguably has been treated more favourably; employer has broadly followed ACAS Code
- Djimon: employer entitled to withhold pay

**Conclude**
- Chris: may complain to the Employment Tribunal
- Fred: automatic unfair dismissal
- Tina: unlikely that her appeal will succeed
- Djimon: no claim against employer

## SUGGESTED ANSWER

### (a) Chris and Fred[1]

Under **s10 of the Employment Relations Act 1999 ('ERelsA')**, a worker who is invited to attend a disciplinary or grievance hearing is entitled to be accompanied by either a trade union official or a fellow worker of their choice. (The term 'worker' is wider than 'employee', which is used in unfair dismissal law, and includes employees and others such as agency workers and home workers: **s13 ERelsA**.) Although the company has not refused his request, its behaviour in refusing to postpone the hearing and in allowing Fred time off to attend it is clearly an infringement of the section. Chris has the right to nominate 'any of the employer's workers' to accompany him (**s10(3)(c)**)

[1] Use the structure implicit in the question to help you write an ordered answer.

and, where the chosen companion will not be available at the time proposed for the hearing and the worker proposes an alternative time within five working days of the proposed hearing date, the employer must postpone the hearing to the time proposed: **s10(4) (b), (c), (5).**

Here, we are told that the hearing is to take place in three days' time[2] and that Fred returns from holiday in four days' time, so it seems that the request by Chris to postpone the hearing until Fred's first day back will be within the five-day period (**s10(5)(b)**), which requires that the alternative time must 'fall before the end of the period of five working days beginning with the first working day after the day proposed by the employer'. It will be a question of fact as to whether the time proposed by Chris satisfies this requirement. Further, under **s10(6)** Fred must be given time off during working hours to accompany Chris to the hearing and the company's refusal to allow this means that Chris may make a complaint to the Employment Tribunal under **s11(1)**. The complaint must be brought within three months of the employer's failure to comply with **s10**, although the tribunal may extend this period where it is not reasonably practicable to present the complaint within this period: **s11(2)**. The remedy is payment of an amount not exceeding two weeks' pay, subject to the statutory limit: **s11(3)**.

Fred has clearly been subjected to a detriment (the dismissal) for a reason connected with his attempt to accompany Chris to the hearing and he may claim under s12. Further, although he has only two months' continuous employment, the reason for his dismissal is an automatically unfair one, for which no qualifying period is required: **s12(3) and (4)**;[3] note that this is one of the very few instances in which a 'worker', as opposed to an 'employee', may bring an unfair dismissal claim.

Under the ACAS Code, which is 'semi-voluntary' in the sense that a failure to follow it does not lead to an automatic finding of unfair dismissal (although compensation may be increased by up to 25 per cent for an unreasonable failure to comply with the Code: see **s207A Trade Union and Labour Relations (Consolidation) Act 1992**), the company should follow a fair procedure, such as that embodied in the ACAS Code as regards both Fred and Chris. The Code recommends[4] that the employer should: (1) carry out sufficient investigation into the problem; (2) provide written details of the problem to the employee; (3) arrange a meeting to discuss the problem (and allow the employee to be accompanied to the meeting where the disciplinary action could lead to (a) a formal warning being issued, (b) the taking of some other disciplinary action, or (c) the confirmation of a warning or some other disciplinary action (appeal hearings)); and (4) arrange an appeal, if requested. Clearly, both (1) and (2) have been complied with in Chris's case,[5] although it seems that the meeting has been delayed because of the problems concerning Fred. The ACAS Code states that 'Employers and employees should raise and deal with issues promptly and should not unreasonably delay meetings, decisions

[2] Repeating the facts briefly draws the examiner's attention to your application of the law.

[3] This level of detailed understanding helps distinguish a strong student from an average one.

[4] The Code is a lengthy document and you will not attract many marks for slavishly copying extracts of it from your statute book! However, briefly summarising the key provisions then relating these back to the question is perfectly appropriate.

[5] Good, clear application to the facts of the case.

or confirmation of those decisions.' Depending on the delay in arranging a hearing, the company may have infringed this requirement.

### (b) Tina

Tina's persistent lateness without justification is clearly a disciplinary matter, and it should be noted that Plinkers' contractual disciplinary procedure is closely based on the ACAS Code. This Code may be particularly important in cases of disciplinary dismissal (see ***West Midlands Co-operative Society Ltd*** v ***Tipton*** **[1986] AC 536, HL**).

Plinkers' contractual disciplinary provisions fairly closely follow the ACAS Code recommendations of a formal procedure, although Plinkers has an oral warning as a first step. The disciplinary action identified in the Code is a first written warning followed by a final written warning where there has been no improvement within a set period, and then dismissal or other sanction. Plinkers' procedure also differs in that it has two written warnings before the final written warning. Further, the company has largely followed its contractual disciplinary procedure for Tina's misconduct, save for the imposition of suspension as the next penalty, rather than dismissal. The sanction of suspension is not provided for in the contractual procedure so such action is technically a breach of contract by Plinkers. However, since the contractual procedure specifies dismissal as the next stage, Tina is in a better position than she would have been had the company strictly followed its procedure. She might lodge an appeal against the suspension, or the period of the suspension, on the ground of breach of contract.

In conclusion, it would appear that Plinkers has committed a breach of contract in suspending Tina. She could appeal to the managing director about this, although she would be in a worse position than if the company had strictly followed its own disciplinary procedure.[6] She could also appeal on the ground that the imposition of the dismissal would be unfair or unreasonable in all the circumstances, but this appeal is unlikely to be successful given that the company has very largely followed its procedure and given her a second chance rather than imposing the dismissal penalty.

[6] This shows a good degree of common sense!

### (c) Djimon

Djimon's action in refusing to carry out all his contractual duties is a breach of the express term of his contract of employment.[7] It is also likely to amount to a breach of the implied terms of obedience, cooperation, and trust and confidence (the first two implied terms may be seen as particular examples of the general obligation implied under the last term). Djimon's refusal to obey a lawful and reasonable order, i.e. to work normally, may justify summary dismissal if it amounts to a repudiatory breach, i.e. one going to the root of the contract (see ***Western Excavating (ECC) Ltd*** v ***Sharp*** **[1978] QB 761, CA**). In ***Laws*** v ***London Chronicle (Indicator Newspapers) Ltd*** **[1959] 1 WLR 698**, Lord Evershed MR said that 'one

[7] This cuts straight to the heart of the issue. Given the time constraints that you are likely to be writing under in a question like this, there is no need to give the examiner a long introduction about industrial action.

act of disobedience can justify dismissal only if it is of a nature which goes to show (in effect) that the servant is repudiating the contract'.

The implied duty of cooperation requires employees to act in such a way as to ensure that nothing is done to obstruct the running of the employer's business. This term was in issue in ***Secretary of State for Employment* v *ASLEF (No. 2)* [1972] 2 QB 455, CA**, in which employees working to rule during an industrial dispute with a view to disrupting the running of the employer's business were held to be acting with a lack of good faith and therefore in fundamental breach of the implied term in their contracts, even though they were not in breach of any express term. In ***ASLEF (No. 2)***, Buckley LJ said that the implied term was one 'to serve the employer faithfully within the requirements of the contract'. Similarly, in ***Ticehurst* v *British Telecommunications plc* [1992] ICR 383, CA**, BT was not acting unlawfully when it refused to allow Mrs Ticehurst, a manager with the company, to work in circumstances where, because of an industrial dispute, she had withdrawn her goodwill and was refusing to work normally (by refusing to sign a declaration to work normally), with the aim of disrupting the efficient running of the business. Mrs Ticehurst was held to be in breach of the implied term to provide faithful service and, as BT was not required to accept part-performance of the contract, it could refuse to accept any performance and withhold wages.

[8] This, and the following sentence, are good examples of how a student can write comprehensively yet succinctly. It says all it needs to say in a clear manner.

Therefore, SupaFast has a choice[8] in the face of Djimon's offer of partial performance of the contract. It may: (1) treat the refusal to work normally as a repudiatory breach, which terminates the contract; or (2) accept partial performance and deduct a sum representing the duties not performed (see ***Sim* v *Rotherham Metropolitan BC* [1987] Ch 216** and ***Miles* v *Wakefield Metropolitan DC* [1987] AC 539**)—this is sometimes summed up in the maxim 'part work, part pay' approach; or (3) indicate that it will not accept partial performance and refuse to make any payment to Djimon (sometimes called the 'part work, no pay' approach: see ***Wiluszynski* v *Tower Hamlets LBC* [1989] IRLR 259, CA**). In the circumstances, the company has taken the third option, and Djimon has no rights to claim against the company.[9]

[9] Strong, clear conclusion leaving the examiner in no doubt of the student's understanding.

## LOOKING FOR EXTRA MARKS?

- In a case such as ***Wiluszynski*** about which there has been much criticism due to the fact that it allows employers to withhold all pay despite partial performance, a line or two about the difficulty with the ratio improves an answer by demonstrating your ability to analyse critically.
- Writing comprehensively but succinctly (as this question requires) is a skill that sometimes takes practice. Working with other students in study groups where you set each other strict time limits for answering questions and then mark each other's answers (you can use this guide to help!) is a great way of practising questions under exam conditions.

## TAKING THINGS FURTHER

- S. Fredman, 'Labour law in flux: The changing composition of the workforce' (1997) 26(4) *Industrial Law Journal* 337

  *Discussion of the emergence of what might be described as a 'two-tier' workforce with differing rights and protections*

- A. Sanders, 'Part One of the Employment Act 2008: "Better" dispute resolution?' (2009) 38(1) *Industrial Law Journal* 30

  *Considers the procedural protections available to employees on dismissal and the ACAS Code of Practice*

## Online resources

www.oup.com/uk/qanda/

For extra essay and problem questions on this topic, as well as advice on revision and exam technique, please visit the online resources.

# 7

# Unfair dismissal

## ARE YOU READY?

In order to attempt the questions in this chapter, you must have covered the following areas in your revision:

- Who is qualified to bring a claim for unfair dismissal
- The meaning of dismissal
- The 'potentially fair' reasons for dismissal
- Whether an employer acted reasonably in deciding to dismiss an employee
- The importance of procedural fairness
- How to bring an unfair dismissal claim
- The remedies an Employment Tribunal can award
- The differences between wrongful and unfair dismissal

## KEY DEBATES

Although the law on unfair dismissal is relatively settled, a number of questions arise in relation to who is qualified to claim unfair dismissal, the procedures that employers should follow, and the impact of outside activities on employment.

**Debate: Qualifying conditions**

Is the requirement of being an employee with two years' service too restrictive? Does it impact on particular groups of workers who may need greater protection?

**Debate: Procedural fairness**

Are the expectations of procedural fairness too lenient or too onerous on employers? Does the law adequately take into account the size and resources of the employer?

**Debate: Outside activities**

How is the expansion of social media impacting employment decisions? To what extent should an employer be influenced by what goes on in an employee's private life?

## QUESTION 1

Alice and Ben are employed by FoodGiant plc, a national supermarket chain, and work on its bakery counter. They are supervised by Cathy. Alice has worked for the company for fourteen months and Ben has been employed for eight years. Last month Ben was given a first written warning for repeatedly arriving late to work.

On Saturday Alice served a difficult customer who overheard Alice remark to Ben that 'I can't stand her'. Alice was not referring to the customer but to a pop star. The customer complained to Cathy who told Alice to 'clear her locker' and leave the store immediately as 'the customer always comes first'.

As Cathy approached the bakery counter to tell Alice to leave, she spotted Ben wearing his outdoor jacket and asked him why he was late for work again. Ben explained that he had arrived at work on time but had been helping another colleague, Dave, bring in some deliveries to the store. Cathy told him that she did not want to hear any excuses and that he could explain himself at a disciplinary hearing on the following Monday morning. When Ben attended the disciplinary hearing, Cathy handed him a letter in which it stated that he would be dismissed with immediate effect due to persistent lateness and would be paid in lieu of notice.

A month has passed since Ben was dismissed and he has received no notice pay. When he called FoodGiant yesterday to ask for his notice pay, Cathy told him that 'he will not receive a penny' as it has since come to light that Ben lied on an expenses claim for a training event he had attended a few weeks before his dismissal.

**Advise Alice and Ben on any claims for unfair dismissal they may have against FoodGiant plc.**

## CAUTION!

- Just because the law on unfair dismissal is relatively settled, that does not mean that it is straightforward. Take care to answer the question in sufficient depth to show the examiner how much you know.
- Be careful not to miss out steps. Take time to consider whether the qualifying conditions have been met, whether there has been a dismissal, and what an employer might argue was the 'potentially fair' reason for dismissal. Remember 'show your working'!
- Read the instructions carefully. In this question the examiner has asked you to consider only unfair dismissal. Had the instruction been to consider '*all* claims and remedies', it would be correct to discuss wrongful dismissal or any other relevant claim including damages.

- In unfair dismissal questions, there may be more than one correct answer depending on how you interpret the facts of the question. By taking time to plan your answer, you can ensure that any conclusion you reach is logical and well argued.

## DIAGRAM ANSWER PLAN

| | |
|---|---|
| Identify the issues | ■ Have Alice and Ben been unfairly dismissed?<br>■ More specifically: do they qualify to bring a claim? Have they been dismissed? What is the reason for dismissal? Has the employer acted reasonably? |
| Relevant law | ■ Sections 86, 94, 95, and 98 Employment Rights Act 1996<br>■ ACAS Code of Practice on Disciplinary and Grievance Procedures<br>■ Key cases of *Burchell*, *Iceland*, and *Polkey* |
| Apply the law | ■ Does Alice meet the qualifying conditions? If not, what is the effect on her ability to claim unfair dismissal?<br>■ Has Ben been dismissed? If so, does the employer have a potentially fair reason (conduct)?<br>■ What procedural steps should the employer take in a conduct dismissal? What is the effect of failing to follow a fair procedure? |
| Conclude | ■ Alice cannot claim unfair dismissal unless she can show that her circumstances fall within the exceptions for automatic unfair dismissal<br>■ Ben may have a claim for unfair dismissal |

## SUGGESTED ANSWER

**Section 94(1) of the Employment Rights Act ('ERA')** provides that an employee has the right not to be unfairly dismissed.[1] Alice and Ben are 'employed' by FoodGiant therefore they are 'employees' **(s230(1) ERA)**.[2] The right not to be unfairly dismissed will not apply unless the employee has been continuously employed for not less than two years ending with the effective date of termination **(s108(1) ERA)**. This preliminary requirement is not a problem for Ben who has been employed for eight years but may be a problem for Alice.

[1] This opening line reassures the examiner that you know the area and can cite relevant authority.

[2] There is no need to discuss the common law tests of employment as it is clear that they are employees. Discussing irrelevant information can waste time and detract from your answer.

[3] Sub-headings can help structure your answer and signpost the key issues.

**Alice v FoodGiant plc**[3]

Alice bears the burden of showing that she is qualified to bring an unfair dismissal claim. There are two possible difficulties that she will encounter: (1) whether she has been dismissed at all; and (2) whether she has the required length of service.

Has Alice been dismissed? The words used by Cathy do not state explicitly that Alice has been dismissed and may have been said in the heat of the moment. In these circumstances, a tribunal will consider what Cathy intended by the words 'clear your locker' and what a reasonable employee would understand those words to mean (***Tanner* v *Kean* [1978] IRLR 110**). Cathy apparently intends to end the employment relationship by telling Alice to remove her items from work. It is therefore likely that Alice has been dismissed due to her contract being terminated by FoodGiant (**s95(1)(a) ERA**).[4]

[4] This paragraph is an example of a confident answer to a subtle point. The facts are discussed briefly, the law is applied, and a firm conclusion is reached.

Where notice has not been given (as is the case here), the effective date of termination will be when it is communicated, i.e. on Saturday (**s97(1)(b) ERA**; ***Kirklees Metropolitan Council* v *Radecki* [2009] ICR 1244**). This can be extended in circumstances where the minimum period of notice has not been given (**s97(2)**). The length of the notice period will be the longer of what (if anything) is specified in Alice's contract or what is provided for under **s86 ERA**. As Alice has been employed for less than two years, she is entitled to a minimum of one week's notice (**s86(1)(a) ERA**). While there may be circumstances of gross misconduct which would justify the employer not giving notice (**s86(6) ERA**), such as theft (***Sinclair* v *Neighbour* [1967] 2 QB 279**), this depends on the facts of each case and it would seem harsh to treat Alice's comment as being sufficient to justify giving no notice. Alice should therefore have been given one week's notice which would extend the termination date by one week (**s97(2) ERA**).[5] This does not help Alice as, in the absence of any circumstances that would point to an automatic unfair dismissal (there is no suggestion of this here), Alice would still have only fourteen months and one week's service and is not qualified to bring an unfair dismissal claim.

[5] A technical point but one which allows you to show off your grasp of detail.

**Ben v FoodGiant plc**

Ben is qualified to bring a claim of unfair dismissal. He is an employee with over two years' service at the effective date of termination and the letter from his employer makes clear that he has been dismissed with immediate effect. He is therefore dismissed within **s95(1)(a) ERA**. The key issues here are: (1) the reason for Ben's dismissal; (2) whether FoodGiant acted reasonably in treating that as a reason to dismiss; and (3) the remedies available.[6]

[6] Clear identification of issues showing the examiner what you will discuss in the remainder of the answer.

FoodGiant has explicitly stated that the reason for Ben's dismissal is persistent lateness. The reason is the set of facts or belief about the employee which caused the employer to dismiss him (***Abernethy* v *Mott, Hay & Anderson* [1974] ICR 323**). For FoodGiant to justify its dismissal, it must show that the reason for the dismissal was one of the prescribed potentially fair reasons. Persistent lateness would fall within the potentially fair reason of 'conduct' (**s98(2)(b) ERA**). Whether it will be considered fair in the circumstances depends on whether FoodGiant acted reasonably (***Mercia Rubber Mouldings Ltd* v *Lingwood* [1974] IRLR 82**).

The question of whether the dismissal was fair must be determined in accordance with equity (i.e. fairness) and the substantial merits of the case, and regard must be had to the size and the administrative resources of the employer (**s98(4) ERA**). FoodGiant is a national supermarket chain.[7] It will likely have a dedicated human resources department, a sophisticated disciplinary process, and sufficient employees to chair disciplinary or appeal hearings.

[7] Good application of law to the context and facts of the question.

***Iceland Frozen Foods Ltd* v *Jones* [1983] ICR 17** remains a highly important authority on how the tribunal will approach the question of reasonableness.[8] The tribunal should direct itself by reference to the words of **s98(4) ERA**, look at the reasonableness of the employer's conduct not at the fairness to the employee, and must not substitute its own decision about what it would have done. The 'range (or band) of reasonable responses' test should be applied. This means that if another reasonable employer may have dismissed, the dismissal is fair even though another employer might have used a lesser sanction. The reasonable responses test has been confirmed by the Court of Appeal in ***Foley* v *Post Office* [2000] ICR 1283**.

[8] Discusses a key authority in this area.

When applying the guidelines in ***Iceland*** to a case of misconduct, the tribunal must also apply the three-stage test laid down in ***British Home Stores Ltd* v *Burchell* [1980] ICR 303, EAT**.[9] Although Lady Hale in ***Reilly* v *Sandwell MBC* [2018] UKSC 16** commented obiter that the Supreme Court had not heard argument as to whether the ***Burchell*** test remains the correct approach, at the time of writing it remains good law. The ***Burchell*** test involves asking three questions. Did FoodGiant have a genuine belief in the misconduct? There is no suggestion that this was not the case. Did FoodGiant have reasonable grounds for that belief? Although Cathy may have jumped to the wrong conclusion, Ben was wearing his jacket and had a track record of lateness. On balance, the tribunal could conclude that there were reasonable grounds to sustain that belief. Did FoodGiant conduct such investigation into the misconduct as was reasonable? This third part of ***Burchell*** needs to be read more broadly: did the employer act in a procedurally fair way?

[9] Another key authority. Here the answer does not discuss the authority in abstract ways but applies each of the questions to the facts and provides an answer to each one.

The leading authority is ***Polkey* v *A. E. Dayton Services Ltd* [1988] AC 344**, which provides that the employer must act in a procedurally fair manner unless it is utterly useless or futile to do so (which would be exceptionally rare). Failing to follow a fair procedure can render an otherwise fair dismissal unfair. It would not have been futile to conduct an investigation. Had FoodGiant spoken to Dave or checked when Ben arrived at work, the true situation would have been uncovered and FoodGiant could have reacted differently. In addition to the lack of investigation, there are other procedural flaws which would contravene the ACAS Code of Practice on Disciplinary and Grievance Procedures. Although breaching the Code is not necessarily fatal to FoodGiant's defence, tribunals can adjust any awards (by up to 25 per cent) for unreasonable failure to comply with the Code. Problematic areas for FoodGiant include giving little notice of the disciplinary hearing and apparently failing to allow Ben to be accompanied to the hearing (had Ben reasonably requested this, he could have been accompanied by a colleague or trade union official: **s10 Employment Relations Act 1999**). Ben appears not to have been given the chance to have his views heard as he was handed the dismissal letter at the hearing and no right of appeal has been given (***Taylor* v *OCS Group Ltd* [2006] ICR 1602**). The dismissal is likely to be unfair for these reasons.

If Ben succeeds in his claim in respect of the reason provided by FoodGiant (persistent lateness), it cannot retrospectively justify an unfair dismissal by referring to a good reason to dismiss which it discovered after the dismissal (such as claiming fraudulent expenses): ***W. Devis & Sons Ltd* v *Atkins* [1977] AC 931**. The conduct can, however, be taken into account when the tribunal considers remedy.

Ben was dismissed one month ago and is within the statutory time limit to claim unfair dismissal (**s111(2) ERA**). If Ben is successful, the potential remedies are reinstatement (same job), re-engagement (similar job), and compensation, which comprises a basic and a compensatory award. The tribunal must look at the remedies in the order stated. Reinstatement within **s114(1) ERA** may be possible on the facts but it is not clear whether Ben would want this (**s116(1)(a)**) or whether it is practicable (**s116(1)(b)**). The tribunal must take into account any contributory fault by Ben (**s116(1)(c)**). Re-engagement to another role would appear possible given the size of FoodGiant (**s115(1)**). If neither remedy is awarded, the tribunal deals with compensation.

The basic award is calculated on a formula based on age, length of service, and week's pay but may be reduced on the grounds of Ben's conduct before the dismissal (**s122(2) ERA**). The compensatory award is calculated according to the headings laid down in ***Norton Tool Co. Ltd* v *Tewson* [1973] 1 WLR 45, NIRC** including loss to the date of the hearing and future loss. 'Loss' means 'economic' loss and does not include compensation for injury to feelings: ***Dunnachie* v *Kingston upon Hull City Council*** **[2005] 1 AC 226**. The tribunal can make a deduction for contributory fault known at the time of dismissal (**s123(6) ERA**). Ben's subsequently discovered misconduct would be taken into account in the general 'just and equitable' provision in **s123(1) ERA**; ***Tele-Trading Ltd* v *Jenkins*** **[1990] IRLR 430**.

## LOOKING FOR EXTRA MARKS?

- Finish the thought! Before you move on to the next issue in a question, be sure to conclude each point by clearly applying the relevant law to the facts and advising the client. Using the IRAC method will help.
- Take care to explore minor points in addition to the more obvious ones. The point about Alice's one week's notice and whether this would have made any difference to her length of service is an example of a small—yet important—point that will allow you to gain extra marks.
- Show the examiner that you realise where there may be more than one answer but take care not to appear insecure or hesitant. Discuss the alternative perspectives then explain which one you prefer and why.

## QUESTION 2

**The courts and tribunals have typically construed the law of unfair dismissal in favour of employers. Discuss.**

## CAUTION!

- Close reading of the question reveals that it invites a discussion of *judicial interpretation* of the law on unfair dismissal. It is not inviting a discussion of the rights and wrongs of the law of unfair dismissal!
- Comparisons with wrongful dismissal and redundancy payments are likely to be otiose.

## DIAGRAM ANSWER PLAN

Judicial interpretation in favour of employees

Procedural fairness

Constructive dismissal

Judicial interpretation in favour of employers

The definition of 'some other substantial reason'

The 'range of reasonable responses' test

## SUGGESTED ANSWER

It may be argued that the **Employment Rights Act 1996 ('ERA')** and its predecessors have, over the years, been construed variously in favour of employees and employers. In this essay, I will begin[1] by discussing how the courts have interpreted the statute apparently in favour of employees, before exploring the evidence that suggests that at times such interpretation has been in favour of employers. In conclusion, I will argue that there is no clear evidence of judicial bias in favour of employers despite the assertion made in this question.[2]

[1] Even under exam conditions, a brief introduction setting out the structure of your essay is necessary. It shows that you have planned what you will say.

[2] Tell the examiner the main argument you will advance.

Sometimes it is clear that interpretation is in favour of employees. An example of this relates to procedural fairness. There is no reference to this concept in **s98(4) ERA**. While the law has fluctuated, a landmark authority was ***Polkey* v *A. E. Dayton Services Ltd* [1988] AC 344, HL**. If the employer dismisses in a procedurally unfair way, that sacking will be unfair unless it would have been futile or utterly useless to undertake a fair process. It may be rare, however, for some element of procedural unfairness not to exist on the facts. It is easy in hindsight to spot flaws in a process as few employers can demonstrate perfection when it comes to procedural fairness. Despite this, the courts have made clear the importance of procedural fairness in an unfair dismissal claim. For example, in ***Charles Robertson (Developments) Ltd* v *White* [1995] ICR 349** an employee had been caught stealing on camera. Nevertheless, Holland J in the EAT was of the opinion that a disciplinary interview had to be undertaken when the employee was long-serving. ***Polkey*** marked the high-water mark of procedural fairness, and the courts and tribunals have arguably retreated somewhat since then. In ***Duffy* v *Yeomans and***

***Partners* [1995] ICR 1**, the Court of Appeal held that the dismissing employer need not act in a procedurally fair manner if a reasonable employer would not have done so. This ruling is one marking something of a return to the 'no difference' rule in ***British Labour Pump Ltd* v *Byrne* [1979] ICR 347** that if going through a fair procedure would make no difference to the decision to dismiss, procedural fairness is not required.

[3] Clear example of critical analysis. The measured tone of this argument shows that the student understands nuance and is evidence of a strong candidate.

It can be added that sometimes interpretation that seemingly has gone in favour of one side or another has subsequently been ameliorated.[3] The best example is the judgment of Lord Denning MR in ***Western Excavating (ECC) Ltd* v *Sharp* [1978] QB 761, CA**. He defined constructive dismissal as a breach of a fundamental term of the employment contract (or evincing an intention no longer to be bound). This determination, based largely on the words of the statute, overruled a line of authority which had held that it was sufficient that the employer acted unreasonably. Since breach of a fundamental term was thought to be harder to show than unreasonableness, which does not require the employee to prove a breach of contract, it was expected that fewer employees than previously would succeed in their claims. However, the development of implied terms over the past thirty years has led to the need for a breach of contract to exist. What would not have seemed a breach, but (merely) unreasonable conduct, may now be a breach of an implied term, particularly that of trust and confidence. Lord Hoffmann in ***Malik* v *Bank of Credit and Commerce International SA* [1998] AC 20, HL**, described this term as a 'default' one, i.e. it applies between all employers and employees. It is now rare for unreasonable conduct not to be a breach of this or some implied term. For example, in ***Hilton International (UK) Ltd* v *Protopapa* [1990] IRLR 316, EAT**, telling off an employee in front of colleagues was a breach of the implied term of mutual respect. The breach must still be of a fundamental term. In ***Cantor Fitzgerald International* v *Callaghan* [1999] ICR 639**, the Court of Appeal said that breach even of a basic term such as that of pay could be insufficient to amount to a breach of a fundamental term where the employer had made a mistake or there had been a breakdown in their technology. It may also occur that what the *employee* thinks is a breach of contract is not. The key example is ***Dryden* v *Greater Glasgow Health Board* [1992] IRLR 469, EAT**.[4] The employer introduced a no-smoking policy. The claimant contended that it had done so in breach of contract. The tribunal held that the change was one of policy not of contract, and therefore there was no breach of contract.

[4] Well-chosen example to illustrate the point.

[5] Good link to the next section of the essay showing that the student has considered both perspectives. This sentence acts as a mini-introduction to the second part of the essay and helps give the essay a clear structure.

Instances of pro-employer interpretation are also evident. Two instances have been chosen to illustrate this:[5] the definition of 'some other substantial reason' and the 'range of reasonable responses' test.

The term 'some other substantial reason' (SOSR) is undefined in the statute but exists as one of the potentially fair reasons for dismissal. Perhaps the most common example of a SOSR dismissal comes from a unilateral change by management to contractual terms as in ***R. S. Components Ltd* v *Irwin* [1973] ICR 535**.[6] Where an employer wishes to amend terms and conditions and cannot obtain the consent of all employees to the variation, it is faced with two options. One is to unilaterally enforce the changes; the other is to dismiss and re-engage the employees on the revised terms. For the purposes of the law on unfair dismissal, the employer is likely to argue that the potentially fair reason for such a dismissal was SOSR; namely, the need to move the employees on to new terms and conditions. These cases demonstrate the width of the category of SOSR and show that even when the employer acts in breach of contract, there may still be a SOSR.

[6] Clear demonstration that the student understands how SOSR is used in real-life situations.

The courts could have restricted SOSR to matters similar to the other potentially fair reasons. After all, the reason has to be 'some other' reason and lawyers should interpret this phrase *ejusdem generis* with the previous items in the list. However, in ***Leach* v *Ofcom* [2012] EWCA Civ 959** the Court of Appeal upheld the SOSR dismissal when it related to a breakdown in trust and confidence. The case concerned an employee who had been arrested but later acquitted of child sex abuse. Notwithstanding the acquittal, Ofcom considered that the trust and confidence between it and the employee had irretrievably broken down and that there would be considerable reputational damage for Leach to continue in the role of International Policy Adviser given the nature of the allegations. The reason must be a 'substantial' one and the Court of Appeal in ***Leach*** was clear that it was not paving the way for employers to use a breakdown of trust and confidence as a convenient excuse for dismissal. That said, sometimes 'substantial' is not given a high threshold. The Court of Appeal in ***Kent CC* v *Gilham* [1985] ICR 227** held that a reason was not substantial only when it was 'trivial or unworthy', a very low hurdle. For example, when dealing with dismissal for efficiency gains, the EAT in ***Chubb Fire Security Ltd* v *Harper* [1983] IRLR 311** asked whether the employer had a reasonable belief that dismissing the employee would be more beneficial to it than the detriment would be to the employee. It would be strange if an employer did not so believe when dismissing in the interests of efficiency. Besides these criticisms, the class of SOSR may be attacked for not being a closed category and for covering instances of dismissal not in accord with modern mores. ***Saunders* v *Scottish National Camps Ltd* [1981] IRLR 277** illustrates both points. The employer dismissed a male homosexual because of its misguided (indeed, offensive) views about gay men and their suitability to work with children. The Court of Session held that the employer had a SOSR despite the lack of supporting evidence but this case was decided before the provisions of the **Equality Act 2010** and the protections on the basis of sexual orientation.

Finally, the 'range of reasonable responses' test found in ***Iceland Frozen Foods Ltd* v *Jones* [1983] ICR 17** gives a wide degree of discretion to employers. If reasonable employers may have dismissed on the instant facts and this employer did so, then the dismissal is unfair, no matter whether the members of the Employment Tribunal think that the dismissal was unfair.[7] There is no reference to this test in **s98(4) ERA**, and over the years the test has come in for trenchant criticism. Nevertheless, it still remains the test, despite favouring employers, and one might have thought that the purpose of the law of unfair dismissal was to favour dismissed employees.

[7] Concise and accurate summary of the test.

As can be seen, the courts and tribunals have neither been uniformly pro-employer nor uniformly pro-employee. On balance,[8] it is suggested that the law itself may be drafted in such a way as to privilege the employer but it would be incorrect to argue that the courts have universally shown pro-employer bias in their judgments.

[8] Effective conclusion. Even if timing is against you in an exam, a brief concluding sentence helps make your essay look polished.

## LOOKING FOR EXTRA MARKS?

- There may well be other examples that you can think of to illustrate arguments for and against the proposition outlined in the question. Rather than rush through a large number of examples with little discussion, limit yourself to two to three points on each side and take the time to analyse each fully. As was shown in this answer, it is perfectly acceptable to say that you have selected only a few key examples to evidence your point.

## QUESTION 3

Hamish has been employed for ten years as a customer services assistant for a large bank in one of its high street branches. He has always had an excellent attendance record but recently has had a number of short-term absences from work due to back pain. Following a referral from his GP to a specialist, Hamish has been diagnosed with sciatica. He tries to manage his condition through regular exercise and taking anti-inflammatory painkillers but when it flares up he finds it difficult to sit for long periods at work. His condition has recently worsened and he is now receiving pain-relieving injections. During his most recent flare-up, his GP completed a 'fit note' in which she informed the bank that Hamish should be fit to return to work in six weeks and that a 'phased return' would be welcome. Ffion, Hamish's line manager, calls him to say that she cannot keep his job open indefinitely and that a phased return is out of the question: 'you are either fit or you are not'. At the end of the six-week period when Hamish is signed off for a further two weeks, Ffion sends him a letter in which it states that he is being dismissed and will be paid in lieu of notice.

**Consider the bank's liability for unfair dismissal, if any.**

## CAUTION!

- Read the rubric! The examiner is not asking you about disability discrimination or wrongful dismissal. Any discussion of irrelevant matters will not score marks, will waste time, and will ultimately create a bad impression.
- One framework that can be used to answer any unfair dismissal question involves the following five steps: qualifications, dismissal, reason, reasonableness, remedy. In other words, does Hamish qualify to bring a claim, has he been dismissed, is there a potentially fair reason, has the employer acted reasonably, and, if not, what remedies are available.

## DIAGRAM ANSWER PLAN

| | |
|---|---|
| Identify the issues | ■ Has Hamish been dismissed for a potentially fair reason, namely capability?<br>■ Has the bank acted reasonably in treating Hamish's absences as a reason to dismiss him? |
| Relevant law | ■ Section 98 ERA<br>■ *Spencer* v *Paragon Wallpapers Ltd*, *BS* v *Dundee City Council*, *East Lindsey District Council* v *Daubney* |
| Apply the law | ■ The bank is likely to demonstrate a potentially fair reason for dismissal, namely capability<br>■ Likely to be unfair dismissal due to bank's unreasonable behaviour |
| Conclude | ■ Advise Hamish that he has good prospects of succeeding in a claim for unfair dismissal |

## SUGGESTED ANSWER

By virtue of **s94 Employment Rights Act 1996 ('ERA')** an employee has the right not to be unfairly dismissed by their employer. The employee bears the burden of showing that they are qualified to bring a claim. The question states that Hamish has been employed (presumably continuously) for more than two years, the qualifying period for unfair dismissal (**s108(1) ERA**). It will be assumed that he is still within the time limit for bringing a claim (three months from the effective date of termination: **s111(2)(a) ERA**, unless to bring it within that time was not reasonably practicable: **s111(2)(b) ERA**). The conclusion is that Hamish is qualified to claim.[1]

The question explicitly states that he has been dismissed by his line manager. This type of dismissal is sometimes called 'direct', 'express', or 'actual' dismissal and falls within **s95(1)(a) ERA**. Since there is an express dismissal, no discussion is needed of any other type of dismissal.[2]

If the bank cannot prove that it had one of the potentially fair reasons for unfair dismissal, it has no defence. The tribunal will, therefore, move to the final stage of remedy. If the bank can prove one of the reasons, it has not (yet) won because reasonableness must be considered.

On the facts, the bank is likely to seek to show incapability under **s98(2)(a) ERA**. In short, it will argue that Hamish is no longer capable of performing the work that he was employed by the employer to do. 'Capability' includes health (**s98(3)(a) ERA**). In ***Sutton & Gates (Luton) Ltd* v *Boxall* [1978] IRLR 486** the EAT advised that tribunals must consider whether the reason is due to the 'sheer incapability' of the employee due to their incapacity or whether the employee was not acting to their full capacity by not fulfilling their talents. In this case, the issue appears to be one of Hamish's incapacity; there is no question that he is lazy or not exercising his talents. A second distinction needs to be drawn between those who are genuinely ill and those who are malingering.[3] As the EAT has held, malingering should be treated as a misconduct issue not a capability issue (***Metroline West* v *Ajaj* [2015] UKEAT0295/15**). Again, there is no question of misconduct here. It is clear that Hamish has been diagnosed with sciatica and has had fit notes to cover his absences.

The reason for the dismissal is 'the set of facts known to the employer or belief held by him which cause him to dismiss the employee': ***Abernethy* v *Mott, Hay & Anderson* [1974] ICR 323**. If a sham reason is given, the tribunal can look behind it. Given the discussion that Ffion had with Hamish before his dismissal, it is likely that the tribunal will conclude that the reason for his dismissal was capability. This is a *potentially* fair reason to dismiss.[4] Whether it was a fair reason in Hamish's case depends on the reasonableness of the dismissal.

The tribunal must consider the reasonableness—fairness—of the dismissal having regard to that reason and to the size and administrative resources of the employer and to equity and the substantial merits of the case. ***Iceland Frozen Foods Ltd* v *Jones* [1983] ICR 17** remains a highly important authority. It makes the points that the tribunal should direct itself by reference to the words of **s98(4) ERA** and must look at the reasonableness of the employer's conduct not at the fairness to the employee. Moreover, it 'must not substitute its decision as to what was the right course to adopt for that of the employer'.

[1] Do not waste time on irrelevant points. This is a confident, no-nonsense start.

[2] Again, this says all you need to say on this issue.

[3] This is a relevant point. Although you can easily discount it, it is important to show the examiner that you have considered (albeit briefly) the question of whether Hamish is malingering.

[4] Shows you understand the significance of **s98(2)** combined with **s98(4)**.

[5] Briefly summarising or paraphrasing a legal rule in your own words can demonstrate understanding.

In other words,[5] it is not open to the tribunal to say that it would not have dismissed Hamish if it were the employer. Instead, it must apply the 'range (or band) of reasonable responses' test. This means if this employer dismissed and a reasonable employer may have dismissed, the dismissal is fair even though another employer might have used a lesser sanction such as demotion, suspension, or loss of pay. This test was abandoned for a brief time but orthodoxy was reasserted by the Court of Appeal in ***Foley* v *Post Office* [2000] ICR 1283**.

As well as acting reasonably in treating an employee's incapacity as a fair reason to dismiss, it is also important that the employer acts in a way that is procedurally fair, which does not appear to be the case here (***Polkey* v *A. E. Dayton Services Ltd* [1988] AC 344, HL**). In cases of long-term ill health, as has become the case here, the procedure to be adopted is quite different from that in other dismissal cases.[6] As ***Welsh National Opera Ltd v Johnston* [2012] EWCA Civ 1046** made clear, it is essential that the appropriate process is used for the scenario in question otherwise a dismissal will be unfair (in that case a musician was unfairly dismissed when a capability process designed for non-musicians was engaged). The leading authority on the procedure to be adopted in long-term ill-health cases is ***Spencer* v *Paragon Wallpapers Ltd* [1976] IRLR 373**. In such a case, the tribunal must consider whether, in all the circumstances of the case, the employer could have been expected to wait much longer for Hamish's return and, if so, how much longer. A number of considerations are implicit in this. First, has Hamish exhausted all the sick pay to which he is entitled? This does not mean that an employer cannot dismiss an employee until sick pay has been exhausted but if, for example, an employer has a contractual sick pay policy that offers full pay for six months, that suggests that the employer is prepared to tolerate a certain level of sickness absence. Second, can alternative temporary cover be provided for Hamish's role? Third, what is the size of the organisation? Here we do not know Hamish's sick pay entitlement. We are told that he has had a number of short-term absences but that the most recent was for six weeks. We do know, however, that Hamish works in a bank in a high street branch and it may be assumed that short-term cover might be provided from an organisation of this size.

[6] The student has spotted that Hamish's absence has now turned into one of long-term absence and the fact that the courts have responded to this differently with different expectations on the employer.

How long should the bank be expected to wait? This involves considering the nature of Hamish's condition. He has sciatica and is receiving treatment for it. He does find it hard to sit for long periods but there is nothing to suggest that he would not be able to continue his role (particularly if he were allowed to move more frequently or stand up from his chair when serving customers). His own GP has indicated that he will be fit to return to work in two weeks and that a phased return with Hamish working his way back to full-time hours would be advisable. It does not appear that Ffion has enquired further of

Hamish or asked for further medical evidence from his GP or specialist to help inform her deliberations (***East Lindsey District Council* v *Daubney* [1977] IRLR 181**). Applying the principles in ***Spencer*** to Hamish's case, it appears that Ffion has acted rashly.[7] No attempt has been made to understand the nature of Hamish's illness or how long his absence might be. Moreover, the fit note is quite clear that Hamish should be able to return to work in a further two weeks. In light of his decade's worth of service to the bank[8] and his previous excellent attendance record, it seems particularly harsh not to wait a further two weeks. No capability hearing has been held and Hamish has not been given the opportunity to appeal the decision to dismiss him. The bank has acted in a procedurally unfair manner and, overall, a tribunal is likely to find that it has acted unreasonably.

[7] Clear use of the IRAC method.

[8] This shows sound commercial awareness and common sense.

The primary remedy[9] for unfair dismissal is reinstatement (same job back); if not, re-engagement in a similar job is the next option (**s113 ERA**). On the facts, reinstatement is possible. It may be what Hamish wishes and it would not seem impracticable for him to get his old job back although the employer's lack of trust and confidence in an employee's capability may be a relevant factor for the tribunal to consider in reinstatement (***Kelly* v *PGA European Tour* [2020] UKEAT0285_18_2608**). The most common remedy for unfair dismissal is the third one the tribunal should consider—compensation—which comprises a basic (**s119 ERA**) and a compensatory award (**s123 ERA**). The basic award is calculated according to a set formula based on Hamish's age, the maximum week's pay, and his ten years of service. The compensatory award is calculated according to principles in ***Norton Tool Co. Ltd* v *Tewson* [1973] 1 WLR 45, NIRC** including loss to the date of the hearing and future loss.

[9] Many students forget to mention possible remedies at the end of a problem question.

## LOOKING FOR EXTRA MARKS?

- When revising, think of simple techniques to help you recall information. One that works for unfair dismissal is to think of the three Rs—reason, reasonableness, and remedy. After dealing with the qualifying requirements and whether there has been a dismissal, the three Rs will give you a structure to deal with any unfair dismissal question and it is easy to remember!

## QUESTION 4

**The statutory law of unfair dismissal has rendered the law on wrongful dismissal obsolete. Discuss.**

## CAUTION!

- This is a quite a straightforward essay question. It is one that may be covered in different ways but essentially is asking you to compare and contrast the two different claims.

## DIAGRAM ANSWER PLAN

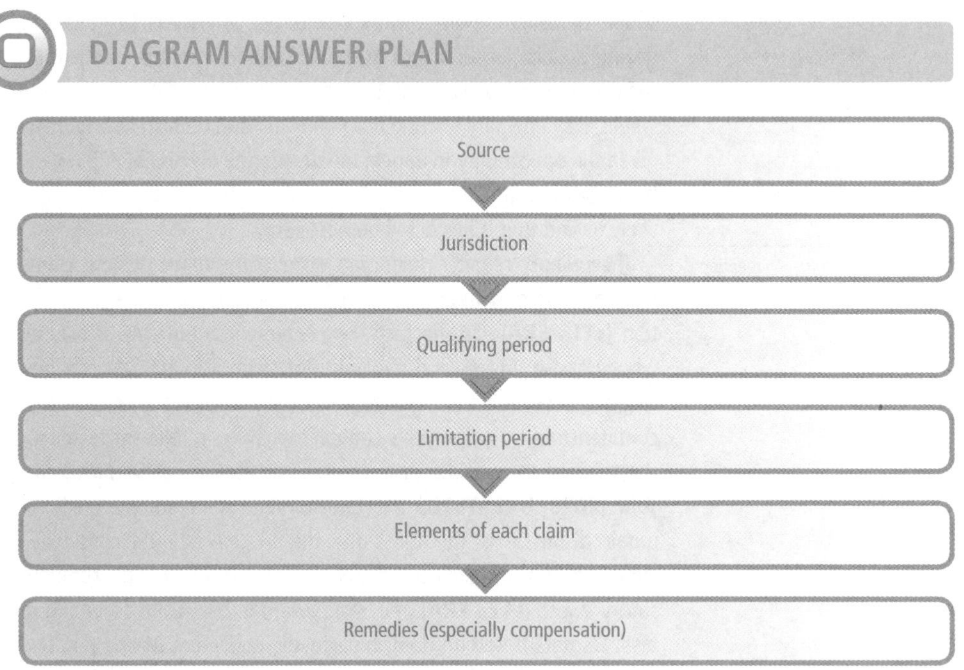

## SUGGESTED ANSWER

In this essay I will compare and contrast the claims for unfair dismissal and wrongful dismissal. While it can be seen that unfair dismissal was introduced in part to counter the drawbacks of a wrongful dismissal claim, that claim still has its place. It would, therefore, be wrong to conclude that it is now obsolete.[1]

Facts can give rise to both claims. For several reasons, it is important to distinguish the claims. Wrongful dismissal is a common law action for breach of contract; unfair dismissal is a creature of statute, originally the **Industrial Relations Act 1971**, now the **Employment Rights 1996 ('ERA')**. One consequence of the different source is that wrongful dismissal was until quite recently[2] only heard in the ordinary civil law courts, the High Court, or the county court, the distinction depending largely on the sum claimed, and unfair dismissal was heard in the Employment Tribunals. However, after lengthy debate, contractual claims for sums of £25,000 and under may now, as a result of the

[1] Every introduction should do two things. State what you will argue and how you will argue it.

[2] When discussing the historical position on any matter, you will need to form a view on how much this is relevant or whether it is unnecessary padding. Here it is relevant to show the development of the claims.

**Employment Tribunals (Extension of Jurisdiction) Order 1994 (SI 1994/1623)**, be heard in the Employment Tribunals. The Law Commission has recently recommended that tribunals be given the power to make awards of up to £100,000 in contract claims to avoid the need for claimants to bring proceedings in two jurisdictions.[3] At present, Employment Tribunals and the ordinary courts have concurrent jurisdiction over such claims. Employment Tribunals can hear claims concerning breaches of the employment contract only if they relate to the termination of the contract, as wrongful dismissal does. They have no jurisdiction over claims arising during the running of the contract. Employers can bring counterclaims against their former employee.

[3] Demonstrates excellent awareness of current debates.

Another consequence of wrongful dismissal's juridical base is that the time limit for bringing a claim in the ordinary courts is six years,[4] whereas for unfair dismissal it is only three months from the effective date of termination, subject to the 'not reasonably practicable' exception, a fairly narrow exception. In legal terms, three months is a short period of time. If a lawyer does not submit the claim form in time, they are liable to be sued for negligence, i.e. the remedy lies against the adviser and the unfair dismissal claim fails.

[4] Limitation periods are vitally important in practice. This shows a student with well-rounded knowledge.

A further consequence of wrongful dismissal being a contractual action is that its foundation is a breach of contract. If there is no such breach, there is no wrongful dismissal. As Lord Evershed MR said in ***Laws* v *London Chronicle (Indicator Newspapers) Ltd* [1959] 1 WLR 698, CA**, 'a contract of service is but an example of contracts in general, so that the general law of contract is applicable'.[5] For the purposes of wrongful dismissal, the dismissal can be express—such as when the employer says, 'I sack you'—or it can be constructive—as occurs when the employer repudiates the contract by evincing an intention no longer to be bound by the contract or they breach a fundamental term entitling the employee to leave. Both forms of dismissal apply to unfair dismissal though repudiation is usually known as constructive dismissal. There is a third type of dismissal applicable to statutory claims only: expiry of a limited-term contract without renewal.

[5] Following **Autoclenz v Belcher [2011] UKSC 41**, employment law contracts appear to be departing even more from general contract law doctrine. This might be worth the briefest of comments but no more; it is not relevant to the question.

For wrongful dismissal, if there is a dismissal it must be 'wrongful'; that is, the employer must have given no notice or insufficient notice. The length of the notice period depends partly on contract, partly on statute.[6] **Section 86 ERA** states that if an employee has worked for under two years, the length is one week; over twelve years, the period is twelve weeks; between two and twelve years, the period increases by a week for every year of employment (e.g. the period is five weeks if the employee has worked for the employer for five years). If, however, the contract provides for a lengthier period, that period applies. The contractual term could be either express or implied; if implied, the

[6] Here knowledge is drawn from different aspects of the course to support the point being made.

period is of reasonable length and what is reasonable depends on the facts. Notice periods form one aspect of the 'floor of rights'; they can be added to by contract but not taken away by contract. However, **s86(6) ERA** provides that notice need not be given if the employer has a cause, a justification, for not giving notice on dismissal. In other words, they may dismiss summarily in certain circumstances. While there is no definitive list of causes, illustrations include[7] theft from the employer (***Sinclair* v *Neighbour* [1967] 2 QB 279**) and disobeying a lawful order (***Macari* v *Celtic Football and Athletic Co. Ltd* [1999] IRLR 787**). A series of incidents can amount to a cause, as in ***Pepper* v *Webb* [1969] 1 WLR 514**. Whether there is a justification depends on the facts of each case.

[7] Examples add interest and demonstrate understanding.

The basis of unfair dismissal is statutory. Therefore, it is governed by statute. In a case where the dismissal is not automatically unfair, the employee must prove that they are qualified and have been dismissed. The burden of proof then switches to the employer to show that they had a potentially fair reason to dismiss such as capability or conduct. If the employer cannot prove that the reason they held fell within one of the prescribed potentially fair reasons, they lose at this stage and the tribunal moves to determine the remedy. If they can, the Employment Tribunal still has to determine fairness, applying **s98(4) ERA**.

One of the reasons for the introduction of unfair dismissal was the failure of wrongful dismissal to remedy a dismissal that was carried out in a procedurally unfair manner.[8] While the emphasis on procedural fairness has changed over the years, the main authority remains ***Polkey* v *A. E. Dayton Services Ltd* [1988] AC 344, HL,** where it was said that a dismissal was unfair if the employer had not acted in a procedurally fair way even though they would have dismissed anyway, unless to go through a fair procedure would have been futile.

[8] This point could even be made earlier if you were to structure your answer by beginning with a discussion of the limitations of wrongful dismissal and the development of unfair dismissal as a claim. There is no right or wrong way to answer this question so this would also be a perfectly appropriate strategy.

There are other important distinctions between both claims.[9] Wrongful dismissal applies to all those working under a contract; unfair dismissal applies only to employees. The qualifying period for non-automatic unfair dismissal is two years' continuous employment. There is no qualifying period for wrongful dismissal. Moreover, the remedy for wrongful dismissal, being a contractual action, is damages aimed at putting the claimant in the position they would have been in had the contract been lawfully performed. The primary remedy for unfair dismissal was intended to be reinstatement, and if not that, re-engagement in a similar job. In fact, the remedy most often used is compensation, consisting of a basic and compensatory award.

[9] This penultimate paragraph shows that you are aware of other differences. If you were merely to list the differences throughout the essay, it would be very descriptive and unlikely to be awarded high marks.

The differences between these two remedies derive from the juridical base of each claim. Unfair dismissal was instituted to remedy the

[10] A very balanced point showing that unfair dismissal is not without its problems.

defects of wrongful dismissal. However, sometimes it can be seen that unfair dismissal is restricted too, particularly the financial cap on the compensatory award.[10] For high earners, the cap means that all losses are not compensated, and there has in recent times been a revival of interest in wrongful dismissal, partly for this reason. It would, therefore, be incorrect to state that wrongful dismissal is an obsolete claim.

## QUESTION 5

Lisa has worked at a local college as an administrator for almost twenty years. Mel joined Lisa's team a few months ago as her line manager. Before taking over Lisa's team, Mel was told by Lisa's former boss John that Lisa 'does just about enough to get by' but that she lacks initiative and organisation. He jokes that he has learned to 'work around Lisa' rather than with her. Lisa's appraisals say little apart from that she meets her objectives with some room for improvement. John confides in Mel that another boss would probably have 'performance managed' Lisa long ago but as she is such a nice person and has been with the college for a long time, it is easier to put up with her. He also comments that it would involve more work for him and 'too much hassle to go down the performance management route'.

Mel has accompanied Lisa to a few meetings with others in the college and has seen how frustrated colleagues get when Lisa cannot answer their questions and also that she is disorganised. She decides that from now on she will attend every meeting with Lisa and has asked Lisa to ensure that every email and letter she sends is checked first by Mel. This has never happened before. Lisa has raised a grievance in which she states that unless this 'bullying' stops, she will have no choice but to resign.

Jenny is a long-standing lecturer at the college and head of the English department. She has recently resigned and is claiming that she has been constructively dismissed. A significant number of students on the foundation degree programme she managed failed their exams, which Jenny marked. The scripts were remarked by two others in the English department and the marks were changed without Jenny's involvement. She was only made aware of this when she attended the exam board a few weeks later. Jenny raised a grievance about these events and an investigation by the college has upheld Jenny's grievance.

**Advise the college on any claims for unfair dismissal that Lisa and Jenny may have.**

## CAUTION!

- The focus of this question is on unfair dismissal only. Although Lisa has alleged bullying, there is little information in the question about issues of stress, for example, so be careful to confine your answer to unfair dismissal.
- Lisa's scenario is often encountered in practice so be discerning before jumping to the conclusion that she will have a sound case for claiming constructive dismissal. If she fails, the law treats her as having simply resigned. From her perspective, she has never been given any indication that there were concerns about her performance so it is understandable that she will be feeling bullied. From the college's perspective, however, it is having to deal with a former lazy manager and a new supervisor who is perhaps trying to be kind but is too overzealous.

## DIAGRAM ANSWER PLAN

**Identify the issues**
- Has Jenny been constructively dismissed? Is it an unfair dismissal? Has the college's investigation acted to cure any breach?
- Will Lisa be entitled to claim constructive unfair dismissal if she resigns? Are there grounds for dismissal for capability/conduct if she does not resign?

**Relevant law**
- Sections 95(1)(c) and 98 Employment Rights Act 1996 ('ERA')
- Relevant cases including *Western Excavating* v *Sharp*, *Courtaulds* v *Andrew*, *Malik* v *BCCI*, *Bournemouth University* v *Buckland*

**Apply the law**
- Jenny's case resembles *Buckland*; likely fundamental breach of implied term of trust and confidence; unilateral action by employer in its investigation will not cure repudiatory breach
- Unclear whether college's behaviour towards Lisa is sufficient to amount to fundamental breach of implied term of trust and confidence; college may have grounds for taking action due to Lisa's poor performance

**Conclude**
- Jenny is likely to have good prospects of succeeding in a claim of constructive dismissal
- Unlikely that Lisa would have sufficient grounds to claim constructive dismissal; any subsequent performance management will need to be handled carefully in light of the fact that her shortcomings have never previously been addressed

## SUGGESTED ANSWER

I have been asked to advise the college on the possible claims that Lisa and Jenny may have for unfair dismissal. In Lisa's case, she has not been dismissed but she has threatened that she may resign. In Jenny's case, she has already resigned and submitted a claim for constructive dismissal. As there is a threat of constructive dismissal for Lisa, I will deal with this issue first for both Lisa and Jenny before briefly addressing the issue of possible dismissal for Lisa's alleged poor performance.[1]

[1] Setting out how you will answer the question is vital in an essay answer but even problem questions can benefit from you explaining your approach.

**Section 94(1) of the Employment Rights Act 1996 ('ERA')** gives an employee the right not to be unfairly dismissed by their employer. This only applies to those employees who have been 'continuously employed for a period of not less than two years ending with the effective date of termination' by virtue of **s108(1) ERA**. Lisa has almost twenty years' service and Jenny is described as long-standing. I am told that both are employed by the college so, in the absence of any evidence to the contrary, I will proceed on the basis that both are potentially eligible to claim. In Lisa's case, there is no effective date of termination as she remains in employment. In Jenny's case, the effective date of termination is unknown. Again, I will assume that Jenny's complaint to the Employment Tribunal has been submitted within the relevant statutory time limit (before the end of the period of three months beginning with the effective date of termination unless not reasonably practicable to present in this period: **s111(2) ERA**) as there is no information to suggest otherwise.[2]

[2] This paragraph deals with important preliminary points but in a succinct way. This shows that you are alive to the issues but are confident enough not to waste time dealing with matters about which you have no information.

For the purposes of unfair dismissal protection, dismissal is not limited to the more usual scenario of when an employer terminates the employment contract (**s95(1)(a) ERA**) but includes where 'the employee terminates the contract under which he is employed (with or without notice) in circumstances in which he is entitled to terminate it without notice by reason of the employer's conduct' (**s95(1)(c) ERA**).[3] This is known as 'constructive dismissal'. In ***Western Excavating (ECC) Ltd* v *Sharp* [1978] QB 761**, Lord Denning set out the approach to be adopted to constructive dismissal and drew from the common law construct of constructive dismissal. For there to be a breach of what is now **s95(1)(c) ERA**, the employer must be guilty of conduct which is a 'significant breach going to the root of the contract' or conduct 'which shows that the employer no longer intends to be bound by one or more of the essential terms of the contract'. In either of those circumstances, the employee is constructively dismissed. Lord Denning went on to caution that the conduct must be sufficiently serious to entitle the employee to leave at once and that the employee must make up their mind soon after the conduct. If they stay, there is a risk that the employee will be regarded as having affirmed the breach.[4]

[3] This question is clearly about the constructive form of dismissal so focus on this rather than spending time giving background information on other forms of dismissal.

[4] This is the seminal case on constructive dismissal so you must understand its ratio.

Turning to Jenny and Lisa's cases, what is the term that is alleged to have been breached? It is likely that both will seek to rely on the implied term of trust and confidence.[5] Breach of the relevant term must be sufficiently serious to amount to a repudiatory breach and any breach of the implied term of trust and confidence has been deemed to amount to such a repudiatory breach (***Courtaulds Northern Textiles Ltd* v *Andrew* [1979] IRLR 84**). The implied term of mutual trust and confidence obliges an employer not to, without reasonable and proper cause, 'conduct itself in a manner calculated and likely to destroy or seriously damage the relationship of trust and confidence between employer and employee' (per Lord Steyn in ***Malik* v *BCCI* [1998] AC 20**). For Lisa and Jenny, they will have to show that the college's conduct is sufficiently bad to amount to a repudiatory breach of a fundamental term of the contract.

[5] This is often the term that will be relied upon in constructive dismissal cases but there may be other fundamental breaches of important terms such as the requirement to pay wages.

The facts of Jenny's case are similar to those in the Court of Appeal case of ***Bournemouth University Corp.* v *Buckland* [2010] EWCA Civ 121**. In that case, a university professor alleged that the remarking of his students' failed scripts by colleagues without his involvement, which led to some of the students passing, undermined his position and was a fundamental breach of the implied term of trust and confidence. The Court of Appeal held that the university's actions amounted to a repudiatory breach of the implied term of trust and confidence. Applying this reasoning to Jenny's case and adopting an objective assessment to the matter as is required by law (***Buckland***), it would appear that Jenny has good prospects of showing that the college's actions amount to a repudiatory breach.

This then leaves the issue of the college's investigation which upheld Jenny's grievance. This, too, is factually similar to ***Buckland***.[6] In that case, the university claimed that the internal investigation which vindicated Professor Buckland had operated to rectify any breach. In other words, the university had put right the alleged breach. The Court of Appeal held that this is not possible. Applying orthodox contractual principles, once a party has committed a repudiatory breach of contract it is impossible for that party unilaterally to rectify the breach. Instead, it is for the employee to choose whether to accept the breach and claim constructive dismissal (as Jenny has done) or affirm the contract. Jenny would therefore appear to have good prospects of showing that she has been constructively dismissed. This does not mean that she will automatically be deemed to have been unfairly dismissed as she still needs to show that the constructive dismissal was an unfair one (***Savoia* v *Chiltern Herb Farms Ltd* [1982] IRLR 166**); but in Jenny's case it is difficult to see how the college could persuade a tribunal that its dismissal was a reasonable one for the purposes of **s98(4) ERA**.[7] The usual unfair dismissal remedies of reinstatement to her old job (**s114 ERA**), re-engagement to another role (**s115 ERA**), and compensation (comprising a basic and compensatory award under **ss119 and 123 ERA**) are potentially available to Jenny. In reality, it is unlikely that Jenny having considered herself dismissed in response to the college's conduct would be keen to work for it again, although the possibility should not be dismissed entirely.

For Lisa, the issue is whether the college is likely to be exposed to a claim for constructive unfair dismissal if she resigns and whether Lisa would succeed with such a claim. Lisa is a long-standing employee who, despite both line managers having misgivings about her performance, has had broadly acceptable appraisals (although some room for improvement was noted) and has never before been informed of any significant concerns about her capability for the role. Regardless of her employer's motivations (whether due to kindness or laziness at the 'hassle' of performance managing), the fact remains that the sudden

[6] This is another key case. The investigation point is a subtle one that gives strong students the opportunity to show their understanding of how contract and statute interact in this area.

[7] One common mistake is to forget that a constructive unfair dismissal involves two separate considerations. Is there a constructive dismissal? If so, is that dismissal a fair one?

change in behaviour by her new supervisor has led to her feeling under scrutiny and bullied. If Lisa were to resign now, would such behaviour by the college amount to a repudiatory breach of the fundamental implied term of trust and confidence? ***Buckland*** makes clear that the issue of whether the employer's conduct is a repudiatory breach should be considered objectively (see also ***Hilton* v *Shiner Ltd* [2001] IRLR 727**). We are not aware of whether Lisa's line manager has instigated the communication review policy with other colleagues. Even if this rule only affects Lisa, the question of whether there has been a breach of trust and confidence is one of degree. One example of conduct that has been held to amount to constructive dismissal is a reduction in salary (***Industrial Rubber Products* v *Gillon* [1977] IRLR 389**), although as Sedley LJ in ***Buckland*** made clear, not paying salary could well be constructive dismissal but the question of whether it was reasonable in the circumstances is a separate question. Other conduct that has been held on the facts to amount to constructive unfair dismissal include accusing an employee of theft without good grounds to do so (***Robinson* v *Crompton Parkinson* [1978] ICR 401**) and failing to provide an employee with safe working conditions (***British Aircraft Corp Ltd* v *Austin* [1978] IRLR 332**).[8]

It is unclear whether Lisa's supervisor's conduct would be sufficient to constitute a fundamental breach of the implied term of trust and confidence. Given that Lisa has yet to resign, the most sensible option would appear to be to respond to Mel's behaviour by suggesting more constructive ways of improving Lisa's performance. This would not cure any breach that may already have happened but may have the effect of preventing Lisa from resigning. There remains, however, the issue of Lisa's performance.[9] This is a sensitive issue, not least because Lisa has not had any performance concerns raised with her in previous years. 'Capability' (or, more accurately, lack thereof) is a potentially fair reason to dismiss (**s98(2)(a) ERA**), as is conduct (or misconduct) if Lisa's behaviour is due to laziness or carelessness (***Sutton & Gates (Luton) Ltd* v *Boxall* [1978] IRLR 486**). It is often unclear when behaviour is the result of a lack of capability or misconduct but this is an important issue to clarify as the college's process to manage the issue will depend on the reason behind the behaviour. Giving Lisa the benefit of the doubt and assuming that this is an issue of capability rather than conduct, the college would generally be required to inform Lisa of the shortcomings in her performance and to give her a chance to improve (with support and training if appropriate), before giving her formal performance warnings and ultimately dismissing if her performance did not improve. Given Lisa's previous broadly satisfactory appraisals,[10] it is likely that the tribunal would expect the college to follow a rigorous capability process before contemplating dismissal on the ground of capability.

[8] This part of the question is testing your skills of analysis. If there is no directly relevant authority, the examiner is looking to see whether you can draw from other cases and come to a reasoned conclusion. In Lisa's case, you may well form another view but you will need to show how you have analysed your way to a sensible conclusion.

[9] A clear link to a minor but relevant issue. As the examiner is asking you to advise generally on unfair dismissal, it would be relevant to discuss the possibility of a claim in the future were the college to dismiss.

[10] This paragraph is a good example of using IRAC within a question. The issue of poor performance is identified, the relevant law is discussed, it is then applied to the facts of Lisa's situation, and the paragraph concludes with clear advice showing good levels of discernment.

## LOOKING FOR EXTRA MARKS?

- Constructive dismissal is a relatively straightforward topic. Its difficulty rests in determining whether any given behaviour is sufficient to get over the line of showing fundamental breach of contract. This can be a difficult call to make and examiners are aware of this. What matters is the process you follow to analyse which side of the line you think the behaviour falls and how you justify the decision you reach.
- Familiarising yourself with the material facts of cases in this area will repay you. Not only does it allow you to spot similar scenarios used in exam questions but it helps you build up a picture of the sorts of behaviour that tribunals will consider gives rise to constructive dismissals—and those that do not.

## TAKING THINGS FURTHER

- A. Baker, 'The "Range of Reasonable Responses Test": A Poor Substitution for the Statutory Language' (2020) 50(2) *Industrial Law Journal* 226

  *Argues that the courts should do away with the range of reasonable responses test*
- Law Commission, *Employment Law Hearing Structures: Report*, HC308 Law Com. No. 390, April 2020

  *Examines the jurisdiction of tribunals and other forums for employment law disputes and contains thoughtful recommendations for reform*
- C. Wynn-Evans, 'Harsh but fair—The "range of reasonable responses" test and the "substitution mindset" revisited: *Newbound* v *Thames Water Utilities Ltd*' (2015) 44(4) *Industrial Law Journal* 566

  *Analysis of a Court of Appeal authority discussing the range of reasonable responses test*

## Online resources

www.oup.com/uk/qanda/

For extra essay and problem questions on this topic, as well as advice on revision and exam technique, please visit the online resources.

# Statutory redundancy payments and consultation procedures

## ARE YOU READY?

In order to attempt the questions in this chapter, you must have covered the following areas in your revision:

- The qualifying period to claim a statutory redundancy payment
- The definition of redundancy
- Questions concerning 'work of a particular kind' and the case law regarding this
- Procedural fairness in a redundancy dismissal
- 'Bumping'
- Suitable alternative employment and the statutory trial period
- How a statutory redundancy payment is calculated

## KEY DEBATES

**Debate: Managerial prerogative**

Is it too easy for employers to structure their businesses in the way they see fit and cut staff numbers?

**Debate: Length of consultation periods**

To what extent do the current periods of collective consultation provide employees with sufficient time to seek alternative employment?

**Debate: Level of redundancy payments**

Do the current levels of statutory redundancy pay adequately compensate employees for losing their jobs through redundancy?

## QUESTION 1

Lite Bikes Ltd, a manufacturer of bicycles of all kinds, announced a week ago that it intended to make some of its employees redundant over the next two weeks. Kieran is employed as a 'hand-painting technician', which involves him hand-painting expensive, lightweight racing bikes. He has only ever carried out this role since he joined the company 103 weeks ago. The company has decided to automate the painting of these bikes. Kieran is told that he will be transferred to work in the bicycle-frame brazing workshop where he would be paid at a significantly lower hourly rate than he is currently on. Kieran feels that he would not be using his skills in the brazing workshop and refuses to transfer. He is dismissed immediately for this refusal and wishes to claim a redundancy payment. At the time of his dismissal, he had worked for Lite Bikes Ltd for 103 weeks.

**Advise Kieran as to his right, if any, to a statutory redundancy payment.**

## CAUTION!

- This question requires an answer confined to a discussion of issues concerning entitlement to claim a statutory redundancy payment. Take care not to stray into a general discussion of unfair dismissal law for the potentially fair reason of redundancy. While some questions may cover both, this will be indicated in the rubric.

## DIAGRAM ANSWER PLAN

| | |
|---|---|
| Identify the issues | ■ Does Kieran have sufficient qualifying service to claim a redundancy payment?<br>■ Is Kieran's role in fact redundant?<br>■ Has he been dismissed?<br>■ Has he unreasonably refused suitable alternative employment? |
| Relevant law | ■ Sections 86, 139, 145, and 155 Employment Rights Act 1996<br>■ Contract/function test debate including *Safeway Stores*, *Murray* |
| Apply the law | ■ With addition of statutory notice, Kieran will have two years' service therefore sufficient qualifying service<br>■ Effect of *Murray* on interpretation of s139<br>■ Effect of pay cut and alternative duties on suitability of new role |
| Conclude | ■ Likely that Kieran would be entitled to a statutory redundancy payment |

## SUGGESTED ANSWER

In order to claim a statutory redundancy payment, an employee must have two years' continuous employment by 'the relevant date': **s155 Employment Rights Act 1996 ('ERA')**. Under **s145 ERA**, where a contract of employment is terminated by notice, the relevant date is the date on which that notice expires. Where the contract is terminated without notice, the relevant date is the date the termination takes effect and, for limited-term contracts, it is the date when the term expires. Kieran has only 103 weeks of continuous employment[1] at the time of his dismissal but, since he has been summarily dismissed without notice, **s145(5) ERA** provides that he may add on the minimum statutory period of notice of one week. This is found in **s86(1)(a)**, which provides that not less than one week's notice is due to be given where an employee has been employed for one month or more but less than two years. This would have the effect of increasing Kieran's length of service to 104 weeks.[2]

[1] When examiners are drafting questions, they take care to ensure that there is sufficient material upon which a candidate can produce a full answer in the allocated time. The question here is short but there is a lot to write about. The point about the qualifying period is one example of this that requires time to explain.

[2] Conclude each point as you go before you move on to examine the next issue.

The right to notice under **s86 ERA** applies only where there has been no repudiatory conduct by Kieran (**s86(6)**). In other words, if Kieran has committed an act of gross misconduct amounting to repudiatory conduct that would entitle the employer to dismiss him summarily, the statutory notice rules will not apply. The next question[3] is, therefore, whether Kieran's refusal to transfer to the new role constitutes such conduct and the answer to that question hinges upon whether he is redundant and has been dismissed on that ground.

[3] Demonstrates a logical, ordered approach.

There is also a further question of whether his refusal to transfer precludes him from claiming a statutory redundancy payment. This depends on whether the job offered is suitable alternative employment. However, where a reference is made to an Employment Tribunal for a statutory redundancy payment, there is a statutory presumption where an employee has been dismissed by their employer that they are, unless the contrary is proved, dismissed by reason of redundancy for the purposes of a statutory redundancy claim: **s163(2) ERA**. It is for the employer to prove that Kieran's dismissal was for a reason other than redundancy or that he is barred from making such a claim for some other reason.

Turning then to Kieran's reason for dismissal, **s139 ERA** provides for a limited number of circumstances where an employee will be taken to have been dismissed by reason of redundancy. Broadly speaking these fall into two categories.[4] The first is whether the business where the employee works is ceasing. The second is where the business is continuing but there is no longer the same need for employees who carry out particular work. In Kieran's case, there is no suggestion that

[4] Shows that you understand the whole of **s139** without slavishly copying out what it says from the statute book. Moving from the general to the specific allows you to focus in detail on the relevant subsection.

the business will be ceasing so his circumstances fall into the second category where it appears that there is less need for his work due to the painting now being automated. More specifically, under **s139(1)(b)(i) ERA**, an employee is dismissed by reason of redundancy 'if the dismissal is wholly or mainly attributable to—the fact that the requirements of that business … for employees to carry out work of a particular kind … have ceased or diminished or are expected to cease or diminish'.[5] Clearly, there is or will be no requirement for employees to hand-paint bicycles given automation. The issue therefore turns on whether Kieran's role as a hand-painting technician is 'work of a particular kind' and whether the job in the brazing workshop is the same kind of work and involves no change in the nature of the job. This is a key consideration as employees are expected to adapt to changing methods of working: see ***Cresswell* v *Board of the Inland Revenue* [1984] IRLR 190**.

[5] This part is worth mentioning explicitly and in detail because it is the key subsection which needs to be analysed.

The courts have traditionally taken two approaches to testing whether a redundancy has arisen under the statutory definition in respect of the meaning of 'work of a particular kind': the 'job function test' and the 'contract test'. Under the former, the approach was to consider what an employee was actually doing (see ***Chapman* v *Goonvean and Rostowrack China Clay Co. Ltd* [1973] ICR 310, CA**); whereas, under the latter, the approach was to consider what the employee could be required to do under the contract of employment. ***Nelson* v *BBC (No. 1)* [1977] IRLR 148, CA**, provides an application of the contract test. In that case, a producer/editor working in the Caribbean Service of the BBC who, under the terms of his contract could be required to work in any capacity in any country and who rejected the offer of alternative work, was held not to be redundant when the Caribbean Service was closed down.

In ***Safeway Stores plc* v *Burrell* [1997] IRLR 200**, the EAT stated that both the contract test and the function test were incorrect approaches and distorted the statutory language. In that case, the claimant was employed as the manager of a petrol station. When that role was removed in a restructure, an alternative role of petrol station controller was offered but with less pay. The claimant refused to take the job, arguing that it was essentially the same as his old role. The tribunal had to consider whether there was a redundancy. The EAT concluded that a three-stage process was required, asking the following questions.[6] Was the employee dismissed? If so, had the requirements of the employer's business for employees to carry out work of a particular kind reduced or were they expected to reduce? If so, was the dismissal of the employee … caused wholly or mainly by that cessation/diminution? When looking at whether work of that

[6] Clear understanding of ratio.

kind has reduced, the EAT said that the only question to be asked is was there a diminution/cessation in the employer's requirement for *employees* to carry out work of a particular kind or an expectation of such cessation/diminution in the future? It was irrelevant at this stage to consider the terms of the claimant's contract of employment. This reasoning was approved by the House of Lords in ***Murray* v *Foyle Meats Ltd* [1999] IRLR 562**, in which it was stated that both the function test and the contract test are an unnecessary gloss on the statute. Instead, the tribunal need only consider whether the business requirements for employees to carry out work of a particular kind has ceased or diminished.[7] In other words, rather than focus on the employee's job in practice or what their contract states, the tribunal should focus on business need. Then, having established that, the tribunal should go on to consider whether the employee's dismissal was wholly or mainly attributable to that.

[7] Another example of a sound grasp of the ratio of the case.

Applying this approach to Kieran's case, he has been dismissed. It seems likely that hand-painting bicycles is 'work of a particular kind'. There is, therefore, clearly a cessation in the requirement for this kind of work due to the introduction of automation.[8] Was Kieran's dismissal attributable to this cessation? Here, it seems that in the absence of a contractual provision allowing it to do so, the employer's instruction to transfer to another role constitutes a unilateral variation of Kieran's contract and Kieran's refusal to transfer would not amount to repudiatory conduct, which would have acted as a bar to him claiming a redundancy payment: **s140 ERA**.

[8] Clear conclusion supported by explanation.

Turning to the final issue, has Kieran unreasonably refused an offer of suitable alternative employment?[9] Underlying the law in this area is the principle that if an employee unreasonably turns down the offer of a suitable alternative job, they forfeit any right that they would have to a redundancy payment (**s141(2)**). Kieran has refused the offer on the grounds that it does not make use of his skills, it is a substantially different role, and it would involve a significant pay cut. In determining the suitability of the role, the tribunal will consider the capacity and place in which the employee would be employed (**s141(3)(a)(i)**). It is not clear whether Kieran would remain at the same place of work but the nature of the role is clearly different. The tribunal will also consider whether the terms and conditions would differ in the new role (**s141(3)(a)(ii)**). Here they would differ and in respect of a fundamental term, namely pay. It would appear that Kieran's refusal of the role is not unreasonable (***Bird* v *Stoke-on-Trent Primary Care Trust* [2011] UKEAT/0074/11**). He would not, therefore, be prevented from claiming a redundancy payment.[10] This would be calculated on the basis of his age and his two years' service.

[9] Asking questions is a nice technique for keeping your focus and getting straight to the heart of the matter.

[10] Definite answer to the question set.

## LOOKING FOR EXTRA MARKS?

- In cases where you are given more detail about the nature of the alternative employment or it is not so clearly unsuitable, discussion of the factors taken into account in the cases in this area would be merited. Here the matter was relatively straightforward given the significant pay cut.
- In a short problem question such as this, take time to ask yourself whether you have missed anything when planning your answer. Bear in mind what was said before that examiners will have written the question carefully to fit the time. If you find that you can answer a question in significantly less time than you are given, check again whether you have missed a point or have dealt with an issue too superficially.

## QUESTION 2

**The UK's law on redundancy protection is drafted to allow employers maximum flexibility in determining how best to structure their organisations. This results in confusion for employees whose entitlement to a statutory redundancy payment may be at risk. Discuss.**

## CAUTION!

- There are a lot of points crammed into this short statement. Underline each point of interest to help you begin considering what you need to cover. Here the examiner is asking you to focus on the UK law, examples of flexibility, what aspects of the law are confusing, and entitlement to statutory redundancy pay.
- Where an essay question is very broad, it is acceptable to say that you will give a couple of clear examples to help focus your answer. What would not be acceptable is to rewrite the question to answer the question that you would far rather the examiner had asked!
- Planning an essay answer takes time. It should not surprise you if you spend at least five minutes of the exam simply reading and planning how you will answer any question.

## DIAGRAM ANSWER PLAN

Entitlement to claim a statutory redundancy payment

↓

Example of flexibility and confusion: place of work

↓

Mobility clauses

↓

Example of flexibility and confusion: bumping roles

Policy underpinning redundancy protection

## SUGGESTED ANSWER

In order to claim a statutory redundancy payment, an employee must establish that they are redundant under the definition in **s139 of the Employment Rights Act 1996 ('ERA')**. This provision does not prevent employers from making roles in their organisations redundant but rather is designed to ensure that employees are compensated (in accordance with a statutory formula) for the loss of their jobs. The very premise[1] behind the UK's redundancy policy is that employers should be free to structure their businesses as they see fit and employees will be compensated for losing their jobs. This essay will begin by exploring briefly the definition of redundancy in **s139 ERA** before considering two distinct areas[2] which can give rise to confusion on the part of employees regarding their entitlement to a redundancy payment. The first relates to how widely the courts are prepared to define an employee's place of work; the second relates to the idea of 'bumping'. As will be argued,[3] these two examples are the result of the law's relatively wide discretion afforded to employers to shape their organisations in the way that best suits their business needs. The essay will conclude by arguing that while the statutory protection seems relatively straightforward, its application has resulted in some confusion over the years.

[1] This shows that you understand the broader industrial relations context and what the law is designed to achieve in this area.

[2] In a broad question, one way of maintaining focus is to say that you will give a few examples.

[3] Tell the examiner at the outset what the key argument of your essay will be.

Turning to the first issue of place of employment, this refers to the wording of **s139(1)(a)(ii) and (b)(ii) ERA.** These provisions require that the dismissal is 'wholly or mainly attributable to' either the fact that the employer has ceased or intends to cease to carry on that business *in the place where the employee was so employed* or the fact that the requirements of the business 'for employees to carry out work of a particular kind *in the place where the employee was employed by the employer* … have ceased or diminished or are expected to cease or diminish' (emphasis added). Critical in both cases is how the courts will define the place of employment.[4]

[4] Focus on the relevant parts of the statute rather than spending time copying out the full section.

There are at least two ways of determining this issue, i.e. by applying the 'contract test' or the 'factual' or 'geographic test'. Until the late 1990s, different courts and tribunals applied one or other of these tests to determine such questions. The former test looked at where the employee could be required to work under their contract, while the latter test focused on the factual aspect of the geographical area within which the employee actually worked.[5] Widely different

[5] Concise summary of the two tests.

answers could be reached depending on which test was used. For example, in ***Sutcliffe* v *Hawker Siddeley Aviation Ltd*** **[1973] ICR 560, NIRC**, Mr Sutcliffe, who worked at RAF Marham, was instructed to move to another RAF station, RAF Kinloss, when Marham closed. A mobility clause in his contract provided that he could be moved anywhere in the UK but he refused to transfer. The court held that the place where he was employed meant the place where he could be required to work under the contract rather than the place where he in fact worked. As there was work at RAF Kinloss, he was not redundant.[6] Similarly, in ***United Kingdom Atomic Energy Authority* v *Claydon*** **[1974] ICR 128, NIRC**, Mr Claydon was employed at the Atomic Energy Authority's (AEA) establishment in East Anglia, under a contract containing a provision that he could be transferred to any of the AEA's establishments in the UK. When the AEA asked Mr Claydon to transfer to its Aldermaston site because it no longer had any need for him in East Anglia, he refused, and the AEA did not invoke its rights under the mobility clause. Instead, it dismissed him and he claimed a redundancy payment. The National Industrial Relations Court (NIRC) followed ***Sutcliffe*** in applying the contract test, under which his 'place of work' was nationwide and, looking nationally at the AEA's establishments, there was no redundancy so the dismissal was not by reason of redundancy. However, the NIRC did state that had the AEA invoked its right to order Claydon to transfer, any refusal on his part to do so would allow the employer to lawfully dismiss him for breach of contract.

[6] Lengthy discussions of the facts of cases should be avoided but here they are appropriate to show how different decisions could be reached depending on the test used.

The EAT in ***Bass Leisure Ltd* v *Thomas*** **[1994] IRLR 104** preferred the factual or geographic test rather than the contract test, although it stated that on either test the claimant in the instant case won. Mrs Thomas was based at her employer's Coventry depot, from where she travelled to various public houses collecting the takings from fruit machines. On the closure of its Coventry depot, Mrs Thomas was instructed to base herself in Birmingham (twenty miles away), pursuant to a contractual mobility clause (this contained two qualifications: first, that the employer should take account of the employee's domestic circumstances; and, second, that, judged objectively, the alternative place of work must be suitable). Mrs Thomas agreed to try the new arrangements but found that they did not suit her so she left and claimed constructive dismissal and a redundancy payment. The EAT held that the correct test to apply was the geographic test, making a factual enquiry 'taking account of the employee's fixed or changing place or places of work, and any contractual terms which go to evidence or define the place of employment' but excluding any mobility clause from consideration. Under this test, she had been constructively dismissed (because the employer had not satisfied the two requirements indicated and was therefore in breach of contract) by reason of redundancy.

*Bass* was approved by the Court of Appeal in ***High Table Ltd* v *Horst* [1997] IRLR 513, CA**. Mrs Horst and other waitresses were employed by High Table as silver service waitresses at Hill Samuel's London office. Although their contracts stated, 'it is sometimes necessary to transfer staff ... to another location', they had in fact worked only at the Hill Samuel office. When Hill Samuel decided to reorganise its catering, they needed fewer waitresses working longer hours, and High Table dismissed all three waitresses. Applying the geographic or factual test, the Court of Appeal found that the waitresses had all been employed, as a matter of fact, at the Hill Samuel offices and, as there was a reduced need for waitresses there, they were all redundant. Peter Gibson LJ[7] (with whom Hobhouse and Evans LJJ agreed) stated, 'If an employee has worked in only one location under his contract of employment for the purposes of the employer's business it defies common sense to widen the extent of the place where he was so employed, merely because of the existence of a mobility clause' (at [22]).

[7] Citing the important part of a judgment shows that you have read and understood the case.

For now, it appears that the factual test of where the employee actually worked prevails when determining their 'place' of work for the purposes of **s139 ERA**.[8] Reliance on mobility clauses in redundancy situations, however, continues to throw up some challenging issues for the courts. In the EAT case of ***Kellogg Brown & Root (UK) Ltd* v *(1) Fitton; and (2) Ewer* [2016] UKEAT0205_16_2111**, the employer's Middlesex site closed and Fitton and Ewer were asked to transfer to Surrey pursuant to the mobility clause in their contracts. Both refused due to the significant increase in commuting times that the transfer would entail. While the Employment Tribunal considered that the subsequent dismissals were unfair for reason of redundancy, the EAT held that the dismissals were unfair but for alleged misconduct, namely the employees' refusal to transfer. This meant that the employees would not be entitled to a statutory redundancy payment.

[8] This 'mini' conclusion summarises your arguments before you begin exploring another issue.

The second issue upon which I wish to focus in this question and one about which there has also been some confusion[9] relates to **s139(1)(b) ERA** where there is a redundancy situation because there has been a reduction in the need for employees to carry out work of a particular kind. While some redundancy situations involve removing a particular role, it is common to see work being reorganised in a particular way such that one employee may be dismissed to make way for another. In those circumstances, can a 'bumped' employee claim that they have been dismissed by reason of redundancy? Established case law suggested that such employees can so claim (***Elliott Turbo Machinery Ltd* v *Bates* [1981] ICR 218, EAT**). In such situations,

[9] Refer back to the question by repeating its wording. This maintains your focus and crucially reminds the examiner that you are answering the question set!

the employee is dismissed not because of a reduction or cessation of *their* work but rather because of a reduction in the need for *another employee's* work. The wording of **ERA** supports this view as **s139** requirements are fulfilled where there is a cessation or reduction in the need for *employees* to carry out work of a particular kind and this need not necessarily be the dismissed employee's work. There must, of course, be a causal connection between the dismissal and the redundancy.

This approach was questioned in ***Church* v *West Lancashire NHS Trust* [1998] IRLR 4**, where the EAT, applying the 'contract test', held that the concept of bumped redundancies was unsound and that an employee was redundant only where there was a reduction in the need for the dismissed employee's work. However, the bumped redundancy concept was approved by the House of Lords in ***Murray* v *Foyle Meats Ltd* [1999] ICR 827**, so the EAT decision in ***Church*** can no longer be considered to be good law. Further, the House of Lords in ***Murray*** approved the approach of the EAT in ***Safeway Stores plc* v *Burrell* [1997] IRLR 200**, in which the EAT approved ***Gimber*** and ***Elliott*** and stated 'In our judgment the principle of "bumped" redundancies is statutorily correct' (per HHJ Peter Clark at [71]). 'Bumped' employees in a redundancy context should, therefore, be able to show that their dismissals were by reason of redundancy.

Is there a requirement on employers to consider bumping in the context of a redundancy consultation? While there may be no absolute rule on an employer that says that it must consider bumping, it may be unfair not to consider this (***Mirab* v *Mentor Graphics (UK) Ltd* [2017] UKEAT/0172/17/DA**).

From the two examples given above, it is clear that the wording of **s139 ERA** has at times caused confusion in its application. The flexibility afforded to employers to deploy staff as they see fit through vehicles such as contractual mobility clauses or internal reorganisations has meant that the factual reality of a situation can be difficult to square with the wording of statute. However, it also appears[10] that in recent years the courts have adopted a common-sense approach to ensure that employees are protected in some way against the business prerogative that allows for organisations to be managed in the way that the employer deems most suitable.

[10] This is a balanced conclusion that fits well with what you have argued in the previous paragraphs.

## LOOKING FOR EXTRA MARKS?

- There is considerable scope in this question for a strong student to do well. Its breadth allows for a creative answer. Try to stand out from the crowd in a positive way by taking a more original approach.
- This type of question would also reward a student who has engaged with the underlying policy behind the UK's approach and who can either cite some academic discussion on the issue or perhaps offer a comparison with another jurisdiction. As long as you explain in the introduction how you will answer the question, treat a wide question like this one as an invitation to demonstrate your full potential to the examiner!

## QUESTION 3

Plimshot Electrical Supplies Ltd is a company employing 120 employees, operating from its only premises in Workton. Today, it received information by email from Wizzo Inc., its parent company in the USA, that Wizzo would cease funding Plimshot. Plimshot has been entirely reliant upon this funding to keep the business going. As a result of the severe financial difficulties Plimshot is facing because of Wizzo's news, it has taken the decision to dismiss all its workforce and close down the business. It proposes to start dismissing employees from next week, with twenty-five employees to be dismissed in the first week, followed by the remaining employees three weeks later. There is a recognised independent trade union, the Electrical, Plumbing and Allied Trades Union (EPATU) to which all of its employees belong. Plimshot seeks your advice as to the correct redundancy dismissal procedure to follow and the risks of failing to follow a correct process.

**Advise Plimshot.**

## CAUTION!

- A number of issues concerning collective redundancies arise in this question despite it being relatively short. Spend some time jotting down all the issues that arise.
- Since the company is in severe financial difficulties, there may also be an issue as to securing actual payment of statutory redundancy pay if the company goes into insolvent liquidation or defaults in payment.

## DIAGRAM ANSWER PLAN

**Identify the issues**

- Is there a redundancy situation?
- Has the employer complied with the requirements regarding individual consultation?
- Is there an obligation on the employer to consult collectively?
- If there has been a breach of collective consultation rules, will the employees qualify for a protective award?
- Rules regarding time off to look for work and payment on insolvency

**Relevant law**

- Section 139 ERA on definition of redundancy, s52 ERA on time off to look for work
- Section 188 TULRCA re collective consultation; *Junk*, *Clarks of Hove*
- Section 189 TULRCA on protective award

**Apply the law**

- Amounts to a redundancy situation; given the number of affected employees there is an obligation to consult collectively
- Employer may plead special circumstances defence due to hasty withdrawal of funding

**Conclude**

- Special circumstances may not succeed; employees likely to be entitled to a protective award for lack of proper consultation
- Employees are entitled to reasonable paid time off work to look for alternative work
- Unpaid wages would amount to a preferential debt on insolvency

## SUGGESTED ANSWER

As Plimshot intends closing down the business entirely, this is a classic example[1] of one of the three main redundancy dismissal situations, i.e. closure, actual, or intended, of the business as a whole: **s 139(1)(a)(i) Employment Rights Act 1996 ('ERA')**. As its only base is Workton, no question arises under **s139(1)(a)(ii) ERA** (closure of the business in one place, where the business has other places of establishment). Plimshot will be potentially liable for unfair dismissal if it fails to follow the correct procedure concerning information and consultation prior to dismissal, at both the collective and individual level. Broadly,[2] this means that Plimshot should give as much warning as possible of the impending redundancies and consult with affected employees and, where there is one, a recognised trade union (there is an obligation to consult with employee representatives where there is no recognised trade union: see **s188(1B)(b) Trade Union and Labour Relations (Consolidation) Act 1992 ('TULRCA')**).

[1] A confident start showing that you can see that there is clearly a redundancy situation here and that you will not waste time discussing irrelevant matters.

[2] Concise summary of what will be expected of an employer.

At the collective level, the company has statutory obligations to inform and consult EPATU, the recognised trade union, about the dismissals. **Section 188(1) TULRCA** places an obligation on employers who are 'proposing to dismiss as redundant 20 or more employees at one establishment within a period of 90 days or less' to consult with 'appropriate representatives of any employees who may be affected by the proposed dismissals or may be affected by measures taken in connection with those dismissals'. Clearly, all three conditions are satisfied here: (1) twenty or more employees; (2) at one establishment; (3) within ninety days or less.[3] In Plimshot's case, the 'appropriate representatives' would be those of the recognised independent trade union, EPATU: **s188(1B)(a) TULRCA**. Consultation must take place 'in good time' and, in any event, subject to minimum periods: **s188(1A) TULRCA**. These periods are: 'where the employer is proposing to dismiss 100 or more employees' within ninety days or less, at least forty-five days 'before the first of the dismissals takes effect': 'otherwise, at least 30 days before the first of the dismissals take effect': **s188(1A) TULRCA**. In ***Junk* v *Wolfgang Kühnel* [2005] IRLR 310**, the (then) ECJ held that under **Directive 98/59/EC (the Collective Redundancies Directive)**, collective consultation must take place before notice of dismissal is given to any employees. This interpretation means that,[4] under **s188**, the words 'proposing to dismiss' mean 'proposing to give notice of dismissal' (see also ***Leicestershire CC* v *Unison* [2005] IRLR 920, EAT**).

[3] Strong example of applying the relevant law to the facts of the case.

[4] Here the EU judgment is applied to domestic law with a clear understanding of what this means in practice.

**Section 188(4) TULRCA** states that the information to be provided for the purposes of consultation must be in writing and state, inter alia: the reasons for the proposed redundancies; the numbers and descriptions of those employees to be made redundant; the total number of employees of that description employed at the establishment; and the proposed method of carrying out the dismissals, having regard to any agreed selection procedure, and the timing of them. The consultation, to be undertaken 'with a view to reaching agreement with the appropriate representatives', must include consultation about ways of '(a) avoiding dismissals, (b) reducing the numbers of employees to be dismissed, and (c) mitigating the consequences of the dismissals': **s188(2) TULRCA**.

If it proceeds with the proposal to dismiss employees, Plimshot will be in breach of these statutory consultation requirements as it proposes to start dismissing employees from next week, with twenty-five employees to be dismissed in the first week, followed by the remaining ninety-five employees three weeks later. However, there is a defence under **s188(7) TULRCA** where 'special circumstances' make it 'not reasonably practicable' for the employer to comply with the consultation requirements under that Act.[5] In this case, the employer must 'take all such steps towards compliance with that requirement as are reasonably practicable in those circumstances'.

[5] Sometimes students will miss this defence. Although it only applies in exceptional circumstances, it is important to consider whether any given set of facts would fall within such an exception.

Here, it would appear that it is not reasonably practicable for Plimshot to comply in full with the collective consultation rules given the sudden withdrawal of crucial funding by its parent company in the USA but Plimshot should still do what it can towards meeting the requirements so as to comply with the requirement to take all reasonably practicable steps towards compliance: **s188(7) TULRCA**. For example, it should inform the EPATU officials immediately today of the proposed redundancies and consult with them in compliance with **s188(2)** although, given the circumstances, there is probably little that can be done to avoid the dismissals, reduce the numbers affected, or mitigate the consequences. However, the union should be given information concerning the proposed method of carrying out the dismissals, the selection procedure, and the timing of them (the question might be, 'Why are twenty-five employees to be dismissed in the first week with the others to be dismissed three weeks later?'),[6] since it may be able to suggest ways to mitigate the effects of the redundancies. The question of whether Plimshot has sought or will seek financial assistance from elsewhere would also arise.

[6] Good demonstration of commercial awareness here.

The EPATU, on behalf of affected employees, may apply to the Employment Tribunal for a protective award on the grounds that the employer failed to comply with the consultation requirements and seek a declaration to that effect: **s189 TULRCA**. The complaint must be presented either before the date of the last of the dismissals or within three months of that date (the tribunal has a discretion to extend that time limit where it considers that it was not reasonably practicable to present the complaint within the three-month period: **s189(5)**). Plimshot may raise the defence set out in **s188(7)**, already discussed. A protective award is a monetary award made where the consultation requirements have not been complied with and where the defence available is not accepted by the tribunal. It relates to the specified employees who have been or will be made redundant over the protected period, up to ninety days (the protected period is what the tribunal considers to be just and equitable, bearing in mind the seriousness of the employer's failure to comply, but the maximum award period is ninety days: **s189(4)(b)**). Every employee to whom the protective award applies is entitled to a week's pay for the protected period. If Plimshot fails to pay the award, the employee(s) affected may present a complaint to the Employment Tribunal within three months of the date of the failure to pay: **s192(1) TULRCA**.

In addition to the consultation requirements, Plimshot must notify the Secretary of State[7] in writing of the dismissals, at least thirty days before the first dismissal takes effect (where between twenty and ninety employees are to be made redundant); the period of notice is at least forty-five days where one hundred or more are to be made redundant: **s193 TULRCA**. If the 'special circumstances' defence (already discussed) applies, Plimshot must take such steps as

[7] Take care not to overlook the notification requirements in a collective redundancy situation.

are reasonably practicable in the circumstances: **s193(7)**. Failure to comply may lead to conviction and a fine.

In addition to the collective consultation requirements, Plimshot should be aware of the possibility of unfair dismissal claims on the redundancy ground from qualifying employees, i.e. generally those with two years' continuous employment: **s108(1) ERA**.

Plimshot must allow affected employees reasonable paid time off during working hours to look for other work, or to make arrangements for training for future employment, before the expiry of the notice period: **s52(1) ERA**.

Finally, Plimshot may go into insolvent liquidation[8] before paying redundancy payments and the protective award (if made). Both of these payments (along with wages, accrued holiday pay, and payment for time off) constitute preferential debts under **s386 Insolvency Act 1986** so that any such payments are given precedence over other creditors' claims. In addition, where an employer is insolvent and has failed to pay, inter alia, a statutory redundancy payment, employees may apply to the Secretary of State for payment out of the National Insurance Fund: **ss166–167 ERA**.

[8] This is an important point that is sometimes missed.

## LOOKING FOR EXTRA MARKS?

- It would not be incorrect for students to discuss the **Collective Redundancies Directive** and/or **Information and Consultation Regulations 2004**. Both have relevance to the question although arguably are not central to it.

## TAKING THINGS FURTHER

- K. Ewing and Lord Hendy, 'Covid-19 and the Failure of Labour Law: Part 1' (2020) 49(4) *Industrial Law Journal* 497

  *Although this paper takes a more general look at the state of labour law in the UK, it is a highly topical discussion in the context of Covid-19 and mass redundancies/use of furlough*

- M. Hall and P. Edwards, 'Reforming the statutory redundancy consultation procedure' (1999) 28(4) *Industrial Law Journal* 299

  *Outlines the historical development of collective consultation rules including empirical evidence that collective consultation can make a difference to managerial decisions*

## Online resources

www.oup.com/uk/qanda/

For extra essay and problem questions on this topic, as well as advice on revision and exam technique, please visit the online resources.

# 9 Equality law

## ARE YOU READY?

In order to attempt the questions in this chapter, you must have covered the following areas in your revision:

- The protected characteristics under the Equality Act 2010
- The different forms of discrimination including direct and indirect discrimination, harassment, and victimisation
- The duty to make reasonable adjustments for persons with a disability

## KEY DEBATES

Equality law is one of the most fast-changing, fascinating, and vast areas of employment law. By its very nature, it has given rise to a number of debates.

**Debate: Theoretical model of equality**

There are a range of approaches to equality. The UK's model of direct discrimination is premised on a model of formal equality, which involves treating like persons alike. Does that adequately address historic disadvantages? Would a model of substantive equality be preferable?

**Debate: Intersectionality**

The model in the Equality Act 2010 is premised on claims being brought on the basis of one characteristic such as sex or race but in reality we each have a number of intersecting characteristics that inform how we are treated. Why might the UK's arguably narrow approach to equality be problematic? Are there other important characteristics, such as socio-economic status, that should also be protected?

**Debate: Tension between characteristics**

In some instances, tensions may arise in protecting different characteristics, such as when some faith groups may hold certain beliefs regarding sexual orientation. To what extent has the Equality Act navigated successfully any tensions that arise when protecting different groups from discriminatory treatment?

## QUESTION 1

Tanisha is the supervisor of area sales representatives for Bigco plc. Her job is to go round all the reps every month and check on their performance. While she was on holiday abroad, she caught a rare disease which made her blind in one eye and partially sighted in the other. As a result, she cannot drive out to all the reps, many of whom work miles away from public transport. Bigco dismisses her for incapacity in that she cannot perform her job.

**Advise Bigco as to its liability for disability discrimination.**

## CAUTION!

- As always, read the rubric. There is a possibility of other claims (such as unfair dismissal) but the question is restricted to discrimination. Discussing unfair dismissal creates a poor impression as it shows that you have not read the rubric.

## DIAGRAM ANSWER PLAN

**Identify the issues**

- Does Tanisha's condition amount to a disability in law? If so, has the company failed in its duty to make reasonable adjustments? Has she been treated less favourably because of a protected characteristic namely disability?

**Relevant law**

- Section 6 Equality Act 2010 ('EA') re definition of disability; s13 re direct discrimination; s15 re discrimination arising from a disability; s20 re duty to make reasonable adjustments; *Goodwin*, *Malcolm*

**Apply the law**

- It is likely that Tanisha's condition amounts to a disability
- Potential breaches of ss15 and 20 given the failure to consider alternatives to driving to supervise; likely that Tanisha can show link between effect of disability and unfavourable treatment
- Unlikely to show that disability itself was cause of treatment (effect of disability appears to be cause) therefore s13 claim may fail

**Conclude**

- Likely that Tanisha would succeed in a claim under ss15 and 20 EA
- More difficult to show direct discrimination under s13

## SUGGESTED ANSWER

Tanisha is likely to be disabled[1] within the meaning of **s6 of the Equality Act 2010 ('EA')**. This provides that a person has a disability if they have a 'physical or mental impairment' and 'the impairment has a substantial and long-term adverse effect on [their] ability to carry out normal day-to-day activities'. Although the **EA** does not define 'impairment', the **Guidance** on the matters to be taken into account in determining questions relating to the definition of disability advises that a disability can arise from a range of impairments including 'sensory impairments, such as those affecting sight or hearing'.[2] Partial sightedness is undoubtedly a physical impairment on the present facts. The first limb of the definition, that Tanisha must have an impairment, has been satisfied.

Turning to the second limb of the definition of disability, does it have a 'substantial' and 'long-term' adverse effect on Tanisha's ability to carry out normal day-to-day activities? In ***Goodwin***, it was emphasised that normal day-to-day activities mean activities that do not relate solely to the claimant's experience but rather to those general daily activities that would be carried out by any person. Again, the **Guidance** is instructive on this matter. Examples include reading, writing, shopping,

[1] In problem questions there is no need for a lengthy introduction. Go straight to the heart of the matter!

[2] Although it may seem obvious that partial sightedness is a disability, supporting your answer with evidence lends weight to your analysis.

getting washed and dressed, and 'travelling by various forms of transport'. All these activities would be carried out in daily life. Driving is likely to be included in the range of normal day-to-day activities. The effect of Tanisha's impairment on her ability to carry out normal day-to-day activities has to be substantial. 'Substantial' means 'more than minor' or 'more than trivial' (***Goodwin* v *Patent Office* [1999] ICR 302, EAT**). Since Tanisha can no longer drive at all, this is clearly a substantial effect.[3] Finally, the effect must be 'long term'. According to **Sch. 1 para. 2 to the EA**, the effect is long term if it has lasted at least twelve months or is likely to last for at least twelve months. There is no suggestion that Tanisha's impairment will improve so it will count as long term as it is likely to last for more than one year. It is, therefore, likely that any Employment Tribunal would hold that Tanisha is a disabled person for the purposes of the **EA**. It should be noted that the decision as to whether a claimant is disabled within the meaning of the statute is for the tribunal, not for the medical staff who give evidence, to determine (see ***Abadeh* v *British Telecommunications plc* [2001] ICR 156, EAT**). Disability is a protected characteristic under **s4 of the EA**.

[3] Be confident in your advice.

Since Tanisha is disabled, the question becomes one of whether she has been discriminated against due to her protected characteristic of disability.[4] There are a number of ways in which a person may be discriminated against under the **EA**. These include direct discrimination, where a person has been treated less favourably because of a protected characteristic. In respect of the protected characteristic of disability, there are a further two grounds of prohibited behaviour. These are 'discrimination arising from a disability' and a failure to comply with the legal duty on an employer to make reasonable adjustments.

[4] This links to the next set of issues to be discussed.

**Section 13(1) EA** provides that a person discriminates against another if 'because of' a protected characteristic A treats B less favourably than A treats or would treat others. In other words, to succeed under **s13** Tanisha would need to show that it is not the impact of her disability that was the cause of her treatment but the disability itself, which is less easy to show.[5] It is not her partial sightedness but the impact of this on her ability to drive that has led to her dismissal. Under **s15 EA**, there is a broader category of prohibited conduct: discrimination arising from disability. **Section 15** provides that discrimination occurs if Bigco treats Tanisha unfavourably 'because of something arising in consequence of Tanisha's disability' and Bigco 'cannot show that the treatment is a proportionate means of achieving a legitimate aim'. This provision was introduced in response to the case of ***Malcolm* v *Greenwich LBC* [2008] UKHL 43**. The EAT has taken a broad approach to the meaning of 'something arising'. In ***Sheikholeslami* v *The University of Edinburgh* [2017] UKEATS/0014/17/JW**, the claimant had work-related stress and depression and was absent from work. Although the university argued that there were other reasons why Professor Sheikholeslami may not wish to return to work, the EAT

[5] Strong analysis showing why direct disability discrimination can be difficult to establish.

held that **s15** contained a 'broad causation question' and so a liberal approach to causation should be adopted. For Tanisha, she should be able to show a causal link between the effect of her disability on her ability to drive and her subsequent unfavourable treatment in being dismissed.[6] Being dismissed from her job is undoubtedly unfavourable treatment. Such discrimination may, however, be justified (**s15(1)(b)**) but Bigco would be required to show that dismissing her was a proportionate means of achieving a legitimate aim. It may well be that Bigco could show that having a supervisor meet area sales reps in person to check on performance is a legitimate aim. However, was the dismissal a proportionate means of achieving that aim? It seems a heavy-handed response[7] when the sales reps could have been able to drive to meet her, there could be other ways of checking on performance (such as telephone calls), or a colleague may have been able to drive Tanisha to meet with other colleagues. These alternative ways around the problem of Tanisha being unable to drive touch upon another form of discrimination—the failure to make reasonable adjustments under **s20 EA**.

Under **s20(3)** where a provision, criterion, or practice puts a disabled person at a substantial disadvantage in comparison with persons who are not disabled, the employer is required to 'take such steps as it is reasonable to have to take to avoid the disadvantage'. Here we can identify the practice of requiring Tanisha to drive to visit colleagues as putting her at a substantial disadvantage.[8] The adjustment must be reasonable and in that equation, as the **EHRC Code of Practice** makes clear, matters such as cost, practicability, and whether any adjustment could avert the adverse effect are important. An example of this can be seen in ***Cordell* v *FCO* [2011] UKEAT/0016/11/SM**. In that case, the EAT held that the FCO had not failed in its duty to make reasonable adjustments for the claimant, a deaf woman, in circumstances where the cost of providing lip-speaker support during a posting to Kazakhstan would be around £230,000 per year. The **Code**[9] gives examples of adjustments such as reallocating duties, transferring the disabled person to an existing job vacancy, modifying equipment, and providing supervision. In Tanisha's case, perhaps Bigco could have moved Tanisha to another job, modified its practices of supervision to allow it to take place by other means, allocated this aspect of her role to another person, or arranged for any necessary information to be provided in an alternative format. On the facts, it appears that Bigco has failed in its duty to make reasonable adjustments.

If Tanisha has a potential claim, she should apply to the Employment Tribunal within three months of the act or omission, unless the tribunal finds it just and equitable to extend the limitation period. If the claim is successful, the tribunal by **s124 EA** may award the normal discrimination remedies including compensation.[10] This includes compensation for injury to feelings, with the law as stated in ***Vento* v *Chief Constable of West Yorkshire* [2003] ICR 318, CA** and ***Da'Bell* v *NSPCC* [2010] IRLR 19**. There is no maximum award.

[6] An example of applying the law to the facts of the case.

[7] This shows your understanding of the justification defence and, by giving some practical examples, also demonstrates your awareness of the provision in practice.

[8] Take care not to miss out steps. Some students might assume (as it is obvious) that there is a substantial disadvantage here but spell it out.

[9] This is an important source and should be mentioned in any question on disability discrimination.

[10] Mentioning remedies, even briefly, is an effective way of concluding your answer to a problem question.

## LOOKING FOR EXTRA MARKS?

- Although it might be tempting to spend time on the development of **s15** and contrast the provisions in the **Equality Act** with those of the previous **Disability Discrimination Act**, focus on what the law is now rather than on what went before.

## QUESTION 2

**Consider the effect EU law has had on the domestic law of sex discrimination.**

## CAUTION!

- This question is very broad in scope so take time to think how you will structure it carefully. Sub-headings may be helpful to guide the examiner through your answer.
- Although the question is drafted to focus solely on sex discrimination, if there are differences in the treatment of other characteristics, you may wish to add one or two comparisons.

## DIAGRAM ANSWER PLAN

Definition of sex

Burden of proof

Definition of indirect discrimination

Free-standing right not to be sexually harassed

Justification for indirect discrimination

Pregnancy as direct discrimination

Removal of financial limit on compensation

## SUGGESTED ANSWER

The UK joined the EEC, as it then was, in 1973. The **Sex Discrimination Act 1975**, now the **Equality Act 2010 ('EA')**, was drafted not in reliance on the EU's **Equal Treatment Directive (76/207/EEC)** since, as can be seen by the dates, the UK statute preceded the EC Directive. However, the UK's impending membership of what is now the EU may well have been a factor motivating the need to provide that discrimination on grounds of sex would be unlawful, and certainly the EU had a significant influence on the development of the domestic law of sex discrimination. In this essay, some of the main influences of the EU on the domestic law in relation to sex discrimination will be considered.[1]

[1] There are many ways in which it can be argued that EU law has influenced the development of domestic law in this area. By highlighting that you will address some of them, you are signalling to the examiner that you will not give an exhaustive discussion but instead highlight the main points.

### Definition of 'sex'

The English statute originally took a strictly biological view of men and women: ***White* v *British Sugar Corp.* [1977] IRLR 121**. The then ECJ, however, in ***P* v *S* [1996] IRLR 346** held that it was sexually discriminatory to dismiss a transsexual person who was undergoing gender reassignment. This decision was applied by the EAT in ***Chessington World of Adventures* v *Reed* [1997] IRLR 556**, which construed the **Sex Discrimination Act 1975** in conformity with the **Equal Treatment Directive (76/207/EEC)**. The Act was itself amended by the **Sex Discrimination (Gender Reassignment) Regulations 1999 (SI 1999/1102)**.

### Definition of indirect discrimination[2]

[2] Sub-headings help structure your answer, particularly when you are discussing a range of factors and it can be difficult to link each factor naturally.

Historically, for indirect discrimination to be shown under domestic law, there had to be a requirement or condition with which fewer women than men could comply, which was to the claimant's detriment and which the employer could not justify. One difficulty was the high hurdle of 'requirement or condition'. A well-known example[3] was ***Price* v *Civil Service Commission* [1977] 1 WLR 1417**. The Civil Service refused a woman of 35 a job because for that job there was an age limit of 17 to 28. Although women between those ages could apply, they may in practice have been prevented from doing so as those were years when women would often have children and be responsible for childcare. It was held that the strict age bar would amount to a requirement or condition. If the employer had, however, expressed the age range merely as a preference[4] rather than a strict requirement or condition, the claimant would have fallen at the first hurdle of showing a potentially discriminatory 'requirement or condition'.

[3] The point that you are making is strengthened by giving a concrete example.

[4] Highlights the problem with the old definition.

What is now needed is a 'provision, criterion or practice', a reduced hurdle for claimants. If a desirable quality constitutes a 'practice', there is the possibility of a case. This change to the law of indirect sex discrimination was as a result[5] of the **Employment Equality**

[5] Refers back to the question to help maintain focus.

**(Sex Discrimination) Regulations 2005** implementing the **Equal Treatment Amendment Directive (2002/73/EC)**. Now, for a claimant to bring a claim for indirect sex discrimination, there has to be a provision, criterion, or practice '(i) which puts or would put women at a particular disadvantage when compared with men; (ii) which puts or would put her at a disadvantage; and (iii) which the employer cannot show to be a proportionate . . . means of achieving a legitimate aim'. These provisions now form **s19(1) of the Equality Act 2010**.

### Harassment

The **Sex Discrimination Act 1975** did not originally refer to sexual harassment. However, ***Porcelli* v *Strathclyde Regional Council* [1986] ICR 564** held that harassment could be a form of direct discrimination because a man would not treat another man in the way that he treated the woman. However, in ***MacDonald* v *Advocate General for Scotland* [2003] UKHL 34** it was held that ***Porcelli*** went too far. The fact that the harassment was sexually based did not mean that there was direct discrimination. The reason for the harassment must be the sex of the victim: unpleasant treatment of a woman is not itself sexual harassment, though it is evidence of it. Following the transposition of the **EU Equal Treatment Amendment Directive** into domestic law in 2005, the definition of harassment was redefined as 'unwanted conduct which has the purpose or effect of (a) violating [a worker's] dignity or (b) creating an intimidating, hostile, degrading or offensive environment . . .'. We have now to distinguish between harassment related to the relevant characteristic of sex and harassment 'of a sexual nature'.

### Justification

The width of the employer's defence in domestic law has varied across the years. For employees, the nadir was reached in the judgment of Eveleigh LJ in ***Ojutiku* v *MSC* [1982] ICR 661, CA**. In that case, justification of potentially discriminatory treatment was assessed on the basis of what was 'acceptable to right-thinking people as sound and tolerable reasons'. The ECJ's higher standard, set in ***Bilka-Kaufhaus GmbH* v *Weber von Hartz* [1986] ECR 1607**, is that there must be a real need for the difference, the practice must be appropriate to fill that need, and the practice must be necessary to achieve that end. The ECJ has held that generalisations are insufficient to constitute a justification (***R* v *Secretary of State for Employment, ex parte Seymour-Smith* [1999] IRLR 253**). The **2005 Regulations** in accordance with EU law, defined justification as 'a proportionate . . . means of achieving a legitimate aim'. This standard of justification of indirect discrimination has been continued into the **Equality Act 2010**.

### Pregnancy

**Section 5(3) of the Sex Discrimination Act 1975**[6] stated: 'A comparison in the cases of persons of different sex or marital status under

[6] In order to be able to discuss the influence of EU law on domestic legislation, it is of course necessary to be able to discuss the previous legislation.

**section 1(1)** . . . must be such that the relevant circumstances in the one case are the same, or not materially different, in the other.' Originally when applying **s5(3)** it was held that discrimination against pregnant women was not sex discrimination because there were no similarly situated men (***Turley* v *Allders Department Stores Ltd* [1980] ICR 66, EAT**): men could not become pregnant. The EAT later, however, held in ***Hayes* v *Malleable WMC* [1985] ICR 703** that a pregnant woman could be compared with an ill man. This decision was the subject of trenchant criticism; pregnancy is not an illness. Finally, the House of Lords referred the issue to the ECJ, which ruled in ***Webb* v *EMO Air Cargo (UK) Ltd* [1994] IRLR 482, [1995] IRLR 645 and [1995] ICR 1021** that discrimination on the ground of pregnancy was sex discrimination and there was no need for a male comparator. **Section 5(3)** was disapplied to that extent. The law was later settled by the **Employment Equality (Sex Discrimination) Regulations 2005**: discrimination on the ground of pregnancy is sex discrimination. The government stressed that this change was solely 'for the purposes of legal clarity' and no change in the width of the law was intended. The current law now found in the **Equality Act 2010** continues this definition. The EU's influence in the area of pregnancy discrimination can also be found in the **Pregnant Workers Directive (92/85/EEC)** and the ECJ case of ***Brown* v *Rentokil Ltd* [1998] ECR I-4185, [1998] IRLR 445**. In that case, it was held that dismissal on the ground of pregnancy/childbirth up to the end of maternity leave is discrimination.

**Remedies**

One final area of influence pertains to remedies.[7] The ECJ ruled in ***Marshall* v *Southampton and South West Hampshire AHA (No. 2)* [1993] ICR 893** that the financial cap on awards for sex discrimination and the lack of interest on awards were in breach of the EU law principles that national measures implementing EU law must be sufficiently powerful and effective to achieve the objective of that law and any loss must be recompensed in full. Domestic law was amended by the **Sex Discrimination and Equal Pay (Remedies) Regulations 1993 (SI 1993/2798)** to comply with EU law. Although **s6(7) of the European Union (Withdrawal) Act 2018** provides that retained EU case law will remain binding on the UK after Brexit, the cap on discrimination remedies is thought to be one area where domestic law might change following January 2021.

[7] This again refers back to the question to show what you are writing is relevant.

**Conclusion**

In conclusion,[8] it may be seen that over the years EU law has led to many changes to the domestic legislation and to the case law implementation of this legislation. Following Brexit, it remains to be seen the extent to which domestic courts will continue to be influenced by the EU in the area of sex discrimination or whether significant divergence will emerge in the UK.

[8] Even if time is a factor in the exam, it is better to include a short conclusion such as this one than no conclusion at all.

## LOOKING FOR EXTRA MARKS?

- One problem in attempting to give many examples of the influence of EU law is that you may not have time to discuss each one thoroughly. This risks your answer reading a little superficially. This suggested answer tries to strike an appropriate balance but you could limit your answer to fewer examples and discuss these in greater detail.
- Another approach for those who have read the academic literature in this area would be to consider the different policy approaches to equality demonstrated by the EU and UK and compare these. This would provide a more theoretical answer. However, if you choose to take this approach, be sure to give concrete examples from the law as this is what the question asks.

## QUESTION 3

Hussain is a Muslim who works for Bloggs Ltd. During a heated exchange with his supervisor (Kevin), Kevin calls him a 'black idiot'. Later that week in the staff canteen, Kevin and some other colleagues are discussing Kevin's forthcoming holiday. Hussain overhears Kevin say that he would ask to move if he was seated next to a Muslim on his flight. A number of colleagues also make comments about 'the state of immigration' in England. When Hussain sits near the group to eat his lunch, the group changes the subject. Hussain has lodged a grievance about Kevin's comment and the fact that he feels uncomfortable at work, claiming that he has been discriminated against on the ground of race. The HR manager of Bloggs Ltd has contacted you for advice on how to deal with the matter.

**Advise Bloggs Ltd.**

## CAUTION!

- This short question invites a lot of discussion. On first glance it might appear that you may have little of substance to write in an exam but there is considerable scope here to discuss a range of issues.

## DIAGRAM ANSWER PLAN

**Identify the issues**

- Has Hussain been treated less favourably because of race and/or religion or belief?
- Does Kevin's comment amount to less favourable treatment?
- Do the comments of Hussain's colleagues amount to harassment?
- Is the employer vicariously liable for its employees' actions?
- What remedies are available?

**Relevant law**

- Section 9 Equality Act 2010 on definition of race; s13 on direct discrimination; s26 on harassment; s109 on vicarious liability; s124 on remedies
- *Mandla* v *Dowell Lee*, *J. H. Walker* v *Hussain*, *Jones* v *Tower Boot*, *Vento*, *Da'Bell*

**Apply the law**

- Likely that comment about colour was an incident of direct discrimination because of race (colour)
- Discussion by colleagues likely to amount to harassment related to religion or belief
- Unclear what steps the employer has done to invoke the defence under s109(4)

**Conclude**

- Hussain is likely to have reasonable prospects of succeeding in claims for direct discrimination because of race and harassment related to religion
- Employer may be vicariously liable and remedies could include compensation for injury to feelings

## SUGGESTED ANSWER

Although Hussain has raised only the prospect of race discrimination in his grievance, it is important to advise Bloggs Ltd on the range of potential claims[1] that he may have including any claims for religious discrimination on account of the comments regarding Muslims. There are two issues raised: (1) the comment made by Kevin to Hussain; and (2) the discussion which Hussain overheard. Each will be considered in turn.[2]

[1] The instruction to you here is a general one to advise the client. This means spotting even those claims that have not yet been alleged.

[2] Problem questions like essays benefit from a brief introduction. The difference with problem questions is that there is no need to set out the relevant background. Instead, go straight to identifying the relevant issues.

**Section 9 of the Equality Act 2010 ('EA')** defines race as including colour, nationality, and ethnic or national origins. Race is not a biological matter. This was made clear in ***Mandla* v *Dowell Lee* [1983] 2 AC 548, HL** where Lord Fraser opined that the word 'ethnic' 'conveys a flavour of race' but that it was not intended to be used in a 'strictly racial or biological sense'. To form part of an ethnic group, Lord Fraser pointed to a number of characteristics that should be shared by the community/group. These include a long-shared history, a cultural tradition, plus other relevant factors such as a shared geographical origin, a common language, a common religion, and a common literature. In ***Mandla***, it was held that Sikhs are a distinct ethnic group as are Jews (***Seide* v *Gillette Industries Ltd* [1980] IRLR 427**). In a later case of ***J. H. Walker* v *Hussain* [1996] ICR 291** it was held, however, that Muslims are not a distinct ethnic group.[3] In respect of the comment made by Kevin to Hussain, it would not therefore be possible for Hussain to plead that this was on grounds of ethnic origins, however the use of the word 'black' by Kevin may open the possibility of Hussain founding a claim on the basis of colour. Hussain has been treated less favourably 'because of' race: see **s13(1) EA** for the definition of direct discrimination. But for his race ('because of'), he would not have been so treated: see, for example, the non-employment case of ***James* v *Eastleigh BC* [1990] 2 AC 751, HL**. Accordingly, the employer seems to have treated him less favourably than it treats or would treat a white person, and has thereby discriminated against him. Kevin would not, presumably, use similar language to a white person. A racial insult is clearly capable of being a detriment[4] (see ***de Souza* v *Automobile Association* [1986] ICR 514, CA**).

[3] This is an important point given that Hussain's grievance generally is one of race discrimination.

[4] This may appear an obvious point but it does no harm to spell it out to the examiner.

Turning to the second point, the group discussion, this is less obviously on grounds of race as Hussain claims but appears to be motivated by Hussain's colleagues' prejudiced views about Muslims. In this case, the comments were not made directly to Hussain but he has clearly overheard them. This conduct may be caught under **s26 EA** as harassment. It was accepted that racial harassment could found a claim of direct discrimination provided it was on the ground of the victim's race (see ***MacDonald* v *Lord Advocate for Scotland* [2003] UKHL 34** on sexual harassment). For a campaign of racial harassment, see ***Tower Boot Co. Ltd* v *Jones* [1997] ICR 254, CA**. One act of harassment is sufficient (see ***Bracebridge Engineering Ltd* v *Derby* [1990] IRLR 3, EAT**). Under **s26(1)**, harassment is defined as when a person 'engages in unwanted conduct related to a relevant protected characteristic' and the conduct has the purpose or effect either of violating another person's dignity or 'creating an intimidating, hostile, degrading, humiliating or offensive environment' for that person. In deciding whether any conduct amounts to harassment, the court will take into account[5] the perception of the person alleging that they were harassed, the other circumstances of the case, and whether it is reasonable for the conduct to have that effect (**s26(4) EA**). Turning to the group discussion, it would appear reasonable for Hussain to feel that the comments of his colleagues are creating both a hostile and offensive environment for him. This is particularly so in light of Kevin's

[5] Hussain appears quite reasonably to have a claim of harassment here but it is important to show the examiner that you have considered the possibility that the tribunal may take into account other factors.

earlier racial insult. While a comment about immigration on its own would be unlikely to amount to harassment[6] (depending, of course, on the language used), the comments about not wishing to sit next to Muslims are clearly degrading and offensive. Harassment applies to the protected characteristic of 'religion or belief' (**s26(5)**) so comments about Muslims would be caught.[7]

It follows that Hussain may have claims based on direct discrimination on grounds of race (colour) and a separate claim for harassment related to religion or belief. The employer is vicariously liable for the actions of its employees done in the course of employment (**s109 EA**) subject to a defence that the employer 'took all reasonable steps' to prevent the employees from doing the thing alleged or anything of that description (**s109(4)**).[8] ***Jones* v *Tower Boot Co. Ltd* [1997] ICR 254** is the leading authority on this point and shows that the courts are prepared to adopt a wide view of what is meant by 'in the course of employment'. Kevin did speak in the course of employment—at work, and it was done by a supervisor to a lower ranked worker. The employer's knowledge of the act is irrelevant. To be able to rely on the defence under **s109(4)**, the **Equality and Human Rights Commission Code of Practice** gives some examples of the sorts of steps that an employer would be expected to take. These include providing training to employees on equality and diversity, and having a robust policy on equality and diversity. A policy of investigating all racial complaints seriously is another way of showing that the employer took such steps.

If Hussain succeeds in his claims of discrimination, the normal discrimination remedies are available. The tribunal may make a declaration that he has been unlawfully discriminated against under **s124(2) EA** and may award compensation, which is assessed using tort principles (***Ministry of Defence* v *Cannock* [1994] ICR 918**) and covers loss of earnings and compensation for injured feelings, the latter being assessed within the guidelines provided in ***Vento* v *Chief Constable of West Yorkshire* [2003] ICR 318**, as amended by the EAT in ***Da'Bell* v *NSPCC* [2010] IRLR 19**. Compensation for psychiatric harm may also be included (see ***Sheriff* v *Klyne Tugs (Lowestoft) Ltd* [1999] ICR 1170, CA**). Finally, under **s124(2)(c) EA** the tribunal may make an appropriate recommendation to the employer.[9] This is a recommendation for the purpose of obviating or reducing the adverse effect on the complainant of any matter to which the proceedings relate (**s124(3) EA**). It would also appear appropriate that the employer consider what disciplinary action it may take against Kevin and any other colleagues for the apparent misconduct in which they have engaged.[10]

[6] This shows a level of discernment.

[7] Not all protected characteristics are covered by the provisions on harassment. This shows that you are aware of this.

[8] This is an important point. Claimants are likely to want to name the employer as a respondent if there is a generally discriminatory culture within the organisation and also because the employer is likely to have greater means than a colleague to be able to pay any compensation ordered.

[9] This remedy is sometimes overlooked but may be a particularly helpful one in circumstances such as these.

[10] As the question asks you to advise HR generally, it is perfectly appropriate to consider what action may be taken against the offending employees.

## QUESTION 4

**Equality law is insufficiently nuanced to recognise that a person may be treated less favourably than another for reasons other than the characteristics that are currently protected. Discuss.**

## CAUTION!

- The key to doing well in a wide question like this is to plan your answer carefully. You have been given plenty of scope in this question to develop an original answer. Think through what you will argue and plan your answer well.
- This wide question can be answered in a number of different ways. You may choose to take a philosophical approach and question why the law has chosen to regard treatment on some grounds as legally (and morally) wrong while some other reasons for differential treatment are permitted. You could explore the idea of intersectionality or consider whether there are other characteristics that ought to be protected. These are all acceptable responses to the question.

## DIAGRAM ANSWER PLAN

Development of the protected characteristics

Problems with current regime: one-dimensional and may require further extension

Intersectionality

Development of protected characteristics—socio-economic disadvantage

Development of protected characteristics—philosophical belief

Conclusion

## SUGGESTED ANSWER

The domestic approach to equality has been to select a number of characteristics where distinguishing (less favourable) treatment on the ground of one of those characteristics will be unlawful. The decision as to which characteristics should be protected from such treatment reflects shifts in societal attitudes (such as the increase of women entering the paid labour market) and has also been influenced by developments in the EU and **European Convention on Human Rights**. The approach adopted by the UK has been to add incrementally to the list of protected characteristics, which can now be found in **s4 of the Equality Act 2010 ('EA')**.[1] They are age, disability, gender reassignment, marriage and civil partnership, pregnancy and maternity, race, religion or belief, sex, and sexual orientation. The difficulty to which this question alludes is that our responses and attitudes to another person may be motivated and shaped by characteristics that are not presently protected or that do not fit neatly within the boundaries of the current list. In this essay, I will consider briefly the development of the current set of protected characteristics before discussing two problems with the current approach where the law is arguably insufficiently nuanced. The first is the law's failure to protect adequately against intersectional discrimination; the second is the relatively limited range of characteristics currently protected.[2] A short conclusion follows.

[1] This is a more elegant way of introducing the topic with a little contextual background rather than starting with a list of the characteristics.

[2] This tells the examiner how you will answer the question, which is essential in a wide-ranging question such as this. It also reassures the examiner that you have thought through the question and should provide a planned and considered response.

Historically, the first characteristic to be protected in the UK was race. This is perhaps understandable given the pace of societal change after the Second World War when many immigrants came to the UK. **The Race Relations Acts of 1965 and 1968** were followed by the **Equal Pay Act 1970** and the **Sex Discrimination Act 1975**. The extension of protection to the characteristic of sex was partly in response to the number of women working in the paid labour market and partly due to the UK's impending membership of what was then the European Economic Community. The next most significant extension of protection came with the **Disability Discrimination Act 1995** and in the 2000s further extensions were made in response to the UK's implementation of the **EU Framework Directive (2000/78/EC)**. Religion or belief and sexual orientation became other grounds to be protected from discrimination, followed by age in 2006 (**Employment Equality (Age) Regulations 2006**).

While it appears that a wide range of characteristics benefit from protection by the legislation, the current regime stands accused of operating within distinct boundaries or 'silos' that leaves those who have experienced less favourable treatment due to the intersection of different characteristics or due to multiple characteristics, without a remedy in law[3] (I. Solanke, 'Putting race and gender together: a new

[3] Engaging with the secondary literature demonstrates your wide reading and helps shape your own views on the issue.

approach to intersectionality' (2009) 72 *Modern Law Review* 723). **Section 14 EA** provided for dual discrimination on the basis of two protected characteristics but this has not been brought into force. This means that the law is ill-equipped to deal with circumstances where, for example, the treatment in question is not on the ground of a woman's gender or race but because of the intersection of the two (***Bahl* v *Law Society* [2004] EWCA Civ 1070**). This would appear to be a missed opportunity for the **EA**. For Hepple, there are a number of advantages to adopting what he describes as a more 'generalised' approach to equality law that moves away from such distinct silos. He suggests that a more 'open-ended' approach to equality would help considerably in proving multiple discrimination where the cause of treatment is due to a combination of a person's characteristics.[4] Moreover, the courts would find it easier to keep pace with changing societal views about the acceptability or otherwise of holding certain attitudes without being limited to finding unlawful only that behaviour which offends a certain protected characteristic (B. Hepple, *Equality: The Legal Framework*, 2nd edn (Oxford: Hart, 2014)).

[4] A good example of how academic authority lends weight to your argument.

The second limitation of the current set of protected characteristics pertains to Hepple's observation that societal attitudes change over time.[5] This raises the question of whether the current list of protected characteristics is too restrictive and ought to be expanded. The law has traditionally taken the view that only those characteristics over which a person has no control should be protected (I. Solanke, 'Infusing the silos in the Equality Act 2010 with synergy' (2011) 40(4) *Industrial Law Journal* 336). This may explain in part the reluctance of the government to enact the provision in the **EA**, which intended to place a 'socio-economic duty' over certain public sector bodies. The provision contained in **s1 EA** (which has not been brought into force) provided that certain public bodies must 'when making decisions of a strategic nature about how to exercise its functions, have due regard to the desirability of exercising them in a way that is designed to reduce the inequalities of outcome which result from socio-economic disadvantage'. While it may appear uncontentious to suggest that poverty or socio-economic disadvantage leads to inequalities of outcomes for persons, two concerns persist about bringing this provision into force. The first relates to how socio-economic disadvantage ought to be defined as it appears a necessarily relational concept. The second is the motivation behind the provision. There exist widely different political views about whether socio-economic disadvantage is best resolved by taking action to address inequality of outcomes (albeit that the **EA** does not go this far—public bodies need only have 'due regard to the desirability' of exercising their functions in a particular way)[6] or whether such disadvantage is best addressed by other measures.

[5] Nice link to the next issue.

[6] Good example of close reading of the text.

One example of where the range of protected characteristics may evolve is with respect to the protection of a belief. **Section 10(2) EA** defines 'belief' very briefly as being 'any religious or philosophical belief'. In ***Grainger plc v Nicholson*** **[2009] UKEAT/0219/09**, a belief in climate change that impacted on how Nicholson led his life was sufficient to amount to a philosophical belief. Burton J set out five conditions that should be met for a belief to be protected under the **EA**: (1) the belief must be genuinely held; (2) it must be a belief and not an opinion or viewpoint based on the present state of information available; (3) it must be a belief as to a weighty and substantial aspect of human life and behaviour; (4) it must attain a certain level of cogency, seriousness, cohesion, and importance; and (5) it must be worthy of respect in a democratic society, be not incompatible with human dignity, and not conflict with the fundamental rights of others.[7] By contrast, the Court of Appeal has recently held that a belief in the moral right to own the rights to one's creative outputs does not constitute a philosophical belief. ***Gray v Mulberry Company (Design) Ltd*** **[2019] EWCA Civ 1720** concerned Gray's refusal to sign a copyright agreement with Mulberry. She believed that it would compromise her writing and film work outside her employment with Mulberry. Mulberry amended the agreement but Gray still refused to sign the altered version. She contended that she was discriminated against because of her philosophical belief namely 'the statutory human or moral right to own the copyright and moral rights of her own creative works and output'. The Employment Tribunal worked through the ***Grainger*** criteria and concluded that her belief was not protected under **s10**. While the tribunal accepted that the claimant strongly believed in the right of ownership to her own creative output, it did not accept that she held that belief as any sort of philosophical touchstone to her life. The EAT and Court of Appeal upheld the tribunal's decision.

The selection of nine characteristics to be protected above others has given rise to certain problems within the law, particularly when it comes to protecting those for whom discrimination is the result of intersecting characteristics or when attempting to capture the vast range of philosophical beliefs or worldviews that may shape a person's experience of the world and how they are treated. In light of this, it might perhaps be time to consider seriously whether the approach of augmenting the list of protected characteristics is the preferred one or whether the list might be removed in favour of a more general prohibition on employers treating an employee for anything other than objective, rational reasons.[8]

[7] In an exam, it would be acceptable to paraphrase these five conditions.

[8] Interesting conclusion suggesting an alternative option. This could even be expanded if time permits.

## LOOKING FOR EXTRA MARKS?

- Do not be put off by what may seem too open-ended a question. The benefit of such questions is that they can be answered in numerous ways, which can allow you to stand apart from others who may be tempted to produce a more standard response to a narrower question.
- Remember to ask yourself 'what is my authority' for making a particular point. Examiners are looking for argument supported by authority, otherwise an essay will just read like an opinion piece!

## TAKING THINGS FURTHER

- S. Atrey, 'Comparison in intersectional discrimination' (2018) 38(3) *Legal Studies* 379

  *Analyses the problem of comparison in cases of intersectional discrimination and examines the use of the South African contextual approach*
- S. Fredman, 'Reversing discrimination' (1997) 113 *Law Quarterly Review* 575

  *An important reflection on how discrimination can be reversed and equality achieved in which the author reveals the flaws with a narrow, formal model of equality*
- I. Solanke, 'Infusing the silos in the Equality Act 2010 with synergy' (2011) 40(4) *Industrial Law Journal* 336

  *Discusses the range of protected characteristics and why certain characteristics are afforded 'protected' status*

## Online resources

www.oup.com/uk/qanda/

For extra essay and problem questions on this topic, as well as advice on revision and exam technique, please visit the online resources.

# 10 Equal pay and family rights

## ARE YOU READY?

In order to attempt the questions in this chapter, you must have covered the following areas in your revision:

- What constitutes 'pay' for the purposes of equal pay
- The sex equality clause
- The three bases upon which an equal pay claim may be founded, i.e. like work, work rated as equivalent, and work of equal value
- The problems concerning selection of an appropriate comparator
- The material factor defence
- The time limits within which equal pay claims must be brought
- Remedies where an equal pay claim is successful, including the period for which arrears may be claimed
- 'Family friendly rights' including the right to request flexible working and the rules on shared parental leave

## KEY DEBATES

**Debate: Gendered models**

To what extent does the law on family rights reflect a gendered male breadwinner/female carer model of family life? Is this an accurate portrayal of modern life?

**Debate: Gendered labour market**

One criticism of our equal pay laws is that they fail to capture the reality of a highly gendered and segregated labour market, which means that it can often be difficult to find an appropriate comparator. To what extent do our laws on equal pay provide a remedy for low-paid women in typically feminised sectors such as caring and cleaning?

**Debate: Reasons for the pay gap**

Numerous and contested reasons for the pay gap have been advanced including occupational segregation, women typically taking on more caring responsibilities and having career breaks to raise children, and feminised and part-time jobs often being poorly rewarded. By contrast, others point to a woman's choice as the key factor in the pay gap. What do you consider to be the main causes of the pay gap? Can law address factors such as occupational segregation?

## QUESTION 1

Supa Kool Fashions Ltd is a company employing twenty employees.

**(a)** Aisha, the company's new marketing director, who was appointed three weeks ago, has discovered that Tom, her immediate predecessor, was paid £75,000 per annum, whereas she is paid £60,000 for carrying out the same duties. She has also discovered that Charles, who was the marketing director but left twelve months ago, was paid £78,000.

**(b)** Rose, a secretary, is paid a basic rate of £10 per hour for a forty-hour week. She wishes to claim equal pay with Harry and Will, two maintenance men, who are paid £12 per hour as a basic rate for a forty-hour week. Rose receives lunch vouchers to the value of £20 per week, which the men do not receive, plus seven weeks' holiday per annum, whereas the men receive only six weeks' holiday.

**Advise Aisha and Rose, who want to bring equal pay claims against the company.**

## CAUTION!

- This question requires a discussion of the equal pay provisions of the **Equality Act 2010**, together with the relevant case law, with reference to EU law where necessary.
- Since the examiner has split the question into two parts, adopt the same approach in your answer. This will help give your answer structure and you should aim to spend roughly the same amount of time on each part.
- It is useful in your revision to have a checklist of the various stages that may arise in an equal pay question in a logical order. Not all aspects in the checklist may arise in the question, but you should identify those that do and then analyse the question in a sequential manner. For example, with Aisha there is no need to spend time examining issues of equivalent work as she is doing the same job as her predecessor whereas with Rose you will need to consider equivalence, particularly whether her role is of equal value to her comparators.

## DIAGRAM ANSWER PLAN

**Identify the issues**

- Aisha: can Aisha rely on a predecessor as a comparator? If so, can she rely on Tom and/or Charles? Would her employer have a material factor defence?
- Rose: is she doing work of equal value to her comparators? Does it matter that overall her terms may be more favourable than those of her comparators? Does her employer have a material factor defence?

**Relevant law**

- Sections 64, 65, 66, 79, and 131 Equality Act 2010; Art. 157 TFEU
- *Macarthys Ltd*, *Rainey*, *Hayward*, *Barber*, *Walker*

**Apply the law**

- Aisha can rely on a predecessor as a comparator
- Rose needs to show her role is of equal value to her comparators; may adopt a term-by-term comparison

**Conclude**

- Aisha can rely on Tom and/or Charles but there is a greater risk of the employer pleading a material factor defence with Charles
- Rose may be able to show that her work is of equal value to her comparators; she may adopt a term-by-term comparison; little information upon which to advise on likelihood of a material factor defence

## SUGGESTED ANSWER

For both Aisha and Rose, equal pay claims are governed by the equality of terms provisions of the **Equality Act 2010 ('EA')**. Provisions of EU law, principally **Art. 157 TFEU (ex 141 EC Treaty)**, may also be relied upon in order to construe the domestic legislation.

### Aisha

**Section 64(1)(a) EA** provides that the relevant equality of terms provisions apply where a person is 'employed on work that is equal to the work that a comparator of the opposite sex . . . does'. Equal work includes work that is 'like work' (**s65(1)(a) EA**), which is further defined in **s65(2) EA** as if the claimant's work is 'the same or broadly similar' to the comparator's work and 'such differences as there are between their work are not of practical importance in relation to the terms of their work'. We are told that the marketing director duties remain the same.[1] Aisha's job is therefore of 'like work' to that of her proposed

[1] As you are told that the duties are the same, there is no need to discuss in detail the case law on the meaning of like work. If you were to do so, it could be regarded as irrelevant.

comparators. The question for her, however, is whether she is able to rely on a predecessor as an appropriate comparator.

The starting point is that Aisha is able to choose her comparator: ***Ainsworth* v *Glass Tubes and Components Ltd* [1977] ICR 347, EAT**. Under **s79(3) EA**, a comparator includes someone of the opposite sex employed by the claimant's employer and working at the same establishment. For Aisha, the only issue then is whether a previous marketing director can be relied upon. The ECJ in ***Macarthys Ltd* v *Smith*** (**[1980] IRLR 210, ECJ**) held that EU law allowed the selection of a predecessor as a comparator. This was endorsed in ***Walton Centre for Neurology & Neuro Surgery NHS Trust* v *Bewley* [2008] ICR 1047**. In that case, Elias J permitted reliance on a predecessor on the basis that had the predecessor remained in employment with the employer, 'he would have received at least the same pay subsequently when the claimant was employed as he had done before she was employed'.[2] Moreover, he opined that this was a legitimate inference to reach on the basis that the employer would be breaching the predecessor's contract if it reduced his pay. Applying this to Aisha's case, it is legitimate to infer that had Tom continued in his employment, he would have continued to be paid £75,000. He was paid this only three weeks before Aisha joined. What Aisha cannot do, however, is to argue that her predecessor would have received pay rises in the future and to hypothesise about what he would have been paid.[3] In other words, she will have to take Tom's salary of £75,000 as the comparison figure.

This then leaves the question of whether Aisha might rely on Charles.[4] He is not her immediate predecessor as he left twelve months previously but he did earn even more than Tom. This is potentially problematic on two fronts. First, there is the question of whether she carries out the same duties as Charles or whether the marketing director role has changed in the period between Charles leaving and Aisha being appointed. The second, and more troubling, issue is whether Aisha's employer might rely on a material factor defence. Once Aisha has established that she is employed on like work to Tom (and possibly also Charles), the 'sex equality clause' takes effect. This clause is imposed into the contract of employment (**s66(1) EA**) and has the effect of modifying the less favourable term of Aisha's contract (in this instance, the term regarding salary) so that it is not less favourable (**s66(2)(a) EA**). The sex equality clause has no effect, however, if the difference is because of a 'material factor' that does not involve treating Aisha less favourably because of her sex (**s69(1)(a) EA**). Here we are not told of what any such factor might be. It may be that Tom and/or Charles had additional qualifications or more experience than Aisha. These would be factors unrelated to sex (***Kenny* v *Minister for Justice, Equality and Law Reform* [2013] IRLR 463**). Market forces might also provide the employer with a material factor defence (***Rainey* v *Greater Glasgow Health Board* [1987] 1 AC 224**).

[2] Shows clear understanding of the ratio of the case. As an actual comparator is needed in almost all equal pay cases, there was concern about whether relying on a predecessor would be akin to relying on a hypothetical comparator. It is not, as Elias J explains here.

[3] A nice point showing discernment.

[4] Clear, logical link. This creates a good impression on an examiner who can see that you are approaching the question in a highly ordered way.

For Aisha, it is unlikely that market forces would explain why Tom was paid so much more than her only three weeks before she joined although this may have been a factor implicated in Charles's pay depending on what the job market was like at the time of his appointment.[5] At what point will a material factor cease to offer a defence? The Court of Appeal considered this question in ***Walker* v *Co-operative Group Ltd* [2020] EWCA Civ 1075**. In this case, the claimant who was HR Director for Co-op compared her work with that of two other directors. The tribunal initially held that material factors existed to explain the difference in pay. These included market forces for one of the directors (he was moving from being a partner in a Magic Circle firm), the fact that the directors had executive-level experience whereas Walker was newly appointed to an executive role, and the fear that these other two directors would leave. However, the tribunal found that at some stage these historical explanations for the pay differential ceased to exist. The Court of Appeal held that the tribunal had erred in its approach. It was not for the tribunal to consider whether the material factor justified the difference in pay, only that it was the cause of the difference. These factors caused the pay differential and provided a material factor defence.

[5] Excellent analysis showing clear application of law to the facts, followed by a brief summary of the merits of the argument.

In conclusion,[6] Aisha would appear to have reasonable prospects of succeeding in an equal pay claim. She can select both Tom and Charles as comparators although she should be advised that it is open to her employer to put forward a material factor defence. In the absence of further information, it is difficult to advise on the likelihood of any such defence succeeding. On that basis Aisha should be made aware that her prospects of success could change when the details of any defence emerge.

[6] 'Join the dots' by giving a brief conclusion to Aisha's query.

## Rose

Rose, as a secretary, is clearly not engaged on like work to maintenance men.[7] In order to claim equal pay with Harry and Will, she will have to show either that her work has been rated as equivalent to their work under a job evaluation scheme (**s65(1)(b) EA**) or that her work is of equal value (**s65(1)(c) EA**). We are not told that there has been a job evaluation study conducted which has rated both roles as equivalent. This is necessary for Rose to claim that the jobs have been rated as equivalent (**s65(4) EA**). This then leaves Rose with the option of showing that although the jobs of secretary and maintenance men are different, they are of equal value to her employer. This means that the work is equal in terms of the demands made by reference to factors 'such as effort, skill and decision-making' (**s65(6)(b) EA**). If it does transpire that a valid job evaluation study had been conducted in which the conclusion was that her male comparators are not doing work of equal value, Rose will not be able to argue that her role is of equal value (**s131(5) EA**) unless a tribunal has reasonable grounds for suspecting

[7] Do not spend time on clearly irrelevant matters. Be confident and discount the issue immediately.

that the evaluation was based on a system that was discriminatory because of sex or is otherwise unreliable (**s131(6) EA**). If Rose wishes to proceed in claiming that her work is of equal value, she should be advised that the process to be followed will involve the appointment of an independent expert to determine whether the two roles are of equal value, and this is often a lengthy and protracted procedure.[8]

[8] You could go into a little more detail on the steps involved in an equal value claim if you have time but be realistic about how much time you will have. It is important that you discuss the central issue of the term-by-term approach so ensure that you leave sufficient time to address this.

If Rose can show that the roles are of equal value, can her employer argue that overall she is better off than her comparators? This argument was used by the employer in ***Hayward* v *Cammell Laird Shipbuilders Ltd* [1988] ICR 464, HL**, which was decided under the previous **Equal Pay Act 1970**. Although Hayward's basic pay and overtime rates were less favourable in comparison, her overall remuneration package was comparable to her comparators (she received sickness benefits, holiday pay, and paid meal breaks, which the men did not receive). The House of Lords held that she could succeed in her claim. Their Lordships held that the correct approach under the **Equal Pay Act 1970** was to examine the claimant's contract clause by clause, and to compare each clause in it with that in the male comparator's. If there was found in the man's contract a term benefiting him but no corresponding term in the woman's contract, then that term would be treated as included in hers (see also ***Brownbill* v *St Helen's & Knowsley NHS Trust* [2011] IRLR 128, EAT**). This follows from the wording of what is now **s66(2)(a) EA** which refers to 'a corresponding term' of the comparator's contract, allowing a term-by-term approach. In ***Barber* v *Guardian Royal Exchange Assurance Group* [1990] IRLR 240**, the ECJ, considering what is now **Art. 157 TFEU** (former **Art. 141 EC Treaty**), confirmed that the term-by-term approach was correct because 'if the national courts were under an obligation to make an assessment and a comparison of all the various types of consideration granted, according to the circumstances of men and women, judicial review would be difficult and the effectiveness of **Article [157]** diminished as a result' (at [34]). Their Lordships in ***Hayward*** acknowledged that this term-by-term approach could lead to 'leap-frogging' claims, i.e. men and women claiming parity with each term of their contract, thereby improving their contractual benefits overall, but the material factor defence could be available to them. It is, therefore, open to Rose to take a term-by-term approach.[9]

[9] Detailed analysis of the law on the term-by-term approach. It is important to spend time on this issue as it is clearly key to this aspect of the question.

Will her employer have a material factor defence to justify the higher hourly rate for maintenance men? We are not told of any factors that could be taken into account so we cannot hypothesise about the likelihood of such a defence. However, it is worth noting a few points. The first is that the factor must be material, i.e. 'significant and relevant' (per Lord Keith of Kinkel in ***Rainey* v *Greater Glasgow Health Board* [1987] 1 AC 224**). Second, the factor must not be tainted by sex (***Glasgow City Council* v *Marshall* [2000] ICR 196**). In conclusion, it would appear that Rose may bring an equal value claim, with Harry and Will as her male comparators, although she may be met with the material factor defence. In the absence of more information about the duties carried out by Rose and her comparators, or the nature of any defence that may be put forward, it is difficult to advise on Rose's prospects of success.[10]

[10] Where you have not been given information, flag this and explain what you would need to know in order to be able to advise. This is better than hypothesising, which risks you straying into 'what ifs' and appearing irrelevant.

## LOOKING FOR EXTRA MARKS?

- If time permits, you could add a line or two to discuss the courts' approach to sex taints and the material factor defence. Be discerning though about how you do this. Making up possible factors that the employer could put forward and discussing the likelihood of success of each one will take you too far off the question and the facts presented.
- Mention remedies. Although these have not been discussed in this answer, a brief line or two about the limited contractual nature of equal pay remedies will go down well with an examiner.

## QUESTION 2

**Successive governments have adopted different approaches in an attempt to achieve a work–life balance for working parents. The resulting framework is a rather confusing patchwork of rights that may not always reconcile paid work with other demands on a worker's time. Discuss.**

## CAUTION!

- This is a broad question and it is for you to frame how you will answer it. The mention of 'successive governments' invites discussion of the historical context but take care not to narrate every change in a very descriptive fashion. Doing so will show knowledge but not analysis whereas demonstrating the ability to analyse will earn you higher marks.
- The question is essentially asking you to analyse whether the various family friendly rights achieve the policy goal of a work–life balance. There is a wide literature on this so support your views with reference to academic commentary.

## DIAGRAM ANSWER PLAN

Older generation of protections: maternity protection and limited rights for fathers

↓

New Labour and its focus on flexibility

↓

Expansion of flexible working but problems with default assumptions

New era of shared parental leave

## SUGGESTED ANSWER

As the question suggests, the UK has adopted a somewhat patchwork approach to issues of work–life balance, with a range of different rights being introduced in a piecemeal way. The result of this approach by successive governments is that the rules regarding issues such as maternity rights, flexible working, and parental leave are found in different statutory instruments and eligibility requirements differ.[1] This essay begins by considering the maternity provisions, which may be regarded as the first of the modern protections on work–life balance. It proceeds by exploring the extensions to family-friendly rights introduced by the New Labour government, before considering the latest government initiative of shared parental leave.[2] It concludes by suggesting that underlying the various rights is a somewhat rigid assumption that most employees will work full time with unbroken service. Moreover, it will be argued that care should be taken in assuming that more flexible employment is necessarily an indicator of a good work–life balance as it may also indicate a more precarious and less secure work situation.

The first generation of family-friendly rights are those associated with the protection from maternity and pregnancy discrimination.[3] The relevant law can be found in **ss71–73 of the Employment Rights Act 1996 ('ERA')** and the **Maternity and Parental Leave Regulations 1999 ('MPLR')**. These provide that an employee is entitled to statutory maternity leave of fifty-two weeks under **regs 4, 5, and 7 MPLR** as amended and **ss71 and 73 ERA**. Historically, the **Trade Union Reform and Employment Rights Act 1993** provided for fourteen weeks' maternity leave but this was increased incrementally until the changes brought in by the New Labour government in the **Work and Families Act 2006**, which set the current period of fifty-two weeks.[4] Statutory maternity pay is available to employees for the first thirty-nine weeks of maternity leave. The rate must be set at a level that will not disincentivise women from taking up their rights to maternity leave (***Gillespie* v *Northern Health Board* [1996] ICR 498, ECJ**). Provided employees comply with the statutory notice requirements (**reg. 11**), they have a right to return to work normally on the same terms and conditions as if they

[1] This introduction shows that you understand precisely the conundrum alluded to by the examiner.

[2] Setting out how you will argue an essay does two things. First, it shows the examiner that you have spent time planning your answer. Second, it tells the examiner that you will present the essay in a logical and structured way. Both create an excellent first impression!

[3] You could give more historical detail but a more convenient way of dealing with this issue is to talk in terms of 'generations' of rights. This allows you to take a more 'bird's eye' view of the issue, which is arguably what the question calls for.

[4] It is not necessary to discuss every increase in entitlement over the years.

had not been absent: **reg. 18(1)**. The right to return to work after Additional Maternity Leave (the first twenty-six weeks of leave is known as Ordinary and the second twenty-six weeks is Additional) is a right to return to 'the job in which she was employed before her absence or, if it is not reasonably practicable for the employer to permit her to return to that job, to another job which is both suitable for her and appropriate for her to do in the circumstances': **reg. 18(2)**. This is in recognition of the fact that after a year of maternity leave, it may not be reasonably practicable to return to the same job. These provisions were considered by the EAT in ***Blundell* v *Governing Body of St Andrews Catholic Primary School*** **[2007] ICR 1451**. In that case, a school teacher returned from maternity leave and was given a different class to teach. Langstaff J concluded that this was not a breach of the statutory right to return. The claimant was able to return to her role as a teacher at the same school, but not to the reception class she previously taught. As Langstaff J concluded, 'a tribunal is not obliged to freeze time at the precise moment [the claimant] takes maternity leave, but may have regard to the normal range within which variation [of precise positions in work] has previously occurred'.[5] A woman also has the right to return 'on terms and conditions not less favourable than those which would have applied if she had not been absent' (**reg. 18A(1)(b)**) and with seniority, pension rights, and similar rights preserved as though she had not been absent (**reg. 18A(1)(a)**).

[5] Discussion of this key case adds depth and shows your understanding.

These maternity rights are further supported by protections against employees from being dismissed or subjected to a detriment or discriminated against because of exercising their rights.[6] Under **s47C ERA**, an employee has the right not to be subjected to a detriment because of, amongst other things, 'pregnancy, childbirth or maternity' (**s47C(2)(a)**) and 'ordinary, compulsory or additional maternity leave' (**s47C(2)(b)**). This is also reflected in **reg. 19 MPLR**. Moreover, under **reg. 20** and **s99 ERA** there will be an automatic unfair dismissal if the reason or principal reason for an employee's dismissal is for a 'prescribed reason' which includes pregnancy, childbirth, maternity, and maternity leave. A further important right is found in **reg. 10 MPLR** which provides that in a redundancy situation during maternity leave where there is a suitable available vacancy, the employee on maternity leave is entitled to be offered this alternative employment. In July 2019, following a consultation, the government announced that it proposed extending this redundancy protection period to six months after the new mother has returned to work. A Bill to enable these changes was unable to complete its passage through Parliament in time for the end of the 2019 session. The Bill was reintroduced to Parliament in 2020 but these provisions have yet to be enacted. Finally, the discrimination provisions in the **Equality Act 2010 ('EA')**

[6] This is a good example of how a lot of material can be covered succinctly.

also offer protection. In ***Webb* v *EMO Air Cargo (UK) Ltd* [1995] ICR 1021**, it was held that dismissal on grounds of pregnancy amounted to direct sex discrimination. The benefit to employees of being able to rely on the **EA** is that compensation for discrimination is uncapped and awards for injury to feelings may also be made.

[7] This paragraph shows excellent critical analysis. By using academic authority, your argument is supported and appears more convincing.

While these maternity rights provide important protections to working mothers, the focus on mothers as care-givers arguably obscures the important role that fathers play.[7] Although the New Labour government took steps to try to redress the balance through the introduction of paternity leave in the **Paternity and Adoption Leave Regulations 2002**, these have been ineffective in encouraging more fathers to take leave for childcare. As Caracciolo Di Torella argues (E. Caracciolo Di Torella, 'New Labour, new dads: the impact of family-friendly legislation on fathers' (2007) 36(3) *Industrial Law Journal* 318), the limited scope of paternity leave made it unattractive to fathers and entrenched the idea that women are and should remain the primary care-givers. For James, the government's promotion of paternity leave as not only a way of caring for the child but also to 'support the mother' lends weight to the idea that mothers bear the primary responsibility for the unpaid labour of care (G. James, 'The Work and Families Act 2006: legislation to improve choice and flexibility?' (2006) 35(3) *Industrial Law Journal* 272).

The New Labour government's commitment to initiatives designed to improve work–life balance can also be seen in the statutory right to request flexible working, which has since been expanded in the **Flexible Working Regulations 2014 ('FWR')**. Put simply, any employee (not only those with caring responsibilities) who has been continuously employed by an employer for a period of twenty-six weeks (**reg. 3 FWR**) may request a contractual variation to work flexibly. This could include changes to hours, times, and place of work. An employer may refuse any application for certain prescribed business reasons under **s80G ERA**. These include the burden of additional costs and a detrimental impact on being able to meet customer demand. While initially appealing, the right is only a right to request flexible working not for it to be granted. Moreover, the default assumption that employees work full time and are requesting a deviation from this norm has the effect of shoring up the notion that the ideal (or certainly default) employee is one who is able to commit full time to a business. Furthermore, the ability of an employer to refuse on business-related grounds prioritises business interests over those of employees.

[8] A nice link to a highly topical debate.

For those with arguably most flexibility, such as those on zero hours contracts, this often comes at a cost. Such flexibility is highly favourable to employers who can recruit staff based on demand without ongoing costs, while workers (they may not meet the definition of employees) risk being engaged in highly precarious work without any guarantee of future employment.[8]

The 2010 Coalition government continued with New Labour's commitment to a flexible workforce by extending the right to request flexible working to all employees (not only those with children under a certain age) and through the introduction of a new right to shared parental leave. This allows a mother to share (or transfer) her entitlement to maternity leave with the father so long as certain qualifying conditions are met. Whilst arguably well intended in scope, it is mothers who, according to Mitchell, remain the 'gatekeepers' of the father's right to participate in childcare.[9] Thus, an ideological commitment to the idea of fathers as breadwinners and mothers as unpaid carers continues to be promoted (G. Mitchell, 'Encouraging fathers to care: the Children and Families Act 2014 and shared parental leave' (2015) 44(1) *Industrial Law Journal* 123).

[9] The shared parental leave provisions are complex. While you have to take care not to suggest to the examiner that you do not understand them by taking a cursory approach, here you maintain an appropriate balance by flagging that you are aware of the qualifying conditions and by discussing relevant critique.

It is apparent that successive governments have taken action to resolve the societal dilemma of how to manage caring obligations with paid employment. While earlier legislation was restricted to providing certain maternity rights to mothers, the scope of these rights has been expanded so that now fathers can play a greater role in care-giving. The problem is that without tackling the deep-seated idea that the rightful role of mothers is to provide unpaid care and that the ideal father is one who is the main breadwinner, fathers will lack the incentive to take up these rights. Furthermore, the different qualifying conditions to access certain rights mean that the full range of rights is only available to employees with a minimum period of qualifying service. In order to tackle the arguably growing problem of caring provision, it appears that more fundamental reform of the female carer/male breadwinner model may be needed.[10]

[10] A well thought-out conclusion. This is clearly not a rushed summary but a measured conclusion drawing together the key arguments and alluding to the need for more fundamental reform. Overall the impression left with the examiner is that this was a thoughtful, analytical response to the question.

## LOOKING FOR EXTRA MARKS?

- There is a vast academic literature on the topics addressed in this question. If you can refer to one or two papers that do not appear on your reading list, you are likely to be able to offer a more original perspective that should reward you with higher marks.
- You need to strike a balance in a question like this between giving sufficient detail of the law to show your learning but without getting too bogged down in the detail such that it stops you reflecting on the broader themes raised. If you feel that you are spending too much time on legislative detail for example, ask yourself 'how is this helping me answer the question?'

## QUESTION 3

Megashop plc is a supermarket chain. Karen works as a check-out operator and Jake works as a delivery driver. Their terms and conditions are governed by different collective agreements, with different unions representing the sales and delivery staff. The sales staff are overwhelmingly female; the delivery staff are exclusively male. Due to an upturn in demand over Christmas and an acute shortage of check-out staff, Megashop has had to recruit check-out operators on a temporary basis, engaging them on three-month contracts to cover the run-up to Christmas and the post-Christmas sales period. Megashop has agreed to pay the temporary employees £1,000 a year (pro rata) more than the existing check-out staff receive. Karen, who is paid £12,000 per year and has worked for Megashop for four years, has been asked to mentor Zafar, a temporary check-out operator in the same store. During a conversation with him, she discovered that he is being paid on a pro rata higher hourly rate. When Karen raised the issue with her local union rep, she was told that Megashop was paying the temporary check-out operators more due to staff shortages. She was also told by her rep that during a recent discussion between the two unions, it came to light that delivery drivers such as Jake who are based at a delivery warehouse a few miles from the store in which Karen works are being paid around £17,000 per year.

**Advise Karen on the possibility of an equal pay claim.**

## CAUTION!

- This is quite an involved question concerning issues such as the scope of comparison and the material factor defence. Take time to scrutinise the question to ensure that you address even minor points. For example, why is the examiner telling you Karen's length of service (hint: historic back pay!)
- Equally, be discerning about what to leave out. With the comparison with Zafar for example, it is clear that he is engaged on like work so there is no need to examine in detail whether he is an appropriate comparator.

## DIAGRAM ANSWER PLAN

**Identify the issues**

- Is Karen entitled to equal pay with Zafar and/or Jake?
- Does her employer have a material factor defence?

**Relevant law**

- Sections 65, 69, and 79 Equality Act 2010; Art. 157 TFEU
- Relevant case law including *Rainey*, *Wilkinson*, *North*, *Lawrence*, *Enderby*, *Gibson and Asda* v *Brierley*

**Apply the law**

- Karen is engaged on like work with Zafar but market forces may provide employer with a material factor defence
- Unclear whether Karen is engaged on work of equal value with Jake; common terms may be observed following *Asda*; she may be able to rely on the single source test under Art. 157

**Conclude**

- Unlikely that Karen will succeed in her claim using Zafar as a comparator
- She may be able to show that Megashop is a single source responsible for her and Jake's pay but she will have to show that they are engaged on work of equal value and it is open for Megashop to plead a material factor defence

## SUGGESTED ANSWER

Karen is employed on exactly the same job as Zafar, which means that she would base her equal pay claim under the 'like work' provision of **s65(1)(a) Equality Act 2010 ('EA')**. This requires that the work of her comparator is the same as or broadly similar to hers and that any differences between their work are not of practical importance. According to the EAT in ***Waddington* v *Leicester Council for Voluntary Services* [1977] ICR 266**, decided under the predecessor **Equal Pay Act 1970**, the correct approach is, first, to ask whether the woman's job is the same as or broadly similar to that of the male comparator and, second, if the answer is 'yes', the tribunal should then proceed to consider whether any differences are of practical importance as regards terms and conditions of employment. It would appear based on the facts of this case that Karen is engaged on like work to Zafar.[1]

[1] This is a strong start. Already you have discussed relevant legislation, case law, and reached a conclusion on a preliminary point.

The next issue is whether Megashop has a material factor defence under **s69 EA**. This requires it to demonstrate that the difference in pay is not due to sex. It needs to be a 'material' factor in the sense of 'significant and causally relevant' (see ***Strathclyde Regional Council* v *Wallace* [1998] ICR 205, HL**). Here, Megashop is likely to argue that the shortage of staff and need to entice employees to work for them for a short period of time has meant that it had to pay a higher rate of hourly pay. In ***Rainey* v *Greater Glasgow Health Board* [1987] ICR 129, HL**, the NHS in Scotland, when setting up a prosthetic service within the NHS, decided to pay employees directly recruited from the NHS on the agreed scale, the Whitley Council scale, but in order to ensure adequate staffing levels, they had to recruit prosthetists from the private sector where they were paid more. Therefore, the NHS offered higher pay to those recruited from the private sector. All of the private sector recruits were men, whereas all but one of the NHS recruits were women. Mrs Rainey, who had been recruited on Whitley Council rates, claimed equal pay with a man recruited from the private sector. The House of Lords agreed with the EAT and the Court of Session that the material factor defence had been made out, and dismissed Mrs Rainey's appeal. Moreover, the Court of Appeal in ***Walker v Co-operative Group Ltd* [2020] EWCA Civ 1075** confirmed that the material factor defence will continue to apply so long as it remains the cause of the difference. It would appear, therefore, that Megashop has a strong material factor defence in any comparison with Zafar on the same lines as the 'market forces' defence offered by the employer in ***Rainey*** and for so long as the staff shortages remain.[2]

[2] Reading the actual cases rather than short textbook summaries will repay you. It allows you to spot analogous factual scenarios.

The second option for Karen is to compare her pay with that of Jake, the delivery driver. She is clearly not engaged on like work with him and, given that their terms and conditions are governed by different collective agreements, it is extremely unlikely that their roles will have been evaluated under the same job evaluation study and rated as equivalent (**s65(1)(b)**). This leaves Karen with the only option of arguing that her work is of equal value to Jake's (**s65(1)(c)**).[3] The complicating factor[4] here, unlike with Zafar, is that **s79 EA** puts limitations on who may be used as a comparator. Either he must be employed by her employer or an associate employer and work at the same establishment (this was the case with Karen and Zafar: **s79(3)**) or Karen must show that Jake is employed by her employer or an associate (**s79(4)(a)**) and that although he works at a different establishment, 'common terms' apply (**s79(4)(b) and (c)**). We are told that Karen and Jake work at different sites. The case is factually very similar to ***Asda Stores Ltd v Brierley* [2019] EWCA Civ 44**. This case involved thousands of predominantly women claimants who worked in the supermarket who were claiming that their roles were of equal value to the (almost exclusively) male employees who were employed in Asda's distribution centres. So far the case has only considered a preliminary issue, namely whether the claimants can rely on the depot employees as comparators.

[3] Here you have quickly discounted the bases of the claim that will not apply, leaving you the space and time to concentrate on the most relevant factor.

[4] Gets straight to the heart of the issue.

'Establishment' is not defined in the **EA**. In ***Edinburgh City Council* v *Wilkinson* [2011] CSIH 70**, it was held that a 'distinct geographical location may, depending on the circumstances, constitute an important definitional element in identifying the establishment'. In that case, females working in schools and libraries for the same council as manual workers working as refuse collectors and in gardens were not employed at the same establishment. A further difficulty for Karen is showing that common terms are observed as her terms are governed by a different collective agreement. In ***Dumfries and Galloway Council* v *North* [2013] ICR 993**, female classroom assistants employed at the council's schools sought to compare themselves with male refuse collectors and gardeners. The terms and conditions of each group were governed by different collective agreements. As Lady Hale argued, 'it is no answer to say that no such male comparators ever would be employed, on those or any other terms, at the same establishment as the women. Otherwise, it would be far too easy for an employer so to arrange things that only men worked in one place and only women in another'. In other words, the tribunal should consider the terms upon which Jake would be employed if he were to be employed at the same establishment as Karen.[5]

[5] This is a difficult case but summarising a key part of the ratio shows the examiner that you have understood it.

There is a second way of broaching the issue of comparison and that is for Karen to rely directly on EU law namely **Art. 157 TFEU**. Rather than insisting that the comparator be drawn from the same establishment or if not the same establishment that common terms are observed, the EU provision requires that there is a 'single source' responsible for pay and crucially one that can take responsibility for putting any disparity right (***Lawrence* v *Regent Office Care Ltd* [2003] ICR 1092**).[6] It is not clear the extent to which matters of pay are delegated to different bodies within Megashop. In ***Robertson* v *DEFRA* [2005] ICR 750**, civil servants working across different departments where pay had been delegated to those departments were unable to show that there existed a single source responsible for pay. In Karen's case, we are merely told that she is employed by the same employer as Jake, albeit that different unions are responsible for negotiating pay. It may be, therefore, that she is able to show that Megashop is the single source responsible such that Jake would be an appropriate comparator. In ***Asda***, the tribunal held that a single source (Asda's board) was ultimately responsible for determining pay and so the claimants could compare their work with those working in the depot under the single source test. At the Court of Appeal in ***Asda***, Underhill LJ gave the leading judgment. Although he concluded that the tribunal had adopted the wrong approach in reaching its decision, he held that the claimants could compare their position with those working in the depot. Adopting a purposive approach to **s79(4) EA**, Underhill LJ clarified that the question of whether common terms applied was to be considered by comparing establishments. In other words, the exercise at this stage was not to compare between terms of the claimant's contract and those of the purported comparator but

[6] It is essential to discuss the different scopes of comparison between domestic and EU legislation.

to ask whether common terms were observed when comparing establishment with establishment. The Supreme Court heard a further appeal in this preliminary matter (**[2021] UKSC 10**).

Even if Karen can show that Jake is an appropriate comparator, the roles may not be of equal value if the demands of the jobs are different. Moreover, it is of course open for Megashop to put forward a material factor defence.

A material factor defence cannot be discriminatory on grounds of sex (**s69(1)(a) EA**). Assuming that Megashop is not crudely deciding that those employed on 'men's work' such as delivery drivers should be paid more than women (if this were the case, it would be direct discrimination), the circumstances of the case show that an exclusively male-dominated group of drivers are being paid more than a predominantly female group of check-out operators. This scenario is often referred to as an ***Enderby*** situation following the ECJ case of ***Enderby* v *Frenchay Health Authority*** **[1994] ICR 112**. This is captured in **s69(1)(b) and (2) EA**. This requires that the employer must objectively justify the material factor by showing that it is a proportionate means of achieving legitimate aim. This is because it is difficult to see how such a statistical gender imbalance where a female group is paid so much less than a male group cannot be tainted by sex (***Gibson* v *Sheffield City Council*** **[2010] ICR 708**).[7] If Karen can show that her work is of equal value to Jake's yet he is paid so much more as are others in his exclusively male group, Megashop will need to objectively justify the difference by showing that it was a proportionate means of achieving a legitimate aim. 'Red-circling' the higher wage-earners' pay for a period with the long-term objective of bringing both groups into line and reducing inequality is always to be regarded as a legitimate aim (**s69(3) EA**) but we are not given any information in this case that can help us advise on the factors that the employer may advance and the credibility of those factors.[8]

The only remaining issue concerning Karen's claim is whether she may claim a remedy (the difference in pay between herself and Jake) for the entire four-year period in which she has been employed. **Section 132 EA** permits arrears to be awarded going back six years, so Karen may claim arrears going back over the previous four years' employment.[9]

[7] Another difficult case allowing you to demonstrate your understanding of a complex area.

[8] Do not hypothesise. This goes far enough to show one possible legitimate aim but do not engage in saying 'what if the employer argued X, Y, or Z' as there is simply not enough information to go on here. If you have dealt with the other issues in detail, you will probably not have time to engage in making up further possibilities!

[9] This rounds off the answer nicely and shows that you have picked up on the four-year point mentioned in the facts.

## LOOKING FOR EXTRA MARKS?

- It pays to keep an eye on current developments, such as the Supreme Court in ***Asda Stores Ltd v Brierley***.
- A mark of a strong student is knowing what to leave out as well as what to put in. Put yourself in the examiner's shoes. If you were to read an answer that strays into irrelevant information, what impression does that create? You might think that it shows the extent of

your revision and knowledge but it can also show someone who does not understand the area so 'tells all you know'.

- There is a lot to equal pay law and much of it is complex. Once you have mastered your revision, think of what you have learned as being like a toolbox. You may not need to use all the tools to answer a particular question but you will have the confidence of knowing that all the tools are there for you and you can choose which ones are appropriate.

## QUESTION 4

**The shared parental leave framework is commendable in its aim of allowing parents to decide how best to share leave between them but its potential to disrupt entrenched gendered stereotypes about care in the family context has not been fulfilled. Discuss.**

## CAUTION!

- You will obviously need to show the examiner that you understand the statutory framework of shared parental leave but the question is asking you to go beyond a mere technical explanation of the rules.
- To do well in a question of this nature, it is important that you engage with the wider academic literature to help support any points you make.

## DIAGRAM ANSWER PLAN

Older generation of protections: maternity protection

Shared parental leave

What are the goals behind parental leave?

Default assumption that workers are full time; problems with pay

Does it entrench or disrupt gender stereotypes?

## SUGGESTED ANSWER

The reconciliation of family life with paid work has, over the years, been tackled via a range of policy solutions. Until relatively recently, most attention has been paid to supporting mothers with maternity leave and pay. While this approach has the advantage of directing resources to the area where it is most needed—it is women, after all, who bear children and typically have primary caregiving responsibilities—one significant drawback is that it arguably perpetuates a model of care-giving mother and breadwinning father that does not reflect modern dual-earner households and risks entrenching gender stereotypes. In this essay, I will provide a brief overview of the key provisions of the **Shared Parental Leave Regulations 2014 (SI 2014/3050)** before critiquing the Regulations from the perspective of whether they help to disrupt gendered stereotypes.[1] The central argument that I will advance is that despite the well-intentioned aims behind the Regulations, on their own they are not sufficient to achieve genuine equality in care-giving between working parents.[2]

The shared parental leave framework applies to all children born on or after April 2015 (**reg. 2(1)**). It is a marked departure from the UK's previous approach to family-friendly rights. As Welden-Johns has noted, policies designed to support working parents can be captured in distinct phases from those that focused on support for mothers (such as maternity leave), those which were extended to carers more generally (such as the right to request flexible working), and those which focused on fathers (such as the right to paternity leave) (G. Welden-Johns, 'The Additional Paternity Leave Regulations 2010: a new dawn or more "sound-bite" legislation?' (2011) 33(1) *Journal of Social Welfare & Family Law* 25).[3] This current policy phase can be characterised by an overarching policy goal of giving families the flexibility to determine for themselves how best to share leave between parents. In this respect, it has the potential to unsettle familiar patterns of care-giving.

Regardless of how long a woman has worked for her employer, she is entitled to twelve months' maternity leave. This includes a compulsory period of two weeks' maternity leave during which the mother must be on leave from work (**s72(1) Employment Rights Act 1996**; **reg. 8 Maternity and Parental Leave etc. Regulations 1999 (SI 1999/3312)**). The **Shared Parental Leave Regulations** follow a similar model with a requirement that the first two weeks of the entitlement of fifty-two weeks must be taken by the mother but thereafter the remainder of the fifty weeks can be split between the parents as they see fit. The Regulations apply in the case of adoption

[1] This briefly sets out how your answer will be structured.

[2] A sophisticated way of telling the examiner what you will argue and demonstrates clear engagement with the question.

[3] Good use of authority to show wider reading.

(**reg. 2(2)**) and references to 'father' can also include the mother's husband, partner, or civil partner at the time of the birth (**reg. 3(3)**).

There are a number of procedural hurdles that must be overcome for parents to enjoy the entitlement to shared parental leave. In summary, for fathers to share parental leave, the mother must first be entitled to statutory maternity leave, pay, or allowance and must have ended or curtailed this right (**reg. 5(3)(c) and (d)**).[4] This means that the right rests with the mother who can choose whether to transfer it to the father. For the father to enjoy the right to shared parental leave, he must show that, apart from the mother, he has the main responsibility for the care of the child (**reg. 4(3)(b)**) and that he can meet the conditions of the employment and earnings test set out in **reg. 36**. This test provides that he must have been employed or self-employed for at least twenty-six of the sixty-six weeks immediately before the expected week of childbirth and that he must earn more than a statutorily prescribed amount (**reg. 36(1)(a) and (5)**). Once these conditions are met, the parents can decide how they wish to share the remaining fifty weeks of parental leave between them (**reg. 6(1)**).

[4] The **SPL Regulations** are complex. While you need to show the examiner that you understand the Regulations, the question is focused more on their impact. It can be tricky to balance showing your knowledge and leaving enough space to analyse.

The right to shared parental leave appears highly progressive. By allowing parents to decide for themselves how best to share parental leave, it acknowledges that modern families may not resemble the traditional model of female carer and male breadwinner. Moreover, if more fathers take extended periods of parental leave, gradually the association between women and care-giving that has been accused of inhibiting women's pay and progression in the workplace can be lessened.[5] In 2015, the UK government and the Equality and Human Rights Commission investigated the experiences of employers and mothers in respect of pregnancy and maternity-related discrimination and disadvantage. While the employers reported being generally positive towards pregnant women and new mothers, 17 per cent of them considered new mothers to be less interested in career progression compared with other colleagues and 7 per cent of employers thought new mothers were less committed to work compared with colleagues (HM Government and EHRC, 'Pregnancy and Maternity-Related Discrimination and Disadvantage: Experiences of Employers' (2015), p. 12). In contrast, 50 per cent of mothers surveyed thought that motherhood had a negative impact on their opportunities, status at work, and even their job security (HM Government and EHRC, 'Pregnancy and Maternity-Related Discrimination and Disadvantage: Experiences of Mothers' (2015), p. 12).[6] The discrepancy in perceptions is interesting with more women than employers perceiving a negative impact on their progression opportunities. Notwithstanding this variance in perception, with almost one in five employers surveyed expressing the view that returning mothers are less interested in progressing with their careers, it suggests that allowing fathers to share parental leave has the potential to break this association

[5] A balanced discussion showing the positive aspects of the Regulations before considering the drawbacks.

[6] Authority can come from a variety of sources including policy and investigation reports.

between caring responsibilities and negative assumptions about commitment to work.

Despite this positive interpretation of the shared parental leave framework and the potential that it offers to disrupt gender stereotypes, there are a number of drawbacks with the Regulations as currently drafted. The first is that the original right rests with the mother who can decide whether to transfer a proportion of her entitlement to the father. By framing the Regulations so that the entitlement 'belongs' to the mother, legislators are arguably implicitly entrenching the idea that caring naturally falls to the mother. A second concern is a pragmatic one. Men generally continue to earn more than women and caring is a factor that has been linked to the gender pay gap (J. Rubery and D. Grimshaw, 'The 40-year pursuit of equal pay: a case of constantly moving goalposts' (2015) 39 *Cambridge Journal of Economics* 319).[7] If the father is the higher earner in the family, there is little incentive for fathers to take leave when their income will be reduced to statutory paternity pay. In the Court of Appeal (permission to appeal to the Supreme Court was refused), in the conjoined cases of ***Ali* v *Capita Management Ltd and Hextall* v *The Chief Constable of Leicestershire Police* [2019] EWCA Civ 90**, the court considered whether it was unlawful to pay a man less than a woman would receive with enhanced maternity pay. In ***Ali***, the employer's policy provided for enhanced maternity pay for mothers but statutory paternity pay only for fathers. A similar workplace policy applied in ***Hextall***. In ***Ali***, the claimant argued that it was directly discriminatory to pay a woman enhanced maternity pay in these circumstances while in ***Hextall*** the claimant framed his case as one of indirect discrimination (although the court found that this should properly have been framed as one of unequal pay). In both cases, the court held that the enhanced payments to mothers were not discriminatory.

The court's rationale reveals the difficulties in attempting to unsettle associating mothers with care. Taking a step back to consider the purpose of shared parental leave, the court had regard to the CJEU decision in ***Commission* v *Luxembourg* (Case C-519/03)**. In that case, the Court drew a distinction between parental leave where the purpose is to provide care for the child and maternity leave where there is a dual purpose. One objective behind maternity leave is to provide a period of recovery for the mother. This logic lies behind the UK's compulsory maternity leave period. The second purpose was, held the CJEU, to protect the 'special relationship' between a woman and her child. This latter purpose reflects the special treatment given to women at both EU and UK levels. On one view, it is important that women are given these protections to protect their health and wellbeing but the risk is that fathers will feel precluded from genuinely sharing care-giving with mothers.

[7] Examiners often give credit for students who can make connections with different aspects of a module. Here, the student is drawing on research on equal pay.

This examination of shared parental leave is an example of a well-intentioned piece of legislation, which ultimately may not fulfil its objective. One reason for this is that it is firmly rooted in the default assumption that mothers will be the primary carers and that they may choose to share leave with fathers. Another reason is that in those workplaces where enhanced entitlements to maternity pay are provided beyond the statutory minimum, the court has held that it is lawful not to extend these to fathers. Arguably, what is needed is a genuine transformation of the workplace that starts with the presumption that everyone cares, with working life then being shaped around this notion.

## LOOKING FOR EXTRA MARKS?

- There are many approaches you could take to answer this question. What matters is that you have a clear argument and you present this persuasively.
- Reading widely helps you canvass a variety of viewpoints and to develop your own opinions on a topic. If you are unsure about where to start, have a look at the footnotes in a paper you are already reading or look up the author's other publications.

## TAKING THINGS FURTHER

- S. Court-Brown, 'Is lower pay for shared parental leave discrimination? *Ali* v *Capita Customer Management Ltd; Hextall* v *Chief Constable of Leicestershire Police*' (2020) 49(4) *Industrial Law Journal* 626

  *Interesting analysis of the combined Court of Appeal cases of* **Ali** *and* **Hextall**
- G. James and E. Spruce, 'Workers with elderly dependents: Employment law's response to the latest care-giving conundrum' (2015) 35 *Legal Studies* 463

  *Provides an important reflection on a topical issue of how the law can respond to the increasing 'conundrum' of how employees can balance paid employment with unpaid elder care*
- R. Russell and A. Masselot, 'Why Do We Care? The Shifting Concept of Care in New Zealand and in the United Kingdom' (2020) 36(1) *International Journal of Comparative Labour Law and Industrial Relations* 81

  *A comparative analysis of New Zealand and UK approaches to the reconciliation of childcare and paid employment*

## Online resources

www.oup.com/uk/qanda/

For extra essay and problem questions on this topic, as well as advice on revision and exam technique, please visit the online resources.

# Statutory rights regulating the employment relationship

# 11

## ARE YOU READY?

In order to attempt the questions in this chapter, you must have covered the following areas in your revision:

- Rights regarding working time including rest breaks and annual leave
- Protections for those who make a public interest disclosure

## KEY DEBATES

**Debate: Protection for whistle-blowers**

To what extent does UK legislation encourage or deter workers from making public interest disclosures?

**Debate: Working time protections**

Compared to the USA, the UK may appear to have generous protections regarding working time specifically with regards to annual leave. Others might argue that more could be done to encourage a better work–life balance. How does the working time legislation protect the interests of both workers and employers?

## QUESTION 1

Hang has been assigned by his employer, Chemical Advisory and Consultancy Services Ltd (CACS), as a project consultant to Winkton Industrial Processes Ltd (WIP), a company supplying chemicals to the metal-finishing industry. The agreement between CACS and WIP stipulates that Hang is to be engaged upon WIP's standard terms of employment and that CACS is to ensure that Hang obeys all instructions issued to him by WIP concerning the work he is engaged upon. Hang has signed an agreement with WIP that states: 'All matters discussed at any management meetings, and all records of such meetings, are strictly confidential.' He has now worked for WIP for fifteen months.

At the last management meeting concerning operational activities, which Hang attended in his capacity as consultant, Shoab, the operations manager, indicated that the Board had decided to save the £100,000 annual cost to dispose safely of the company's highly toxic waste by discharging it directly into the local river. Hang makes his concerns about this proposal known at the meeting but is told by Shoab that the decision has been taken at a higher level and that he should not create any problems. Hang again raises the matter with Gina, the managing director, who says, 'Just forget about it. By the way, all matters discussed at management meetings are confidential. If you want to continue to work here, you'll remember that.' Hang informs Gina that he is very concerned that what is proposed is illegal, to which Gina replies, 'We may need to have a word with CACS if you create problems for us.'

Hang has informed the Environment Agency of WIP's proposed pollution of the river. Two weeks later, CACS withdraws Hang from the WIP work because of complaints about his poor timekeeping (Hang was ten minutes late for work on two occasions). CACS has encountered great difficulty in placing Hang with other clients. He was told by CACS's managing director that this could be because of WIP's actions as Gina had told CAC's managing director that she would 'make sure that Hang never works in the chemical industry again'.

**Advise Hang of any protection afforded to him by employment law in this situation.**

## CAUTION!

- You are asked to advise Hang regarding employment law so you should not discuss any protections that you may have learned about in other modules such as environmental law.

## DIAGRAM ANSWER PLAN

| | |
|---|---|
| Identify the issues | ■ Has Hang made a qualifying disclosure?<br>■ Is it a protected disclosure?<br>■ Has he been subjected to a detriment on the ground that he has made a protected disclosure? |
| Relevant law | ■ Sections 47B, 43A, 43B, 43C, 43F, 43J, 43K, and 49 Employment Rights Act 1996<br>■ Relevant case law including *Bolton School*, *Babula*, *Chesterton*, *Gilham*, *Kilraine*, and *Fecitt* |
| Apply the law | ■ Hang qualifies to bring a claim due to the extended definition of worker for these purposes<br>■ Has made a qualifying disclosure to a relevant person therefore it is a protected disclosure<br>■ Should be able to show causative link between disclosure and subsequent treatment |
| Conclude | ■ Hang has been subjected to a detriment on the ground that he has made a protected disclosure<br>■ No suggestion that he has acted in anything other than good faith therefore any compensation should not be reduced |

## SUGGESTED ANSWER

The key issue raised[1] by Hang's circumstances is whether he has been subjected to a detriment on the ground that he has made a protected disclosure, contrary to **s47B(1) of the Employment Rights Act 1996 ('ERA')**. This protection applies to 'workers' and for the purposes of the whistle-blowing protection this is given a particularly broad definition (**s43K ERA**; ***Gilham* v *Ministry of Justice*** **[2019] ICR 1655**). **Section 43K(1)(a)** provides that a worker, for these purposes, includes a person who 'works or worked for a person in circumstances in which he is or was introduced or supplied to do that work by a third person, and the terms on which he is or was engaged to do the work are or were in practice substantially determined not by him but by the person for whom he works or worked, by the third person or by both of them'.[2] Hang was supplied to WIP by CACS (the third person) and works under WIP's terms of employment. CACS must ensure that Hang obeys all of WIP's instructions and there is also a personal

[1] This opening sentence shows the examiner that you understand the area under discussion. It creates a good first impression by reassuring the marker.

[2] The wider definition of 'worker' for the purposes of whistle-blowing protection is a key feature of the protected disclosure regime so you need to be familiar with the definition.

agreement by Hang to do so. Therefore, Hang works on terms that are 'in practice substantially determined ... by the person for whom he works', i.e. WIP. He is, therefore, a 'worker' for the purposes of engaging the whistle-blowing (public interest disclosure) legislation.

Hang is only protected if he has made a 'protected disclosure'. This means that it must be: (1) a 'qualifying disclosure'; and (2) that is made in certain prescribed ways (**s43A ERA**).

[3] Clear, logical link to the next issue.

Is there a qualifying disclosure?[3] According to **s43B(1) ERA**, this means 'any disclosure of information which, in the reasonable belief of the worker making the disclosure, is made in the public interest and tends to show [one or more categories of wrongdoing]'. These categories include situations where, in the reasonable belief of the worker: (1) 'a criminal offence has been committed, or is being committed or is likely to be committed': **s43B(1)(a)**; (2) 'that a person has failed, is failing or is likely to fail to comply with any legal obligation to which he is subject': **s43B(1)(b)**; (3) 'that the health or safety of any individual has been, is being or is likely to be endangered': **s43B(1)(d)**; (4) 'that the environment has been, is being or is likely to be damaged': **s43B(1)(e)**; or (5) 'that information tending to show any matter falling within any one of the preceding paragraphs has been, or is likely to be deliberately concealed': **s43B(1)(f)**. The nature of the alleged wrongdoing would be captured by one or more of these categories.

[4] There are four key aspects (or ingredients) of a qualifying disclosure. Write a brief comment on each.

Taking each of the remaining limbs of the qualifying disclosure in turn,[4] has there been a disclosure of information? Yes: he has told Shoab of his concerns, reported the matter to Gina, and latterly informed the relevant regulatory body. The Court of Appeal in ***Kilraine* v *Wandsworth LBC* [2018] ICR 1850** held that the distinction in ***Bolton School* v *Evans* [2007] IRLR 140** between a mere allegation and disclosure of actual data/information was an unhelpful gloss on what the legislation required by way of disclosure. Rather than focus on the form of disclosure, the Court of Appeal held that the focus should be on whether the disclosure contains sufficient and specific factual content. In this case, it appears that Hang has disclosed concerns about the 'proposed pollution', suggesting that the disclosure meets the requisite standard.

Does Hang hold a 'reasonable belief' that the information 'tends to show' wrongdoing? The courts and tribunals must decide what constitutes a 'reasonable belief'. In ***Babula* v *Waltham Forest College* [2007] IRLR 346**, the Court of Appeal held that provided the belief (objectively considered) is reasonable, it is irrelevant if it turns out to be wrong. For example, even if it subsequently transpired that Hang was misguided in his belief that an environmental breach had occurred, what matters is Hang's reasonable belief.[5] At the time of making the disclosure, it seems that Hang does indeed hold such a reasonable belief and it is likely that the information tends to show

[5] An important case, the ratio of which is then applied to the facts here.

that: (1) is satisfied in that it is likely that a criminal offence will be committed if the chemicals are discharged into the river, as proposed; under (2), WIP is a person likely to fail to comply with its legal obligations concerning the discharge; under (3), if discharged, the chemicals are likely to endanger the health and safety of individuals; under (4), the environment is likely to be damaged in that the river will be polluted; and under (5), given the behaviour of WIP's senior employees, it seems that information relating to these matters is likely to be deliberately concealed. Moreover, Hang's expertise in this area is a factor that is entitled to be respected when determining the reasonableness or otherwise of his belief in the alleged wrongdoing (***Korashi* v *Abertawe Bro Morgannwg University Local Health Board* [2012] IRLR 4**).

Finally, is the disclosure in the 'public interest'? The issue is clearly one that extends beyond Hang's personal interests to wider issues of public environmental concern and so is likely to be in the public interest (***Chesterton Global Ltd* v *Nurmohamed* [2015] IRLR 614**).[6] Although we are not told about the specific complaints raised by Hang, the court will consider what was in his mind at the time of making the disclosure and whether he thought the issue raised concerns that were of wider interest to the public (***Ibrahim* v *HCA International Ltd* [2020] IRLR 224**).

Hang has made a qualifying disclosure but for it to be 'protected' it must be disclosed in one of a narrow range of prescribed ways.[7] Hang first makes the disclosure to Gina, the managing director of WIP (a third party), rather than to his employer, in accordance with **s43C(1)(b)**. As the matter is the responsibility of WIP, rather than CACS, this is an internal, third-party disclosure. It is, therefore, a protected disclosure. Hang has gone on to make a disclosure to a prescribed person. The Secretary of State may prescribe certain persons for these purposes (the Environment Agency is prescribed for environmental matters) under the **Public Interest Disclosure (Prescribed Persons) Order 1999 (SI 1999/1549)**. For it to be a protected disclosure to a prescribed person, Hang must show that he reasonably believes that the failure falls within the description of matters in respect of which the Agency is prescribed and reasonably believes that the information is substantially true: **s43F(1)(b)**. These provisions would appear to be satisfied in Hang's case.[8]

Hang has the right not to suffer a detriment for making the protected disclosure: **s47B**. If a reasonable worker might consider themselves to have been disadvantaged, this may amount to a detriment (***Jesudason* v *Alder Hey Children's NHS Trust* [2020] EWCA Civ 73**). The trickier issue is whether the detriment was 'on the ground that' he has made a protected disclosure (***Tiplady* v *City of Bradford MDC* [2020] IRLR 230**). He clearly has suffered a detriment, first, in

[6] This looks like an obvious point but shows that you have explored all aspects of a qualifying disclosure.

[7] This links to the second issue: can Hang 'convert' a qualifying disclosure into a protected one? Again, be logical and work through each person to whom he has disclosed.

[8] Summarise as you go by giving mini-conclusions on each issue.

being withdrawn from the assignment with WIP and, second, through the inference that WIP has used its influence to prevent other persons in the industry from engaging him. It must, however, be established that the detriment is suffered because he made the disclosure rather than because of his lateness. There must be a link between the act and the protected disclosure (***Vivian* v *Bournemouth BC*** **[2011] UKEAT 0254/10**). In ***Fecitt* v *NHS Manchester*** **[2012] ICR 372**, Elias LJ opined that **s47B** will be infringed if the protected disclosure 'materially influences' the employer's treatment. Given Gina's comments, it would be reasonable to conclude that WIP's actions were 'on the ground that' Hang made a protected disclosure.

This leaves the issue of the contractual confidentiality provisions prohibiting disclosure of matters discussed at management meetings. Such a provision is void 'in so far as it purports to preclude [Hang] from making the protected disclosure': **s43J ERA.**[9]

[9] A neat, contained point but one that must be dealt with given that the examiner has included this information in the question.

Hang may complain to the Employment Tribunal that he has been subjected to a detriment. If the claim is well-founded, the tribunal may make a declaration to that effect and order compensation to be paid (**s49(1) ERA**). If it appears to the tribunal that the disclosure has not been made in good faith, the tribunal may 'if it considers it just and equitable in all the circumstances to do so, reduce any award it makes to the worker by no more than 25 per cent' (**s49(6A) ERA**). There is no suggestion that Hang has acted in anything other than good faith.

## LOOKING FOR EXTRA MARKS?

- Although the provisions on whistle-blowing appear complex, they are actually highly structured and formulaic. Think of the provisions like a flowchart. First, you need a qualifying disclosure—work logically through each of the four limbs of the definition (disclosure of information, reasonable belief, public interest, tends to show wrongdoing). Then to convert it to a protected disclosure, it needs to be made to a particular person.
- When it comes to converting a qualifying disclosure to a protected disclosure, remember that the further outside the organisation you disclose, the more the law demands.

## QUESTION 2

'The UK's working time policy has been motivated by the need to protect workers' health and safety from the harm that can be caused by working long hours without sufficient rest.'

**Analyse this statement with respect to the key provisions of the Working Time Regulations 1998.**

## CAUTION!

- This question is asking you to 'analyse' so this means evaluating the statement and putting forward evidence in support or against the claim made.
- Remember that the examiner is testing your ability to analyse and evaluate so it does not matter whether they agree with you. What matters is that you can discuss the main legislative provisions and case law, and put forward a convincing case in support or against the statement.

## DIAGRAM ANSWER PLAN

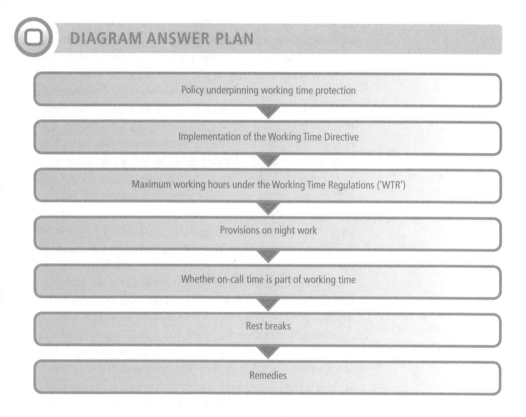

Policy underpinning working time protection

Implementation of the Working Time Directive

Maximum working hours under the Working Time Regulations ('WTR')

Provisions on night work

Whether on-call time is part of working time

Rest breaks

Remedies

## SUGGESTED ANSWER

The **Working Time Regulations 1998 ('WTR')** implement the **Working Time Directive (93/104/EC)**. The **Working Time Directive** was enacted as a health and safety measure. It proved controversial and was opposed by the UK in ***United Kingdom* v *Council of the European Union (Working Time Directive)*** **(Case C-84/94)**. Interestingly, in that case the ECJ took a wider view of 'health and safety' as not merely being about preventing work-related accidents but included a more holistic notion of worker 'well-being'.[1]

[1] This addresses specifically the idea of the policy intention behind the legislation.

The resulting implementation of the **Working Time Directive** in the **WTR** is a curious mix of measures which allow limits to be placed on the number of hours worked in a week and provide minimum entitlements to rest. These protections will be examined in turn insofar as they affect adult workers (young workers have additional protections: (**reg. 5A**)). These protections must, however, be seen in the context of managerial control and the pressure (albeit that it may be implicit) on workers to contract out of certain protections.[2]

[2] Demonstrates that you understand the industrial relations context in which the **WTR** operates.

The **WTR** cover not only employees but also those who personally perform work or provide services: **reg. 2(1)**. Perhaps the most well-known protection is the legal limit set out in **reg. 4(1)**, which provides that unless the employer has 'first obtained the worker's agreement in writing', working time shall not exceed an average of forty-eight hours over seven days. The ability to 'opt out' of the limits on the working week (**reg. 5**) was introduced in the **Working Time Directive** following representations from the UK government and is arguably the most controversial aspect of the working time regime. While on one view it allows individual workers autonomy to determine the hours they wish to work, another view holds that it is too easy for employers to pressure workers to sign an opt-out. Workers may appear to be consenting freely in signing an opt-out but the risk is that such consent may not be completely unfettered.[3] The number of weekly working hours is generally calculated over a reference period of seventeen weeks (**reg. 4(3)**), which allows for peaks and troughs in the hours of work. An employer must take all reasonable steps to ensure that this limit is complied with: **reg. 4(2)**.

[3] A good example of analysis. A descriptive treatment of the opt-out provision would simply state what it is. An analytical treatment goes deeper and assesses its repercussions. The ability to analyse is key to doing well.

The **WTR** recognise the additional demands that are made on a worker who works unsociable hours.[4] **Regulation 6(1)** provides that a night worker's normal hours of work shall not exceed an average of eight hours in every period of twenty-four hours. A night worker is defined in **reg. 2** as someone who either: (1) as a normal course, works at least three hours of their daily working time during night time; or (2) 'who is likely, during night time, to work at least such proportion of his annual working time as may be specified … in a collective agreement or work force agreement'. Under (1), a person works hours 'as a normal course … if he works such hours on the majority of days on which he works': **reg. 2**. In ***R* v *Attorney General for Northern Ireland, ex parte Burns*** **[1999] IRLR 315**, the Northern Ireland High Court held that a worker who worked for at least three hours during the night on one week in each three-week cycle was a night worker. It further held that 'as a normal course' meant 'as a regular feature'. Night time is defined as a period of 'not less than seven hours, and which includes the period between midnight and 5 a.m.': **reg. 2**. In default of any relevant agreement, this period is between 11 p.m. and 6 a.m.: **reg. 2**.

[4] Consider how you will link different topics. One sign of a strong candidate is an elegant writing style so it is worth spending a little time on the language you use so that your essay flows well.

[5] You will not have time to consider all the provisions of the **WTR** so focus on those that are most important/controversial.

One issue that has vexed the courts and which is particularly problematic for night workers is how to interpret 'on-call' time.[5] The problem with on-call time is that the worker is not entirely free to rest; the employer retains some control over the worker's time. However, the nature of on-call work can differ. While some workers may be required to be present at their place of work, others merely need to be contactable in case of an emergency. The difficulty this presents is how such time is to be regarded when calculating the hours of work for the **WTR**. Put simply, is a worker 'working' while on call? Under **reg. 2**, 'working time' includes any period when a worker is 'working, at his employer's disposal and carrying out his activity or duties'. In ***Sindicato Medicos Publica* v *Valenciana* (Case C-303/98) [2001] ICR 1116**, the ECJ held that time on call at the place of work counts as 'working time', but not if the worker is not at the place of work. This was upheld in the EU case of ***Landeshaupstadt Kiel* v *Jaegar* (Case C-151/02) [2003] IRLR 804** despite the worker being given a place to sleep during on-call time. More recently, the ECJ considered the question of on-call time where there was a requirement to be on standby. In the cases of ***D. J.* v *Radiotelevizija Slovenija* (Case C-344/19)** and ***R. J.* v *Stadt Offenbach am Main* (Case C-580/19)**, the ECJ held that a worker could be working if they were on standby and needed to be contactable but only if their ability to pursue their own leisure was 'objectively and significantly' impacted by the need to be on standby. Although the UK is no longer bound by the ECJ's judgments pursuant to **s6(1) European Union (Withdrawal) Act 2018**, it can still look to these for interpretation. Applying the EU's jurisprudence to the question of on-call time, it would appear that a crucial factor in determining whether the time on standby should be counted as 'work' will include the extent to which a worker can genuinely pursue their own interests or whether the requirement that they have to be at work very soon after receiving a notification means that their freedom to pursue their own leisure is significantly curtailed.

[6] A good example of how some thought has been given to how to link different topics in an elegant way.

In addition to setting limits on the number of weekly working hours, the **WTR** protections provide for certain minimum periods of rest. These include rest breaks during the working day and week, and the right to holiday during the year.[6] **Regulation 12(1)** provides that a worker is entitled to a rest break where their daily working time is more than six hours. Details regarding the rest break may be contained in a collective agreement (**reg. 12(2)**) but, subject to this, a rest break should be 'an uninterrupted period of not less than 20 minutes, and the worker is entitled to spend it away from his workstation if he has one' (**reg. 12(3)**). In ***Network Rail Infrastructure Ltd* v *Crawford* [2019] EWCA Civ 269**, the Court of Appeal held that in special cases where an uninterrupted break of twenty minutes cannot be taken, the compensatory rest need not be an uninterrupted break of twenty minutes but could be more frequent, shorter breaks. In each period of twenty-four hours, a worker is entitled to a rest period of not less than eleven consecutive hours (**reg. 10(1)**) and generally a rest period of twenty-four hours in a seven-day week (**reg. 11(1)**).

The most significant period of entitlement to rest is annual leave, i.e. holidays. A substantial body of case law has been generated on this issue.[7] In the UK, a worker is entitled to 5.6 weeks' annual leave based on a worker's normal working week (**regs 13 and 13A**). Importantly, the right is to paid leave (**reg. 16(1)**). This is understandable given the intention behind the **Working Time Directive** that it is to protect workers' well-being. The rationale is that if workers were not paid during holidays, they would be less inclined to use their annual leave entitlement. The importance of this right was made clear in the case of ***Robinson-Steele* v *R. D. Retail Services Ltd* (Case C-131/04) [2006] ICR 932**. In that case, the employer paid 'rolled up' holiday pay. This meant that holiday pay was added to the hourly rate of a worker rather than being paid during the holiday period. The idea was that the worker would then budget this sum from their hourly rate to cover periods of leave. The ECJ held that this was unlawful. It may be unrealistic to expect all workers to budget from their hourly pay in this way, meaning that if they were not to be paid during annual leave (on the basis that the payment was rolled up into their usual pay), they would be less likely to take holidays.

A further area which has generated a body of case law has been what should happen when a worker is sick during annual leave. Perhaps unsurprisingly given the policy intention behind the Directive, it is not appropriate for an employer to equate a period of sick leave as rest for the purposes of annual leave. This means that a worker on sick leave may choose to take annual leave during this period (***Stringer* v *Revenue and Customs* (Case C-520/06) [2009] ICR 932**). Moreover, if a worker has been unable to take their full annual leave entitlement due to sickness, unused holiday can be carried forward to the next leave year (***Schultz-Hoff* v *Deutsche Rentenversicherung Bund* (Case C-350/06) [2009] IRLR 214**) and if a worker falls sick during their holiday or before they go on holiday, they are entitled to postpone their annual leave and take the time off as sick leave instead (***Pereda* v *Madrid Movilidad SA* (Case C-277/08) [2009] IRLR 959**).

The rights under the **WTR** are underpinned by protections against unfair dismissal for asserting these rights. In certain circumstances, where dismissal of an employee is for a reason (or, where there is more than one, the principal reason) relating to rights conferred by the **WTR**, it will be automatically unfair: **s101A Employment Rights Act 1996 ('ERA')**.[8] These circumstances include: (1) the refusal

[7] There is much that can be written on paid annual leave including how pay is determined. You need to consider how much to include. While an important issue, aim for balance in the context of the whole essay.

[8] Although this right falls outside the **WTR**, it is a good example of how you can use your knowledge from another part of the module in an effective and relevant way. This demonstrates your grasp of the wider subject area.

(or proposed refusal) of the employee to comply with a requirement that the employer imposed (or proposed to impose) in contravention of the Regulations; or (2) the refusal (or proposed refusal) of the employee to forego a right conferred on them by the Regulations: **s101A(a) and (b)**. In addition to these rights, where a worker has suffered a detriment for, inter alia: (1) refusing (or proposing to refuse) to comply with a requirement that the employer imposed (or proposed to impose) in contravention of the **WTR**; or (2) refusing (or proposing to refuse) to forgo a right conferred on them by the Regulations, they may bring a claim for detriment under **s45A ERA**.

This exploration of key provisions of the **WTR** has shown that workers are entitled to a number of safeguards designed partly to encourage a greater work–life balance but primarily to protect health and safety.[9] The EU has been particularly influential in this regard, choosing to take a broad view of what amounts to health and safety to include the wider issue of worker well-being. Given the UK's initial reluctance to adopt the **Working Time Directive**, it will be interesting to see the extent to which the UK and EU will diverge post-Brexit in their approaches to the protection of working time. From the review of the protections in the **WTR**, it is clear that a tension exists between an employer's wish to have as much flexibility to organise their human resources as possible and a worker's right to time off. This has manifested itself in claims about payment during holidays and more fundamentally in the option for workers to contract out of the protection of a limit to the working week. It is curious that such an important right to limit the working week is essentially voluntary in nature and appears to contradict the aim of safeguarding worker health and safety.

[9] Comprehensive summary of the issues you have discussed.

## LOOKING FOR EXTRA MARKS?

- Examining some of the academic literature in this area would lend a further layer of analysis to your discussion.

## TAKING THINGS FURTHER

- V. Abazi, 'The European Union Whistleblower Directive: A "Game Changer" for Whistleblowing Protection?' (2020) 49(4) *Industrial Law Journal* 640

  *Analysis of the recent EU Directive in which the author questions whether the Directive will be a 'game changer' and suggests that the protection is more limited than this claim maintains*

- M. Fodder, J. Lewis, and J. Bowers QC, 'Whistleblowing Detriment and the Employment Field: Has the Court of Appeal Taken a Wrong Turn?' (2020) 49(3) *Industrial Law Journal* 397

  *Considers the decision in* **Tiplady** *that detriment must be suffered in the work capacity rather than in any other capacity in which the worker may be in relationship with the respondent*

- D. McCann, 'Travel time as working time: *Tyco*, the unitary model and the route to casualisation' (2016) 45(2) *Industrial Law Journal* 244

  *Examines the CJEU case of* **Tyco** *on the question of how travel time should be addressed for the purposes of working time, set in the context of increasingly casual forms of work relationships*

## Online resources

www.oup.com/uk/qanda/

For extra essay and problem questions on this topic, as well as advice on revision and exam technique, please visit the online resources.

# Trade unions and industrial action

# 12

## ARE YOU READY?

In order to attempt the questions in this chapter, you must have covered the following areas in your revision:

- The nature and role of trade unions
- Membership of a trade union including the rules on expulsion and exclusion of members
- Balloting and notice rules regarding industrial action
- Picketing
- Tort liability for industrial action including the rules regarding statutory immunity

## KEY DEBATES

**Debate: The function of a trade union**

Trade unions are about much more than representing workers in the workplace. Given the relatively low levels of trade union membership in the UK, how are the functions of unions changing/developing?

**Debate: Ballot thresholds for industrial action**

Do you agree that the ballot thresholds are a necessary protection for employers or are they an attempt to undermine worker power?

**Debate: Industrial action in public services**

What justifications lie behind the additional requirements regarding industrial action in the context of important public services? Do these requirements go too far or not far enough?

## QUESTION 1

A trade union's ability to exclude, expel, or discipline any of its members has been severely curtailed by statutory and judicial intervention.

**Critically consider this statement.**

## CAUTION!

- In a question like this, it is sometimes difficult to resist the use of detailed analysis of statute. Remember that you are unlikely to be awarded many marks for repeating great chunks of legislation.

## DIAGRAM ANSWER PLAN

Introduce relevant statute

↓

Issues related to exclusion/not being admitted to membership

↓

Issues related to expulsion and the Bridlington Principles

↓

Issues related to discipline including suspension and unjustifiable discipline

↓

Conclusions re curtailment

## SUGGESTED ANSWER

Until the **Industrial Relations Act 1971** there was little statutory regulation limiting a trade union's powers to admit, discipline, or expel a member. **Section 65** of this Act introduced rules against arbitrary exclusions or expulsions and unfair or unreasonable disciplinary action. Although this section was repealed in 1976, it was re-introduced in the **Employment Act 1980** as part of the new government's response to the closed shop (where every employee would have to join a particular union) and reinforce the idea that unions are voluntary associations. The rules on exclusion, expulsion, and discipline are now contained in the **Trade Union and Labour Relations (Consolidation) Act 1992 ('TULRCA').**[1]

An individual may not be excluded or expelled from a trade union, except for four specific reasons: **s174 TULRCA**. Exclusion in this case means not being admitted to membership (see ***NACODS* v *Gluchowski* [1996] IRLR 252**). These reasons include when an individual does not satisfy an enforceable membership requirement (**s174(2)(a)**). This means a restriction on membership as a result of employment being in one specific trade, industry, or profession; or of an occupational description such as a particular grade or level; or of the need for specific trade, industrial, or professional qualifications or work experience (**s174(3)**). It also includes when the exclusion or expulsion is attributable to the individual's conduct (**s174(2)(d)**).

The leading modern authority[2] on trade union membership is the European Court of Human Rights case of ***ASLEF* v *United Kingdom* [2007] IRLR 361**. In that case, the ASLEF union had expelled a member of the British National Party (BNP) on the basis that the racist views promoted by the BNP and its members were at odds with ASLEF's objectives and principles. The BNP member challenged his expulsion on the basis that domestic legislation provided that individuals who were expelled from a union by virtue of membership of a political party could claim compensation from the union. ASLEF, however, contended that it had rights of freedom of association under **Art. 11 of the European Convention on Human Rights** and this included being able to decide with whom it should associate. The ECHR agreed with ASLEF, concluding that it would run counter to the idea of freedom of association if it had no control over its membership and was obliged to allow those with contrary or conflicting values to join. It was, therefore, entitled to expel the BNP member on the ground that his membership was incompatible with the objects of the union.

This case has relevance for **s174(2)(d)** which provides that it is permissible for a union to exclude or expel a person due to their conduct.[3] This provision is a somewhat complex one. First, it provides for certain conduct to be 'excluded' meaning that a member cannot be excluded or expelled for conduct that falls under **s174(4)**. This includes being or ceasing to be a member of another union (**s174(4)(a)**). This revises the original 'Bridlington Principles'. These were a set of recommendations agreed at the 1939 Trades Union Congress (held at Bridlington). They were designed to minimise disputes over membership questions. They laid down the procedures by which the TUC dealt with complaints by one trade union against another and were designed to stop inter-union disputes over membership and representation. Excluded conduct also includes being or ceasing to be employed by a particular employer at a particular place (**s174(4)(b)**).

[1] This brief introduction sets the scene for what is a very politically motivated area. There is no need to say much more about the history of the legislation.

[2] This is a seminal case and examiners will expect you to mention it in answer to a question on membership.

[3] Links back to the earlier discussion.

Perhaps the most contentious provisions relate to membership of a political party and these rules have been amended following ***ASLEF***.[4] A union may exclude or expel a member for membership of a political party but only if membership of that party would be contrary to a rule or objective of that union (**s174(4C)**) and provided that certain procedural requirements are complied with.

[4] There is a wide literature on the *ASLEF* decision but this question is about more than political membership so think about how much to say on this point so that you present a balanced answer.

An individual may present a complaint to an Employment Tribunal if they have been excluded or expelled in contravention of **s174 TULRCA**.[5] Compensation can be reduced if the union member is partly at fault. In ***Saunders* v *The Bakers, Food and Allied Workers Union* [1986] IRLR 16**, an applicant resigned from the union over a disagreement about an unofficial strike. The individual later reapplied for membership and the application was refused. An appeal was made to the national executive committee in writing but the individual failed to attend the appeal in person. The EAT agreed with the Employment Tribunal when it stated that the individual could have done more to help himself by attending the meeting of the national executive committee. Compensation was reduced as a result of this. It is the trade union's duty to put the member back into the position that they were in before the wrongful expulsion (see ***NALGO* v *Courtney-Dunn* [1992] IRLR 114**).

[5] Remedy is an important aspect of many answers.

The second main area addressed in this question pertains to a union's right to discipline an existing member.[6] Like any organisation, unions will have certain rules of membership with which members are expected to comply. **Section 64(1) TULRCA** states that an individual who is, or has been, a member of a trade union has the right not to be 'unjustifiably disciplined' by that trade union. A person is disciplined by a trade union if the action takes place under the rules of the union or is conducted by an official of the union or by a number of persons who include an official. **Section 64(2) TULRCA** provides a list of six meanings of 'disciplined'. These include expulsion from the union, payment of a sum to the union, depriving the individual of access to any services or facilities that they would be entitled to by virtue of belonging to the union, encouraging another union or branch not to accept the individual into membership, and subjecting the individual to some other detriment.

[6] Introduces a new discussion.

The meaning of 'unjustifiably disciplined' is set out in **s65 TULRCA**. This provides a further list, this time of ten different items of conduct for which any resulting discipline will be 'unjustified'.[7] This conduct includes failing to participate in or support a strike or other industrial action, or indicating a lack of support for, or opposition to, such action. In the case of ***Knowles* v *Fire Brigades Union* [1996] IRLR 617**, the complainants failed in showing unjustifiable discipline because the pressure exerted on employers by the union did not amount to industrial action.

[7] Do not list all types of conduct even if you have the statute in front of you. All this shows is that you can copy from a book!

[8] Concludes with further discussion on remedy.

An individual who claims to have been unjustifiably disciplined may present a complaint to an Employment Tribunal within three months of the infringement, unless it was not reasonably practicable for the complaint to be presented in that time.[8] Additionally, if there is a delay resulting from an attempt to appeal against the discipline or have it reviewed or reconsidered, the three-month limit may be extended: **s66(2)(b) TULRCA**.

## LOOKING FOR EXTRA MARKS?

- It is not unusual to see questions devoted solely to exclusion/expulsion due to membership of a political party. To do well in a narrower question, you will need to discuss ***ASLEF*** in detail including academic and ILO commentary on the legislative provisions regarding political party membership.

## QUESTION 2

The Unloading Co. Ltd employed 500 people unloading ships at Seaside docks. During a recession, it decided to dismiss as redundant 150 of its employees. This was announced to the workforce on a Monday, with the dismissals to take effect on the following Friday.

All the employees belonged to the Dockworkers Union. The branch committee of the union called a mass meeting of the employees on the Wednesday and obtained a vote in favour of strike action. This was done by a show of hands. After the meeting, the branch committee informed the company that unless the dismissal notices were withdrawn immediately, the employees would go on strike from the Friday. The employer refused to withdraw the notices and a strike commenced, forcing the closure of the docks.

The employer has informed the general secretary of the union that they are to take legal action and seek compensation for damages.

**Advise the national executive committee of the union on its legal position.**

## CAUTION!

- You are being asked to comment on the actions of the branch committee and the trade union, not on the legal implications of the employer's actions. This means that discussion of the law on collective redundancies and the employer's obligation to consult is not relevant.

## DIAGRAM ANSWER PLAN

**Identify the issues**

- Is the union immune from liability for inducing a breach of contract?
- Has it complied with the appropriate balloting requirements?
- Has it given sufficient notice to the employer?
- What are the consequences for the union of any breach of balloting/notice requirements?

**Relevant law**

- Relevant provisions of TULRCA as amended by the Trade Union Act 2016 including ss20–21, 226–227, and 234
- Relevant case law including *London Underground* v *ASLEF* and *Balfour Beatty*

**Apply the law**

- Statutory immunity from tort liability is only available if certain balloting and notice provisions are complied with
- A show of hands vote would not meet the strict balloting requirements
- Forty-eight hours' notice of a strike is insufficient

**Conclude**

- The union would not be immune from liability unless the union takes steps to repudiate action purportedly done in its name

## SUGGESTED ANSWER

The starting point is that there is no general right to strike in domestic law. This means that a trade union, as the organiser of a strike, could be liable for certain economic torts (most obviously the tort of inducing a breach of contract).[1] However, the law provides that a union will be offered immunity from liability provided that certain conditions are met. The question for the union in this case is whether those conditions have indeed been met.[2]

[1] Discussing whether there should be a right to strike or how the UK's position compares with other international instruments goes too far beyond the scope of this question and would be irrelevant here.

[2] This is the key issue—does the union qualify for statutory immunity?

**Section 219(1) of the Trade Union and Labour Relations (Consolidation) Act 1992 ('TULRCA')** provides that an act done by a person 'in contemplation or furtherance of a trade dispute' is not actionable in tort on the ground only that it induces another person to break a contract or interferes/induces another to interfere with its performance, or that it consists in threatening such breach or interference. The question of whether action is 'in contemplation or furtherance of a trade dispute' is to be assessed subjectively from the viewpoint of the strike organiser (***Express Newspapers Ltd* v *McShane* [1980]**

**AC 672, HL**). The meaning of 'trade dispute' is set out in **s244(1)** and includes a dispute between workers and their employer which relates wholly or mainly to '. . . termination . . . of employment . . . of one or more workers' (**s244(1)(b)**). The intended redundancies would therefore qualify.[3]

[3] This summarises the point that the union would prima facie be entitled to claim immunity but for its breach of notice and balloting requirements discussed later.

**Section 219(4)** makes clear that a trade union will lose its protection from tort liability under **s219** if it induces a person to take part or to continue to take part in industrial action that is not supported by a ballot and the rules concerning notifying the employer about the ballot. There are two concerns here: (1) the show of hands vote two days before the strike; and (2) telling the employer of the intended strike two days in advance.[4]

[4] Gives structure for the remainder of your answer.

First, the decision of the union to induce a strike must be supported by a ballot (**s226(1)**). Voting at mass meetings by raising a hand is not permissible. Every member entitled to vote must be given a voting paper which must state the name of the independent scrutineer and clearly specify the address to which it is to be sent and the date by which it must be sent: **s229**. The voting paper must also contain at least one of two questions, depending upon the industrial action envisaged. The first question is whether the voter is prepared to take part in, or to continue, a strike. The second is whether the voter is prepared to take part in, or to continue, industrial action short of a strike. If the union wishes to pursue both options, then it must ask both questions. The questions need to be in such a form that the members can vote either yes or no.[5]

[5] This cuts through much of the detail regarding how ballots should be conducted. The law in this area is very technical so raise only the main points.

There are strict rules governing ballots which must be complied with. The entitlement to vote is to be given only to those members of the trade union whom it is reasonable at the time of the ballot for the union to believe will be induced to take part in, or to continue to take part in, the industrial action (**s227(1)**). No one else has any entitlement to vote (see ***University of Central England* v *NALGO* [1993] IRLR 81**). There is a difference between 'taking part in industrial action' and 'being on strike'. **Section 227 TULRCA** refers to the former, and this means that the ballot is not necessarily restricted to those who will actually go on strike (***British Telecommunications plc* v *Communication Workers Union* [2004] IRLR 58**). This occurred in ***London Underground* v *ASLEF* [2012] IRLR 196**, where the union balloted other people in the same grade as those who would actually be called out on strike.

There are problems for trade unions in organising ballots that meet the statutory requirements. ***Balfour Beatty* v *Unite the Union* [2012] IRLR 452** concerned a claim that union members who were entitled to vote were left out of the ballot, despite the union spending hundreds of hours of employees' time to try to track down all those entitled to vote. The court refused the employer's application for an injunction because the union had gone to 'considerable lengths to ensure democratic legitimacy' and it would not have been reasonable to expect more.

There are also strict rules applied to the ballot itself. As far as is reasonably practicable, voting must be done in secret (**s230(4)(a)**), which would exclude the sort of vote that was taken in this case. Every person who is entitled to vote in the ballot must be allowed to do so without interference from the trade union or its officials. They need to have a voting paper sent to them by post to their home address or any other address to which the individual has requested the union to send it. Moreover, **s2 of the Trade Union Act 2016** has inserted an additional requirement into **s226(2)(a)(iia) TULRCA** to the effect that industrial action will only be regarded as having the support of a ballot if at least 50 per cent of those entitled to vote in the ballot did so.[6] The show of hands vote taken on Wednesday would not fulfil the strict balloting requirements laid down in **TULRCA**.

[6] This level of precision when citing statute will likely only be expected if you have access to the statutes in the exam. Otherwise, it will usually be sufficient that you know the rule.

Furthermore, an act done by a trade union to induce a person to take part in, or to continue, industrial action will not be regarded as protected unless the trade union gives a relevant notice to the affected employer or employers, within seven days of having notified the employer of the balloting result as required by **s231A TULRCA**. This notification of the ballot result is in addition to the notification under **s234A** to give notice of the industrial action that will take place including lists of the categories of affected employees (**s234A(3A)**). Moreover, the changes introduced by the **Trade Union Act 2016** mean that two weeks' notice of action must be given to the employer (**s234A(4)(b)**). Notifying the employer on the Wednesday of action forty-eight hours later would be in breach of this provision.[7]

[7] Refers back to the question to maintain relevance.

The Dockworkers Union has failed to follow any of these procedures, so it is unlikely that the action would be protected from liability in tort, unless it repudiates the action of the branch committee and the members on strike.[8] Trade unions are to be taken as having endorsed or authorised an act if it was authorised or endorsed by, first, any person who is empowered by the rules of the union to authorise or endorse such action; second, by the executive committee, the president, or general secretary of the union; or, third, by any other committee or official of the union: **s20(2) TULRCA** (see ***Express & Star Ltd* v *NGA* [1985] IRLR 455**). For the purpose of this last category, a committee of the union is any group of persons constituted in accordance with the union's rules and an act is to be taken as authorised or endorsed by an official if it was authorised or endorsed by a committee of which the official was a member and the committee had as one of its purposes the organising or coordinating of industrial action (see ***Heatons Transport (St Helens) Ltd* v *TGWU* [1972] IRLR 25**).

[8] Remember who you are advising so it is appropriate to advise on how the union might repudiate the actions.

It is possible for a trade union to avoid this liability for the actions of members, in this respect, by the executive, president, or general secretary repudiating the act as soon as is reasonably practicable after it came to their knowledge. For such a repudiation to be effective, the union must give, without delay, a written notice to the committee or official in question and do its best, without delay, to give the notice to every member that the union believes might be involved with the action and to the employer of every such member: **s21 TULRCA**.

It is only by following this procedure that the union can avoid liability for the act and its consequences.[9] There is a requirement for strict compliance with a repudiation for the union not to be held liable for further breaches. **Section 21(5) TULRCA** provides that an act will not be treated as being repudiated if, subsequently, the executive, president, or general secretary of the union acts in such a way that is inconsistent with a repudiation. Thus it is not enough to issue a written repudiation and then continue as before (see ***Richard Read (Transport) Ltd* v *NUM (South Wales Area)* [1985] IRLR 67**).

[9] Summarises clearly the advice to your client.

If the Dockworkers Union wishes to avoid liability for the payment of damages it will need to take the necessary action to repudiate the actions of its branch committee and members.

## LOOKING FOR EXTRA MARKS?

- Another issue that you could mention is whether the employer might seek an injunction to stop the strike and its likelihood of success in obtaining one.
- Look carefully at the nature of the business affected. This case concerned dockworkers. Since the coming into force of the **Trade Union Act 2016**, an additional threshold of 40 per cent support for industrial action must be obtained in 'important public services'. Under **s3** of the 2016 Act, this includes health, education of those under 17, fire, and transport.

## QUESTION 3

**Assess the protection provided in s219 TULRCA 1992 from 'certain tort liabilities'. Specifically consider this protection in relation to picketing.**

## CAUTION!

- There are two aspects to this question. It asks you first to consider the protection from certain tort liabilities offered by **s219 TULRCA**. It is a conditional protection and you will need to examine the qualifications for a union to receive the protection.
- The second aspect of the question requires some critical discussion of this protection in relation to picketing.

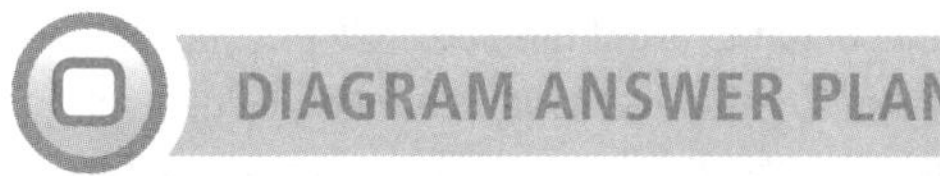

## DIAGRAM ANSWER PLAN

Section 219 immunity from certain liabilities in tort

Example: tort of inducing breach of contract

Qualified protection offered

Picketing and secondary action

## SUGGESTED ANSWER

As the question observes, protection is given to trade unions against certain potential liabilities in tort by operation of **s219 of the Trade Union and Industrial Relations Act 1992 ('TULRCA')**. Examples of tortious acts for which trade unions and individuals may be liable, without statutory immunity, include the common law torts of inducing a breach of contract and interference with a contract or with business. The most obvious tort that would apply in the context of industrial action is the tort of inducing a breach of contract.[1] In ***OBG Ltd* v *Allan* [2007] UKHL 21**, the House of Lords laid down certain elements that must exist for this tort to be demonstrated: a breach of contract, knowledge that a breach is being procured (or a deliberate failure to enquire), and intention to induce a breach. Applying that to industrial action such as striking, it is clear how the tort may be committed. Withdrawing labour is a breach of contract, the union will have knowledge of this in official action and intention can usually be demonstrated.[2]

[1] Although it may be tempting to work through the various common law torts, the question asks you to focus on **TULRCA** so contain your answer to that.

[2] This shows how easily an economic tort could be committed in these circumstances and why the statutory immunity regime exists.

The immunity from liability under **s219** is on the grounds that the act, first, induces another to break a contract or interferes, or induces another to interfere, with the contract's performance and, second, that it consists in threatening these actions. Any agreement or combination of two or more persons to do, or procure, the doing of an act in contemplation or furtherance of a trade dispute will not be actionable in tort if the act is one that would not have been actionable if done without any agreement or combination.

There are three requirements in respect of this protection.[3] First, the act done should be in 'contemplation or furtherance of a trade

[3] This breaks down the provision into more manageable chunks and allows you to structure the paragraphs that follow.

dispute'; second, it must be a trade dispute between workers and their employer; and, third, it must relate, wholly or mainly, to a number of specific issues. These include terms and conditions of employment, allocation of work or the duties of employment between workers, and matters of discipline (**s244**).

[4] Concrete examples lend weight to the points you make and add richness to your answer.

The phrase about relating 'wholly or mainly to' is intended to direct attention to what the dispute is about, or what it is mainly about (***Mercury Communications Ltd*** **v** ***Scott-Garner*** **[1983] IRLR 494**). In that case, a dispute about government policy was outside the scope of protection.[4] 'Wholly or mainly' means a consideration of more than the event that caused the dispute and includes the reasons why there is a dispute. This, in turn, perhaps means investigating the motives of a trade union and whether there are other reasons that might be perceived as the real ones, such as possible political motivations, as in ***University College London Hospital*** **v** ***Unison*** **[1999] IRLR 31, CA** where action to protect employees' terms and conditions was caught up with the union's principled objections to hospital privatisation.[5]

[5] A good example of how political motivations may become entwined with those relating to the particular workplace.

The term 'in contemplation or furtherance of a trade dispute' requires a subjective judgement as to how widely it should be interpreted. The question is whether the union genuinely and honestly believed that the action was in contemplation or furtherance of a trade dispute. In other words, did the union think that this action would act to further the cause (***Express Newspapers Ltd*** **v** ***McShane*** **[1980] AC 672, HL**)? While it may seem odd to adopt a subjective approach, the alternative is that the courts would be placed in the position of having to make an objective assessment of the merits of any action, which risks them being drawn into workplace (and potentially wider) politics.[6]

[6] This shows a level of maturity and understanding. It may seem counter-intuitive to take a subjective view (after all, would anyone admit that they did not think that it was in furtherance of a dispute?) but the alternative might have unfortunate repercussions.

The dispute must be between existing workers and their current employer. It is not possible to conduct a dispute, within the protection of **s219 TULRCA**, about the contracts of employment of future workers (see ***University College London Hospital*** **v** ***Unison*** **[1999] IRLR 31, CA**).

[7] Provides a link to the second aspect of the question.

Turning to the issue of picketing, this is where a group of union members gather as a further form of protest during a strike.[7] This may be done partly to raise awareness of the strike taking place (it is not uncommon to see those picketing with placards and posters about the reason behind the industrial action) but it may also be done to interrupt the employer's business particularly if it has the effect of deterring other workers from crossing the picket line to enter work.

As well as the economic torts mentioned briefly above, pickets are potentially liable for other torts, such as trespass to the highway, the tort of private nuisance, and the tort of public nuisance which consists of an act or omission that causes inconvenience to the public in the exercise of their common rights, such as the unreasonable obstruction of the highway (***News Group Newspapers* v *SOGAT '82* [1986] IRLR 337**).

There is no immunity from actions in tort for acts done in the course of picketing unless they are done in accordance with **s220 TULRCA**. This provides that it is lawful for a person, in contemplation or furtherance of a trade dispute, to attend at or near their own place of work for the purpose of either peacefully obtaining or communicating information or peacefully persuading any person to either work or abstain from working. The same provision allows an official of a trade union to accompany, for the same purposes, a member of the union, whom the official represents, at or near their workplace. There is no precise definition of what is meant by 'at' or 'near' the place of work. May LJ declined to provide one as the number of circumstances that one might have to provide for were so variable as to make it impossible to lay down a test (***Rayware Ltd* v *TGWU* [1989] IRLR 134, CA**).[8] The court suggested the use of a common-sense approach. The issue had been whether a group of workers picketing at the entrance to a private trading estate and not directly at the workplace were 'at' or 'near' the place of work. The picket had been set up there as it was as close as the picketers could get to the place of work. The word 'near' was to be an expanding word not a restraining one. The meaning of the word was to be expanded to give effect to the purpose of the legislation. This purpose was to give a right to picket and in ***Rayware*** picketing at the entrance to the industrial estate was 'near' the place of work.

The picket must be 'peaceful'. While physically forcing people from crossing the picket line might be an obvious example of picketing that is not peaceful, there are grey areas particularly when it comes to the numbers of people involved in a picket. The legislation does not prescribe the number of pickets who are to be allowed at or near the place of work. It may be that picketing by large numbers of individuals may be intimidating enough for it no longer to be seen as peaceful. ***Thomas* v *NUM (South Wales Area)* [1985] IRLR 136** concerned fifty to seventy strikers on a picket line at the gates of a number of collieries in South Wales during the 1984 miners' strike. It was held to be tortious because of its nature and the way that it was carried out. The reasoning behind the judgment was that such a large number of people could not be involved in communicating peacefully. In contrast, however, a more recent judgment noted the right to freedom of assembly and cautioned against imposing a limit on numbers (***Gate Gourmet London Ltd* v *TGWU* [2005] EWHC 1889 (QB)**).[9]

Secondary action is not lawful picketing: **s224**. Secondary action is defined in **s224(2)** as an inducement to, or a threat to, break or interfere with a contract of employment where the employer in that contract is not party to the dispute. An employer shall not be regarded as party to a dispute between another employer and the workers of

[8] An important case on the right to picket.

[9] Bear in mind that older cases would have been decided before the **Human Rights Act 1998**. The impact of the **European Convention on Human Rights** (particularly **Art. 11**) is important in this topic and later cases such as this show the influence that **Art. 11** has had.

that employer and, where more than one employer is in dispute with its workers, the dispute between each employer and its workers is to be treated as a separate dispute.

Since the introduction of the **Trade Union Act 2016** further restrictions have been placed on picketing. Under **s10** of that Act, **s220A** has been introduced to **TULRCA** providing that a picket will not be lawful unless a picket supervisor is appointed. The union or picket supervisor must take reasonable steps to tell the police the picket supervisor's name, where the picketing will be taking place, and how to contact the supervisor (**s220A(4)**). During the picket, the supervisor must be easily identifiable as such and must be present when the picket is underway.[10]

[10] This is an important feature of the post-2016 Act rules. Indeed, if time permits in an exam this point could be expanded by reference to some of the recent academic critiques in this area.

## LOOKING FOR EXTRA MARKS?

- Consider **Art. 11** and its influence in this area. Is there evidence of a change in approach since its adoption?

## TAKING THINGS FURTHER

- A. Bogg, 'Beyond Neo-Liberalism: The Trade Union Act 2016 and the authoritarian state' (2016) 45(3) *Industrial Law Journal* 299

  *Part of a special edition of the Industrial Law Journal on the* ***Trade Union Act 2016****, this paper argues that the legislation is an example of 'a more authoritarian style of Conservative ideology and statecraft'*
- K. Ewing, 'The implications of the *ASLEF* case' (2007) 36(4) *Industrial Law Journal* 425

  *Detailed analysis of the* ***ECHR*** *decision of* **ASLEF *v* United Kingdom**
- M. Harcourt, G. Gall, N. Novell, and M. Wilson, 'Boosting Union Membership: Reconciling Liberal and Social Democratic Conceptions of Freedom of Association via a Union Default' (2020) *Industrial Law Journal* (online)

  *Written from the perspectives of the UK and New Zealand, this paper explores the possibility of a default system of union membership and its implications*

## Online resources

www.oup.com/uk/qanda/

For extra essay and problem questions on this topic, as well as advice on revision and exam technique, please visit the online resources.

# 13 Collective bargaining

## ARE YOU READY?

In order to attempt the questions in this chapter, you must have covered the following areas in your revision:

- Inequalities of power in the employment relationship
- The status and function of a collective agreement
- The statutory right for a union to receive certain information
- Time off for trade union members

## KEY DEBATES

**Debate: The relevance of trade unions**

Although trade unions are less present in the private compared to the public sector, is it fair to suggest that trade unions are irrelevant to the private sector?

**Debate: Trade union power**

UNISON took judicial review proceedings against the UK government's introduction of Employment Tribunal fees. IWGB more recently brought a judicial review against the government's flawed implementation of the EU's Health and Safety Directive. In what other ways might trade unions be creative in using their powers outside industrial action and collective bargaining?

**Debate: Inequality of bargaining power**

To what extent does the law recognise inequalities of bargaining power in the employment relationship by allowing for terms and conditions to be bargained collectively? How easy is it for collective labour to obtain concessions from management?

## QUESTION 1

**The provisions contained in the Trade Union and Labour Relations (Consolidation) Act 1992 that compel an employer to disclose information to trade unions are totally inadequate. Critically consider this statement.**

## CAUTION!

- Although it would be tempting to write an emotional response to this question given the claim that the provisions are 'totally inadequate', it is important to give a balanced view. Even if you ultimately agree with the statement, you need to show that you have considered the provisions carefully.
- Take care in the language you use. You may well feel strongly in support or against the statement but using temperate language will allow you to make your argument far more forcefully.

## DIAGRAM ANSWER PLAN

Statutory duty of employer to provide information

Test for relevance of information

ACAS Code of Practice

Exceptions to duty to disclose

## SUGGESTED ANSWER

**Section 181(1) of the Trade Union and Labour Relations (Consolidation) Act 1992 ('TULRCA')**[1] provides a general duty for an employer, who recognises an independent trade union, to disclose certain information for the purposes of all stages of collective bargaining. This is an important aspect of collective bargaining as a trade union can only meaningfully discuss matters with the employer if it is privy to up-to-date and relevant information. Despite this recognition in **s181(1)**

[1] Beginning your answer with a clear statutory reference reassures the examiner that you understand the area and have good attention to detail.

of the importance of information to the collective bargaining process, there is a concern that this and associated provisions are limited.[2] This essay will explore the duty to provide information and its effectiveness.

[2] This linking sentence shows that you understand the problem raised in the question.

The duty relates to the descriptions of workers for whom the trade union is recognised as representing them for collective bargaining purposes (**s181(1)**). For example,[3] if the trade union is only recognised for staff of a particular grade or separate unions are recognised for manufacturing as opposed to administrative staff, the information will only relate to the relevant group. The information must be disclosed to representatives of the union, who are defined as officials or other persons authorised by the union to carry on such bargaining (**s181(1)**). According to ***R* v *Central Arbitration Committee, ex parte BTP Oxide Ltd*** **[1992] IRLR 60**, these provisions envisage that there may be alternative types of relationship between employers and unions (rather than just collective bargaining) that entitle a union to information. The information to be disclosed is information that relates to the employer's undertaking and is in the possession of the employer (**s181(2)**).

[3] Rather than simply copying out the words of the statute, this example shows that you understand their meaning.

There is a two-fold test[4] in **s181(2)** to decide the relevance of the information. It must be information without which the trade unions would be 'to a material extent impeded in carrying on collective bargaining' (**s181(2)(a)**) and, second, information the disclosure of which 'would be in accordance with good industrial relations practice' (**s181(2)(b)**).

[4] Although the statute does not use the language of 'two-fold test', summarising the provisions in this way is arguably more elegant than simply copying from the statute book.

There is an ACAS Code of Practice on the disclosure of information to trade unions for collective bargaining purposes. Paragraph 11 of this Code provides examples of information that might be relevant in certain collective bargaining situations. These examples are information relating to the undertaking about pay and benefits, conditions of service, manpower, performance, and financial information. Although the Code is an important guide, it is not intended to exclude other evidence that might accord with good industrial relations practice. The request for information by the trade union must be in writing, if the employer so requests, as must the employer's reply if requested by the trade union (**s181(3)**).

To determine what information is relevant, regard will be had to the subject matter of the negotiations. As is made clear in para. 9 of the ACAS Code, trade unions would be significantly impeded in the course of collective bargaining if they did not have access to material and relevant information. Paragraph 10 continues that what is relevant will depend on the circumstances including the subject matter of the negotiations and the level at which they are taking place. For example,[5] if the negotiations concern pay rises, it would appear relevant to provide the union with information regarding current pay systems and structures, earnings and hours of work, and grading criteria for affected jobs.

[5] This is a good example of applying the ACAS Code to a real-life hypothetical scenario, which adds colour to your answer.

There are a number of situations in which an employer is not required to disclose information. These are set out in **s182**. They include if the disclosure would be against the interests of national security or could not be disclosed without contravening a statutory prohibition. This list of exceptions contributes to making the legislation ineffective. One particularly contentious exception[6] is contained in **s182(1)(c)** which provides that the employer need not disclose information 'which has been communicated to him in confidence, or which he has otherwise obtained in consequence of the confidence reposed in him by another person'. The need for confidentiality could result in important and relevant information not being disclosed to a trade union. In ***Sun Printers Ltd* v *Westminster Press Ltd*** [1982] **IRLR 292, CA**, a widely circulated document about the future of a company was held not to be confidential, but it was suggested, obiter, that the stamping of the word 'confidential' on the document would have been enough to allow wide circulation while retaining confidentiality. Perhaps of more concern to trade unions is the difficulty shown in obtaining pay information concerning parts of a business that are put out to competitive tender. In ***Civil Service Union* v *CAC*** [1980] **IRLR 274**, a trade union was stopped from obtaining information about a tenderer's proposed wage rates on the basis that they were given in confidence and that it was information the lack of which could not be held to impede, to a material extent, the union's ability to carry out collective bargaining.

[6] There is no need to list every exception as that simply shows the examiner that you can copy from the statute book! It is better to analyse a couple of exceptions in more detail supported by case law.

There are further limitations on the obligations of employers to disclose information contained in **s182(2)**. An employer is not required to produce any documents or extracts from documents, unless the document has been prepared for the purposes of conveying or confirming the information, and the employer is not required to compile or assemble any information that would involve an amount of work or expenditure out of proportion to the value of the information used in the conduct of collective bargaining.

All these exceptions place important limitations on the right of trade unions to make employers disclose information. It is, perhaps, of significance[7] that during the period of the 1980s and early 1990s, when Conservative governments were introducing legislation to limit the power of trade unions, this particular piece of legislation remained untouched. The remedy for trade unions[8] for failure to disclose is to make a complaint to the Central Arbitration Committee (CAC) **(s183)**. The CAC will refer the matter to ACAS if it thinks that there is a reasonable chance of a conciliated settlement. If this fails, the CAC will hear the cases of all sides and make a decision on whether the complaint is well founded. If it does so, then the employer is given a period of not less than a week to disclose the information. If the employer still fails to disclose, then the trade union may present a further complaint to the CAC, which will hear all sides and decide whether the complaint is well founded and specify the information in respect of which it made that decision (**s184**). The CAC may then make an award in respect of the employees specified in the claim. This award will consist of the

[7] Without straying too far into discussion of politics, this demonstrates to the examiner that you are aware of the wider political context of industrial relations and provides a nice example of a balanced yet analytical commentary.

[8] Brief discussion of remedy will gain you marks in most answers as it is a point often missed by students!

terms and conditions being negotiated and specified in the claim, or any other terms and conditions that the CAC considers appropriate. These terms and conditions can only be for matters in which the trade union is recognised for collective bargaining purposes.

[9] An overall conclusion finishes off your answer nicely.

In conclusion,[9] while it may be incorrect to say that the provisions in **TULRCA** are 'totally inadequate', the exceptions to when information must be disclosed mean that trade unions are on the 'back foot' when attempting to obtain information for the purposes of collective bargaining.

## LOOKING FOR EXTRA MARKS?

- Being able to weigh up both sides of an argument is an important skill in essay writing. Even if you want to argue strongly from one side of the debate, think about the counter-arguments that can be made against you and address these.
- Showing the examiner that you are aware of the wider industrial relations context will add depth to your answer. In this question, it would be perfectly appropriate to reflect on the very narrow scope of **s181**, that it only relates to information related to collective bargaining, and the fact that even where unions are present in the workplace they may not be recognised for collective bargaining purposes. This is all important contextual information helping you write an informed answer about why these provisions may be regarded as weak.

## QUESTION 2

Rumpa and Steve are employed as flight attendants by Alba Airways, which operates flights from mainland Scotland to the Scottish islands. Both are members of Solidarity, a union recognised by Alba for the purposes of collective bargaining. Rumpa is also an elected union official for her local branch. Rumpa and Steve have contacted you, an in-house solicitor with Solidarity, seeking advice.

Alba has announced that to save money it intends to reduce the number of crew members on its Glasgow to Stornoway service from three to two. The relevant term of the collective agreement between Alba and Solidarity states that 'All crew complements will be agreed between Solidarity and Alba from time to time and will not be reduced below the current agreed minimum of three'. Steve works on this service and is concerned that these changes will potentially compromise passenger safety and lead to him doing significantly more work on each flight.

Rumpa is also concerned that her new line manager appears hostile to her work as a union official. Whereas Rumpa's previous line manager allowed her to use one of the meeting rooms for union business, she has now been told that her union work cannot be done during work time or on work premises. Rumpa has also asked to attend a training event on negotiation skills organised by Solidarity but has been told that if she wants time off, she needs to complete a holiday request form and take annual leave.

**Advise Steve on the effect of the collective agreement on his terms and conditions, and Rumpa on any support to which she is entitled as a trade union official.**

## CAUTION!

- There are two clear issues raised in the question: (1) Rumpa's entitlement to time off and facilities for her union work; and (2) the effect of the collective agreement on Steve's contract. With Steve, it may be tempting to discuss other matters such as whistle-blowing, whether there might be grounds for constructive dismissal, or whether a reduction in crew complements could lead to a redundancy situation. Stick to what the examiner has asked you as there is plenty to discuss on the collective agreement issue alone without straying into other areas.
- This question does not state how marks will be allocated between discussion of Steve and Rumpa so assume that the examiner will want you to devote roughly equal amounts of time to both parts. It may seem obvious but if you can only answer one aspect of the question, attempt another question! A brilliant answer to only half a question will not score you high marks overall.

## DIAGRAM ANSWER PLAN

| | |
|---|---|
| Identify the issues | ■ Steve: can he rely on the terms of the collective agreement? What is the effect of the collective agreement on his individual contract of employment?<br>■ Rumpa: is she entitled to time off during work time to undertake her trade union duties? Should the employer provide her with facilities at work for her to undertake her duties? |
| Relevant law | ■ Steve: s179 TULRCA 1992; *Alexander* v *Standard Telephones Ltd (No. 2)*; *Malone* v *British Airways plc*<br>■ Rumpa: s168 TULRCA 1992; ACAS Code of Practice; *Skiggs* v *South West Trains Ltd* |
| Apply the law | ■ Steve: is the term 'apt' to be included in the individual contract of employment?<br>■ Rumpa: has she been denied the right to reasonable time off? There are no rights to facilities to be provided although it would be good practice to provide these |
| Conclude | ■ Steve: following *Malone*, it is unlikely that the term would be considered apt to be included in the contract of employment<br>■ Rumpa is entitled to reasonable time off work, although she and her employer may disagree on what amounts to 'reasonable'; there are only legal rights to facilities in respect of collective redundancy and TUPE consultations |

## SUGGESTED ANSWER

### Steve

For Steve, the key issue[1] is whether he can rely on the terms of a collective agreement, which state that crew numbers will be agreed between his employer and union, and that in any event the crew numbers will not drop below three. The starting point for Steve is **s179(1) of the Trade Union and Labour Relations (Consolidation) Act 1992 ('TULRCA')**, which provides that a collective agreement will be presumed not to have been intended by the parties to be a legally enforceable agreement unless it is in writing and it contains a provision stating that the parties intend it to be a legally enforceable contract. The reason for this is due to the nature of collective agreements. They perform two functions. One is that they regulate at a collective level the relationship between the union and the employer. It follows that[2] those provisions in the agreement which govern how Alba and Solidarity act in respect of the other would not be something that Steve would expect to form part of his individual contract of employment. The second function of a collective agreement relates to its status as a source of rules which govern the individual employment relationship. For example, it may contain provisions regarding pay or hours of work. The question for Steve, then, is whether the term regarding staffing levels can be relied upon by him.[3]

We are not told that the collective agreement has been expressly incorporated into Steve's individual contract. **Section 1(4)(j) of the Employment Rights Act 1996** states that the initial statement of employment particulars must include details of any collective agreements which directly affect the terms and conditions of employment. As the question is silent about this,[4] we will assume that there is no express incorporation of the terms of the collective agreement into Steve's contract. There is, however, the possibility that Steve may argue that the terms should be implied into his contract. This turns on its facts and the intention of the parties alone is not enough; what requires to be shown also is that the term upon which Steve is seeking to rely is 'apt' to be incorporated into the individual contract (***Alexander* v *Standard Telephones Ltd (No. 2)*** **[1991] IRLR 286**). The courts have distinguished between matters that regulate the collective relationship between the union and employer, such as procedures for resolving disputes between the two parties, and individual matters, such as pay. It is only those individual matters that would be apt to be incorporated. The difficulty for Steve is determining into which category a provision regarding crew complements will fall. Is this a collective matter or one which affects his individual contract of

[1] A confident start showing immediately that you understand what is being asked of you.

[2] A clear example of IRAC in use. The general rule about the function of collective agreements is stated, immediately followed by it being applied to the facts of the case.

[3] This gets to the heart of the question about the extent to which certain terms of a collective agreement will be 'apt' to be incorporated. It sums up what has been discussed and links nicely to the following, more detailed, discussion of aptness.

[4] If a question is silent about material facts you can either say if X is the case, then Y follows but if A is the case, then B follows. Alternatively, as is the case here, you can say that you will proceed on the basis that the facts are as given. The crucial point here is that you should not spend too much time hypothesising as that risks distracting from your answer.

employment? In ***Malone* v *British Airways plc* [2010] EWCA Civ 1225**, the Court of Appeal had to consider on which side of the line a very similar term in a collective agreement fell.[5] In ***Malone***, the Court of Appeal focused on the 'disastrous consequences' for British Airways were such a term to be capable of enforcement by an individual, suggesting that it substituted a question of 'aptness' for a more subjective test of 'appropriateness'[6] (R. Russell, '*Malone* v *British Airways plc*: protection of managerial prerogative' (2011) 40(2) *Industrial Law Journal* 207). Although there is some merit in the argument that the number of staff working alongside Steve is a matter which might be apt for inclusion in his contract of employment, following ***Malone*** it appears unlikely that Steve will be able to rely on this term.

[5] This repays a student who has read the material facts of a previous authority!

[6] You need to think carefully when using academic authority in a problem question. In most cases, it is better to leave it out as it may risk your answer veering away from the problem in hand to more academic discussions. This example here is a good example of where it can be used carefully to help analyse case authority.

### Rumpa

In accordance with **s168(1) TULRCA**, Rumpa (as an official of an independent trade union recognised by her employer) should be permitted to take time off during her working hours for the purpose of carrying out her duties as a union official. These duties include negotiations for the purposes of collective bargaining (**s168(1)(a)**). Importantly for Rumpa given that she wants to attend a training course on negotiation skills, **s168(2)** allows Rumpa to take time off during working hours for the purpose of undergoing training in aspects of industrial relations relevant to carrying on her duties and approved by the TUC or her union. Given that the course is organised by Solidarity and relates to negotiation, it is likely that Rumpa would be able[7] to show that this was relevant training for which she should be permitted time off work to attend.

[7] Another example of IRAC. The law is stated, it is applied to the facts, and a conclusion is reached in which Rumpa is advised that she should be permitted time off work to attend the negotiation training.

The extent to which Rumpa may be permitted time off will depend on 'what is reasonable in all the circumstances' (**s168(3)**). The ACAS Code of Practice on Time Off for Trade Union Duties and Activities provides some guidance on what might be considered reasonable. This includes time off for attending negotiation meetings with the employer and time off afterwards to communicate with employees about the outcome of those meetings. While the use of the word 'reasonable' suggests that there is a spectrum[8] of what might be regarded as reasonable time off, in Rumpa's case it appears that her employer is refusing to provide her with any time off during working hours, which would be in breach of **s168**. Moreover, the time off should be paid at the usual rate (**s169**).

[8] Careful discussion of the wording used in the statute shows excellent attention to detail and sound analytical ability.

In the first instance, it would be advisable for Rumpa to seek to agree reasonable time off with her line manager. It may be that an agreement can be reached between them as to what would amount to 'reasonable' time off for Rumpa to carry out her duties. In the event that she and the employer cannot agree (and this may be likely given that her employer's starting position is that she is not entitled to any time off work for trade union duties), Rumpa may complain to the Employment Tribunal that her employer has failed to allow her time off (**s168(4)**) and/or that her employer has not paid her for this time off (**s169(5)**). If Rumpa succeeds, she is entitled to compensation for being denied time off—***Skiggs* v *South West Trains Ltd* [2005] IRLR 459**. A further difficulty that Rumpa may encounter in practice, however, is that the right in **s168** is for the employer to permit Rumpa to take time off for carrying out her duties. Implicit in this, is that Rumpa must seek her employer's permission—***Ryford Ltd* v *Drinkwater* [1996] IRLR 16**. This means that Rumpa will need to take care not to disobey a reasonable management instruction or commit a disciplinary offence by taking time off regardless. The safest option in the circumstances[9] if her employer will not agree to any time off for trade union duties, is to seek a declaration from the tribunal as to what would be reasonable and, in the meantime, not to be absent from work in case she risks the employer taking disciplinary action for unauthorised absence.

[9] This whole discussion about time off shows a mature understanding of the area. An answer that stopped by advising Rumpa to complain to the tribunal would not be wrong but this answer shows a level of understanding of how different aspects of employment law fit together that would typically be displayed by a stronger candidate and is likely to be reflected in the marks awarded.

Turning to Rumpa's final concern,[10] she would like some facilities at work to be provided to allow her to carry out her duties. This is understandable given that if Rumpa has to communicate the outcome of negotiations to those she represents she will need a room in which to meet with members and/or a forum in which she can notify members of any union news. When it comes to collective redundancy consultation, **TULRCA** expressly provides in **s188(5A)** that the employer shall allow the appropriate representatives access to affected employees and shall afford them such accommodation and other facilities as may be appropriate. Although there is no general statutory right to be provided with facilities, para. 46 of the ACAS Code of Practice provides examples of what facilities might reasonably be provided by an employer and include a noticeboard, access to rooms (including a dedicated office should the volume of work require it), access to a telephone, and a confidential space where a union official can meet with members who may have a complaint or grievance about work.

[10] This indicates the final legal issue for consideration in your answer.

## LOOKING FOR EXTRA MARKS?

- The ability to spot more subtle nuances in a problem will lift your answer. For example, the discussion of why it will not be in Rumpa's interests to take time off work without permission or the later discussion about the facilities that it may be good practice to provide all show a command of the area that goes beyond a simple understanding of the statutory right.
- Reading case commentaries are important to help you develop your ability to analyse a case. In this example, an average student would discuss the test of aptness for incorporation and may even be able to spot the similarity with ***Malone***. A strong student, however, can go further and mention whether the Court of Appeal has confused 'aptness' with 'appropriateness'.

## QUESTION 3

**Collective agreements are not, normally, legally enforceable. Consider ways in which the terms can become part of the contractual relationship between employer and employee.**

## CAUTION!

- A strong answer will go beyond merely listing the ways in which terms of the collective agreement can form part of the individual contract of employment to explore the various problems that have arisen in determining whether a term is apt for inclusion in the individual contract of employment.
- To attempt this question, you will need a sound appreciation of how collective agreements differ from other agreements and why there are limits to the enforceability of the law in the area of industrial relations.

## DIAGRAM ANSWER PLAN

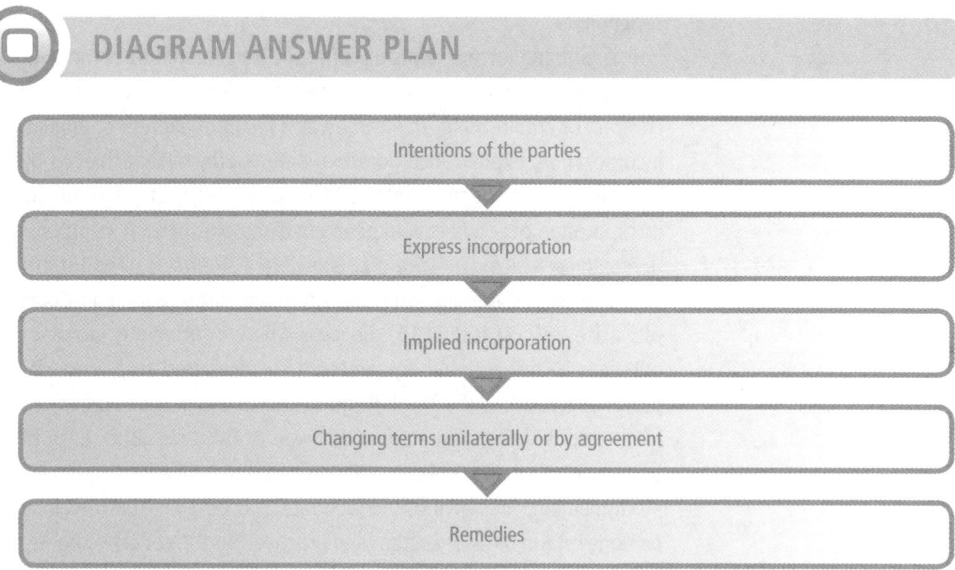

## SUGGESTED ANSWER

According to **s179 of the Trade Union and Labour Relations (Consolidation) Act 1992 ('TULRCA')**, a collective agreement shall be conclusively presumed not to have been intended by the parties to be a legally enforceable agreement unless it is in writing and it contains a provision which states that the parties intend that the agreement shall be a legally enforceable contract. As such, the intention of the parties appears to be crucial.[1] Unless that intention to enter into a legally enforceable agreement is clear, then there is likely not to be such an agreement. The collective agreement needs to show that, at the very least, the parties have directed their minds to the issue of legal enforceability and have decided in favour of such an approach. ***National Coal Board* v *National Union of Mineworkers* [1986] IRLR 439** concerned whether an agreement on consultation was legally binding or not. The court held that there would need to be evidence that the parties had at least directed their minds to the question and decided on legal enforceability.

[1] This paragraph outlines the first key issue to be considered—the parties' intentions.

Without this, there will be an insufficient statement of intent for the purposes of the statute. The court may take into account the surrounding circumstances and even the general climate of opinion about this issue when the agreement is made. In ***Ford Motor Co. Ltd* v *Amalgamated Union of Engineering and Foundry Workers* [1969] 2 QB 303**, the court found the generally unanimous climate of opinion was relevant. This view was that collective agreements were binding in honour and were subject to social, rather than legal, sanctions.

It is possible for the terms of collective agreements to become legally binding through the route of incorporation into the individual contract of employment. This can be as a result of express or implied incorporation. Express incorporation is most effectively achieved by including a term of the contract of employment that refers to the incorporation of a collective agreement. Examples of such incorporation[2] can be seen in ***Parkwood Leisure Ltd* v *Alemo-Herron* [2010] ICR 920**, where the Supreme Court referred to the European Court of Justice (**[2013] ICR 1116**) the issue whether future pay increases pursuant to the national agreement had transferred to a new employer as a result of the **TUPE Regulations**. If a collective agreement is not expressly incorporated in this way or by some other form of agreement, then the courts may be prepared to impliedly incorporate an agreement, thus giving it legal effect. It is possible that this may be done on the basis of custom and practice, but the collective agreement would need to be well known and established practice and need to be 'clear, certain and notorious' (see ***Duke* v *Reliance Systems Ltd* [1982] IRLR 347** and ***Garratt* v *Mirror Group Newspapers* [2011] IRLR 591**).

[2] The point concerning express incorporation is dealt with by reference to case authority.

***Alexander* v *Standard Telephones & Cables Ltd* [1991] IRLR 286** concerned a claim that a redundancy procedure had become incorporated into individuals' contracts of employment. The High Court summarised the principles to be applied in deciding whether there had been incorporation of a part of the collective agreement.

[3] This is an important point about the extent to which the terms of a collective agreement can be implied into the individual contract.

The key question to consider is whether the term is 'apt' for incorporation into the individual contract of employment.[3] The question of aptness stems from the fact that collective agreements have two functions. On one level, they regulate the relationship between the union and employer. Terms that govern the relationship may include redundancy consultation procedures or mechanisms for resolving complaints between the parties. These terms are not in keeping with those that would be found in the individual contract of employment and thus not apt for incorporation. There is, however, a second function of collective agreements, which is to operate as a source for collectively agreed rules about the individual contract. These could include provisions on pay rates for grades of jobs, rules about hours of work, and entitlement to holiday. These would be apt for incorporation in the sense that it can more readily be seen that the parties would have intended these provisions to be legally enforceable by an individual employee. One difficulty that arises is where it is not clear into which group a provision falls.[4] For example, in ***Malone* v *British Airways plc* [2010] EWCA Civ 1225** a term in the relevant collective agreement regarding the number of crew members on flights was held not to be apt for incorporation despite the fact that the number of colleagues sharing a person's workload is arguably a matter affecting the individual employment relationship. Moreover, while the test of aptness should be judged objectively, the Court of Appeal in ***Malone*** appeared to give weight to the fact that making this term enforceable would have disastrous consequences for the employer. Rather than focusing on whether the term is sufficiently individual in nature, Russell has argued[5] that the Court of Appeal appeared to take into account further considerations of whether it would be desirable for a given term to have contractual effect (R. Russell, '*Malone* v *British Airways plc*: protection of managerial prerogative' (2011) 40(2) *Industrial Law Journal* 207).

[4] Discussion of aptness in this paragraph follows the PEA method.

[5] This goes beyond statute and case law to show your wider reading. In doing so, it allows you to analyse the case in much more depth by drawing on and acknowledging the views of others.

Once the collective agreement has become incorporated[6] into the contract, it is not open to the employer to alter it unilaterally (see ***Gibbons* v *Associated British Ports* [1985] IRLR 376**). It is only when terms are varied collectively by agreement that the individual contracts of employment could be varied. If the collective agreement is unilaterally varied or the employer withdraws from it, the contracts of employment containing the provisions are likely to remain intact. The possible exception to this is when there are provisions that allow the employer to vary the terms. If there is a collective agreement that allows an employer to vary part of the contents unilaterally, then the fact that it has become part of the contract of employment will not inhibit this option (see ***Airlie* v *City of Edinburgh DC* [1996] IRLR 516**).

[6] This paragraph links to the next issue to be discussed.

To protect the collective bargaining process, **s145B TULRCA 1992** provides that a worker who is a member of an independent trade union that is recognised (or seeking to be recognised) by their employer has a right not to have an offer made to them that would have the result that their terms of employment (or any of those terms) will not (or no longer) be determined by collective agreement negotiated by the union (**s145B(1) and (2)**). These provisions, therefore, make it unlawful for an employer to seek to induce a worker away from having their terms determined by collective bargaining. In ***Kostal UK* v *Dunkley* [2019] EWCA Civ 1009**, the collective bargaining process had broken down so the employer, as a one-off, made a pay offer directly to the employees. Was this an unlawful inducement? The Court of Appeal held that it was not. The court considered the main purpose behind **s145B** and the employer's motivation. It concluded that the main purpose of the employer making this particular offer was not to induce employees to relinquish their trade union membership or to forego collective bargaining rights. This is a significant case and permission has been granted for an appeal to the Supreme Court, which will be heard in May 2021.

In certain situations, the courts are willing to be assertive in their remedies.[7] ***Anderson* v *Pringle of Scotland Ltd* [1998] IRLR 64** concerned a decision about whether an agreed redundancy procedure should be followed as a result of incorporation or whether the employer could introduce a more selective method. In order to stop the employees being made redundant under the new procedure, the court was willing to grant an interdict (injunction) restraining the employer from changing the selection procedure, even though this might amount to an order for specific performance which would not normally be granted by the courts when intervening in the employment relationship. In this case, the court felt that there was still no lack of trust and confidence in the employee by the employer. There may also be some judicial reluctance to imply terms into collective agreements when they are found wanting in relation to particular issues.[8] Where a collective agreement leaves a topic uncovered, the inference is not that there has been an omission so obvious as to require judicial intervention; the assumption should be that it was omitted deliberately for reasons such as the item being too controversial or too complicated (see ***Ali* v *Christian Salvesen Food Services Ltd* [1997] IRLR 17, CA**).

[7] This is a subtle way of showing your own opinion about the case law in this area.

[8] Clarity and sophistication of language is usually a sign of a strong student!

## LOOKING FOR EXTRA MARKS?

- This question calls for an understanding of how collective agreements differ from other agreements. While the cases may appear to be rather technical in nature, it is important that you understand why the parties to a collective agreement may not always wish their terms to have contractual effect.

## TAKING THINGS FURTHER

- A. Bogg and K. D. Ewing, 'Collective Bargaining and Individual Contracts in *Kostal UK Limited v Dunkley*: A *Wilson and Palmer* for the Twenty-First Century? (2020) 49(3) *Industrial Law Journal* 430

  *In-depth analysis of the Court of Appeal judgment in* **Kostal**

- O. Kahn-Freund, 'Collective agreements' (1941) 4 *Modern Law Review* 225

  *A seminal paper on the effect of collective agreements on individual contracts of employment*

- M. O'Sullivan, T. Turner, M. Kennedy, and J. Wallace, 'Is employment law displacing the role of trade unions?' (2015) 44(2) *Industrial Law Journal* 222

  *Interesting discussion in light of the claim that employment law is often focused on individual rights; considers whether the body of employment law is taking the place of trade unions*

## Online resources

www.oup.com/uk/qanda/

For extra essay and problem questions on this topic, as well as advice on revision and exam technique, please visit the online resources.

# 14 Mixed topic questions

## ARE YOU READY?

Most legal problems do not occur in isolation. If a corporate client wishes to sell one branch of its business, it is likely that advice will be required on matters as diverse as the disposal of land and assets, staffing issues, and contract. Law firms are often 'multi-service' for this reason; one law firm can provide advice on every aspect of a client's legal problem. Even within a single area of law, such as employment law, there may be a number of interconnected issues upon which you are asked to advise. A client seeking advice on her entitlement to a redundancy payment may involve enquiring into matters of continuous service, whether a redundancy situation exists, and whether there has been a dismissal. Should the client then mention in passing that she suspects that she has been selected for redundancy because she now works part-time due to her childcare commitments, other equality law claims would then merit consideration.

While it may be unlikely that a single employment law exam question will require you to cover the whole range of material covered in your module (not least for reasons of time!), you may well encounter questions that are 'mixed' to some extent, meaning that they will deal with more than one topic. This may be due to the interconnected nature of much of employment law; dismissal without notice, for example, may well raise issues of breach of contract, wrongful dismissal, and unfair dismissal which are often dealt with in different parts of the syllabus. It may also be a deliberate tactic of the examiner. One feature of a strong answer is its ability to make connections with different parts of the course by spotting not only the major issue under examination but also the minor but relevant side issues. 'Mixed' questions therefore offer an opportunity for students to show their comprehensive grasp of the topic.

To help you prepare for mixed questions remember:

- As a general rule, mixed questions reward students who have covered the course comprehensively and who are able to show both their depth and breadth of knowledge.
- To help achieve this level of understanding, it is important that you do not question-spot! While it is important that you familiarise yourself with previous exam papers and the nature of the topics examined, it is dangerous to limit your revision to a few key topics or to assume that certain topics will always be examined in a particular format, for example that unfair dismissal will always appear as a problem question.

- When it comes to revising, if topics appear connected, study both/all! Mind-maps can help you see the connections between different areas and how a topic relates to others. Once you are comfortable with the topics and how they fit together, you can start to make these connections in the exam.
- Think of your revision in terms of building a toolbox of knowledge that you can use. If you have a thorough knowledge of case and statutory law together with the hot topics and academic debates in any area, you can go into the exam confident that you will be able to select whatever 'tool' to deal with what the examiner asks of you.
- Spend time looking at how topics have appeared in previous papers to see how certain topics can be given a different emphasis depending on the question. If you are well prepared, you should be confident that you can apply your knowledge to any given situation.

## QUESTION 1

Clare, a solicitor, seeks your advice on whether she is entitled to a redundancy payment. She has been employed by Big Law for two and a half years as an associate. She has spent much of the past year on secondment to one of her clients and has been off work with the flu for the last five working days. During her secondment, she continued to be paid by Big Law and was subject to its terms and conditions. When Big Law was particularly busy, she was also required to help Big Law with its other client work in addition to her work for the client on secondment. Following a meeting with the firm's HR manager as part of the individual consultation process, Clare was told that she may not be entitled to a redundancy payment as her year on secondment may not 'count' and her time off sick may also not be included. Clare thinks that the HR manager is incorrect. She is also suspicious that her selection for redundancy was announced soon after she told her head of department that she was pregnant. Clare has always received excellent appraisals but in her most recent appraisal, before she announced her pregnancy, she was graded 'meets expectations' rather than her usual mark of 'exceeds expectations' for the attribute of 'loyalty'. She queried this as she feels that she has been loyal—she has cancelled many personal engagements for work reasons, has never looked for other jobs while at Big Law, and is a regular participant in the extra-curricular activities organised by the firm's social society. The relevant partners told her that this rating was given to everyone in the team. When Clare mentioned this to Steve, another associate at Clare's level, he said that he was given a rating of 'exceeds expectations' for loyalty and will soon be promoted to senior associate. Steve told Clare that he had received an offer of senior associate with a rival law firm and when he told the partners at Big Law, they offered him promotion on the spot. Appraisals were a factor that the firm took into account when deciding on who should be selected for redundancy.

**Advise Clare.**

## CAUTION!

- Although Clare is seeking your advice on her entitlement to a redundancy payment, you have been asked to advise her generally. Clearly, you should therefore advise her on all possible claims. It is your job as the adviser to spot any other relevant claims.
- Think about how much depth and weight to give each part of the question. Take care to pick up on major and minor issues.
- Take an extra couple of minutes when planning an answer to a mixed question to reread the question and ask yourself 'is there anything I have missed?' In the pressure of an exam, it can be surprising how much information can be missed the first time you read through a question.

## DIAGRAM ANSWER PLAN

**Identify the issues**

- Has Clare been treated less favourably than Steve in her appraisal because of sex?
- Has Clare been selected for redundancy because of her pregnancy?
- Will the dismissal be unfair due to the selection criteria used?
- Does Clare have sufficient length of service to claim a redundancy payment?

**Relevant law**

- Sections 13 and 18 Equality Act 2010, reg. 20 Maternity and Parental Leave Regulations, ss98, 99, 135, 136, 139, and 212 Employment Rights Act 1996
- Key cases including *Shamoon*, *James*, *Nagarajan*, and *Williams*

**Apply the law**

- While Clare has been treated less favourably than Steve in her appraisal, it may be difficult for her to show that the 'reason why' was because of sex
- There may be sufficient information to pass the burden of proof to the employer to show that Clare was not selected for redundancy because of her pregnancy but it is difficult to advise without seeing all her scores
- The appraisal score appears subjective but may be only one of a number of criteria used
- Clare has over two years' continuous service

**Conclude**

- Clare is entitled to claim a redundancy payment
- Whether she has been unfairly dismissed or discriminated against is less certain

## SUGGESTED ANSWER

Although Clare is seeking advice on her eligibility for a redundancy payment, I will advise her on all possible claims. She raises a number of issues: (1) her grading of 'meets expectations' for loyalty when a male colleague was graded 'exceeds' and whether this may amount to a detriment; (2) her selection for redundancy shortly after announcing her pregnancy; (3) the use of appraisals as part of the criteria for selection; and (4) whether she has sufficient length of service to be eligible to receive a redundancy payment. I will deal with each of these in turn.[1]

[1] A strong introduction showing that you have spotted the key issues raised by the question.

Sex is a protected characteristic for the purposes of equality legislation (**s4 Equality Act 2010 ('EA')**). This is defined as being a reference to a man or a woman (**s11 EA**). If, because of a protected characteristic, Clare has been treated less favourably than a person treats or would treat others, this would amount to direct discrimination under **s13(1) EA**. On a comparison of cases for the purposes of **s13 EA**, there must be no material difference between the circumstances relating to each case (**s23(1) EA**). There are two possible instances of less favourable treatment here—the lower appraisal rating than a male colleague and the selection for redundancy. Dealing with the appraisal first, Clare appears to have been treated less favourably than Steve when it comes to her score. Clare's concern over the rating appears to be more than an unjustified sense of grievance (per Lord Hope in ***Shamoon* v *RUC* [2003] ICR 337**) but rather might reasonably be regarded as amounting to a detriment. Clare can point to an actual comparator in Steve who is an associate at the same level as her but who is of the opposite sex. We are not told of what other considerations might have led to the difference in appraisal ratings but, on the face of it, it appears odd that Steve's behaviour which may be characterised as less loyal than Clare's was met with a higher rating. Clare will, however, have to show that this less favourable treatment when compared with Steve was 'because of' sex.[2] The employer's motive or intention is irrelevant.

[2] Shows an ordered mind dealing with both steps—is there less favourable treatment and is this because of sex?

Over the years, the courts have taken different approaches regarding how to determine whether an employer's behaviour is because of a protected characteristic. In ***James* v *Eastleigh Borough Council* [1990] 2 AC 751**, Lord Goff held that in cases of direct discrimination, the simple question to ask to determine causation was would the claimant have received the same treatment from their employer but for their sex? Applying the 'but for' test strictly, it would appear that all Clare needs to show is a difference in sex and a difference in treatment to succeed in a claim of direct discrimination (***King* v *The Great Britain-China Centre* [1992] ICR 516**). If this is the case, the risk is that it would be too easy for anyone to complain of direct discrimination. For this reason, Lord Nicholls in ***Nagarajan* v *London Regional Transport* [2000] 1 AC 501** held that the better test is to ask why the claimant received the treatment they did, i.e. the reason why test.[3] In light of the limited facts given, it is difficult to advise with certainty about what caused the employer to act as it did (see judgment of Lady Hale in ***R* v *Governing Body of JFS* [2009] UKSC 15**). Motive is irrelevant and unconscious biases may feature (e.g. views that mothers are less committed or less loyal to the firm). On its own, it may be difficult to show that the lower appraisal rating was because of sex, particularly as the appraisal was conducted before she announced her pregnancy.[4]

[3] The correct approach to causation in discrimination is a complex issue. This paragraph shows that you understand the key cases in this area.

[4] Get into the habit of concluding on each point before moving on to the next one.

The second area where Clare's sex may be an issue relates to her selection for redundancy which was announced after she told the partners of her pregnancy. While Clare may also attempt to show that this amounts to direct discrimination because of sex, it is also open to her to argue that she has been treated unfavourably because of her pregnancy (**s18 EA**). This has the advantage that the test is one of unfavourable treatment not less favourable treatment and so there is no need for a comparator. Showing that the pregnancy is a cause of treatment (it need not be the sole or main cause) should be assessed objectively (***O'Neill* v *Governors of St Thomas More RCVA Upper School* [1996] IRLR 372**). The timing appears suspicious but there is little further information on which to advise Clare with certainty. If Clare could show that she was dismissed for a reason connected with pregnancy, this would be an automatically unfair reason for dismissal (**s99 Employment Rights Act 1996 ('ERA'); reg. 20 Maternity and Parental Leave etc Regulations 1999 ('MPL')**).

One issue that may be worth exploring with Clare is precisely when the redundancy will take effect. **Regulation 10 MPL** provides that where, during an employee's maternity leave, it is not practicable to continue to employ her, she is entitled to be offered a suitable available vacancy. This only applies during her period of maternity leave, although in 2019, following a consultation, the government announced that it proposed to extend this right to women who have returned from maternity leave in the previous six months. It appears that Clare is relatively early on in her pregnancy if she has only recently announced it and so this right may not be available to her.

Even if Clare might struggle in the absence of further information to show sex or pregnancy discrimination, she may still contest the fairness of the redundancy selection.[5] Redundancy is a potentially fair reason for dismissal for the purposes of **s98(2) ERA**. Whether the dismissal is fair or unfair depends on whether in the circumstances (including the size and administrative resources of the employer's undertaking) the employer acted reasonably or unreasonably in treating it as a sufficient reason to dismiss Clare, and shall be determined in accordance with equity and the substantial merits of the case (**s98(4)**

[5] A nice link to the next issue.

[6] Demonstrates careful reading of the question.

[7] Good application of case law to the facts of the question.

**ERA**). In Clare's case, we are not told how many employees are at risk of redundancy or how many roles will be redundant. It is reasonable to assume that more than one role will be redundant and that there is some form of selection from a pool of potential candidates given the reference in the question to selection criteria.[6] For Clare, she should be pooled together with other employees who are doing work of a kind for which Big Law's need has diminished (**s139(1)(b) ERA**). It is clear that Big Law will continue to operate so there is no question here of the business ceasing. In Clare's case, it would seem that she should be pooled together with other associates in her area of law. It is not clear whether Steve was included in the pool although it is clear that he was not selected. It is not for the tribunal to determine how Big Law should construct its pool for selection unless, applying the range of reasonable responses test, it is clear that the selected pool is outside the range of reasonable pools that a reasonable employer would have picked (***Capita Hartshead Ltd* v *Byard* [2012] ICR 1256**). Selection criteria should then be applied to those within the pool to decide which employee(s) should be redundant. As Browne-Wilkinson J made clear in ***Williams* v *Compair Maxam Ltd* [1982] ICR 156**, the criteria should as far as possible not depend solely on the opinion of the person making the selection but should be capable of being checked objectively against matters such as experience, attendance, etc. We are told that appraisals only form one part of the selection criteria but the problem with the appraisal as it currently stands is that loyalty is a somewhat subjective assessment.[7] It would seem difficult to check whether an employee has been 'disloyal' in speaking to other firms, for example, and the higher rating given to Steve who obtained an offer from a rival firm and used this as a bargaining chip suggests that there is an element of subjectivity in the assessment. It seems, objectively, difficult to reconcile his score with that of Clare's. Subjective selection criteria can lead to a procedurally unfair dismissal (***Watkins* v *Crouch (t/a Temple Bird Solicitors)* [2011] IRLR 382**). Moreover, although tribunals will generally not examine the scoring process too closely, if there is a mistake or clear inconsistency in scoring this may provide further grounds for an unfair dismissal (***Northgate HR Ltd* v *Mercy* [2008] ICR 410**). It would be advisable for Clare to ask to see her scores (***Alexander* v *Brigden Enterprises Ltd* [2006] ICR 1277**) and it is open to a tribunal to see the scores of all employees in the pool (***King* v *Eaton Ltd (No. 2)* [1998] IRLR 686**).

Turning to the final issue raised by Clare, is she entitled to a redundancy payment? **Section 135 ERA** provides that an employer shall pay a redundancy payment to an employee if the employee is dismissed by reason of redundancy. Clare is an employee and it appears that she is about to be dismissed by Big Law terminating her contract of employment (**s136(1)(a) ERA**). The reason for the dismissal is unclear. If it is due to her pregnancy, this will be automatically unfair although, as discussed above, we would need further information. Taking Big Law at its word and in light of what we are told about the redundancy consultation and selection criteria, it would appear that the requirements of Big Law's business for work of a particular kind or work of a particular kind at the place Clare is employed have ceased or diminished, which would amount to redundancy (**s139(1)(b) ERA**).[8] Clare is only entitled to a redundancy payment if she has been continuously employed for a period of not less than two years (**s155 ERA**). Clare has over two years' service unless her secondment and illness operate to break her continuous service. It is clear that during Clare's secondment her contract of employment continued. The only difference was that she carried out her duties at a client's place of business. Under **s212(1) ERA**, any week during the whole or part of which an employee's relations with their employer are governed by a contract of employment counts in computing the employee's period of employment. This will include any week where the employee is incapable of work in consequence of sickness or injury (**s212(2)(a) ERA**), so long as the absence is less than twenty-six weeks.[9] Clare has only been absent for five days which would not break her continuous service.

[8] This is an excellent example of maintaining clear relevance and going straight to the heart of the matter. It is an essential requirement for a redundancy payment that there is a redundancy but there is no need to discuss in detail the different forms of redundancy in this case.

[9] A small but important point that allows a strong student to stand out.

In summary, Clare would be entitled to a redundancy payment. A statutory redundancy payment is calculated based on her age and length of service (**s162 ERA**). Big Law may also offer an enhanced redundancy payment scheme. As for her selection for redundancy,[10] there is a risk that the dismissal will be procedurally unfair if wholly subjective criteria have been used but this is far from certain if the appraisal is only one of a number of factors. There is also a possibility of an automatic unfair dismissal if she can show that her selection was because of her pregnancy and a possible claim of direct sex discrimination if she can establish that her lower rating was because of sex. These latter two claims appear more tenuous based on the limited facts that we have, although taken as a whole they may allow Clare to prove facts from which the tribunal could infer that discrimination has occurred and thus the burden of proof would pass to Big Law (***Igen Ltd* v *Wong* [2005] IRLR 258**).

[10] This paragraph ties together the discussion that has gone before and takes a realistic view on the prospects of succeeding with the different claims identified.

## LOOKING FOR EXTRA MARKS?

- There is a lot of ground to cover in this question so get into the habit of writing succinctly yet comprehensively to ensure that you complete your answer in good time. The best way of doing this is to set a timer and practise a past paper question. If you struggle to complete it on time, look over what you have written and think about any bits of 'padding' you can cut. Have you included too much background or 'scene-setting' information that meant that you had no time to tackle certain issues? Perhaps you wasted time repeating the facts of the case at the outset—this is a common mistake! You can try doing this exercise with a friend and give each other feedback. Once you can spot some potential pitfalls in each other's work, it becomes much easier to spot them (and avoid them!) in your own.

## QUESTION 2

The New Labour government's employment law agenda can best be summed up by its 'family friendliness' as demonstrated by its introduction of the right to request flexible working. This was arguably the most important reform introduced during the New Labour period. Discuss.

## CAUTION!

- The mixed nature of essay questions may not be explicit and instead the examiner is testing your ability to make connections. A sophisticated answer will identify how different areas of the law interact.
- What is this essay about? It is tempting to say 'the right to request flexible working' but the examiner is inviting you to discuss much more than this. If we interrogate this question more deeply, the examiner is asking you to explore the history of employment law and particularly to reflect on New Labour's employment law agenda. Was being 'family friendly' really its defining characteristic? What else might be relevant? What other reforms were introduced in this period? An answer that simply reflects on the importance of flexible working would not be incorrect but if you 'stop there' you risk not giving a full answer.

## DIAGRAM ANSWER PLAN

Brief introduction of right to request flexible work

Other important reforms between 1997 and 2010

Family-friendly rights including right to request flexible work

National minimum wage as another example of an important right

Conclusion that there is evidence that New Labour was 'family friendly' but the right to request flexible work may not have been most important reform

## SUGGESTED ANSWER

The New Labour government governed from 1997 until 2010. During this period, a number of employment law reforms were introduced. One of these was the introduction of a statutory right to request flexible working. An employee always had the ability to request a variation in their pattern of work but this was now placed on a statutory footing with the introduction of the **Flexible Working Regulations 2002**. This right is an important one in the sense of giving an insight into the ideology of 'New' Labour, which was branded in such a way as to distinguish it from the 'old' Labour of the past, which had been characterised as pro-worker and anti-business. New Labour intended to appeal to businesses by showing that it could work in partnership with workers and flexible working was one initiative that was perceived as having benefits to both groups. However, this was not the only reform of this period. Instead, in this essay I will suggest that the period of 1997–2010 witnessed a wide number of changes to the employment law landscape, with the statutory right to request flexible working being just one. In this way, it might appear misleading to characterise all the New Labour initiatives as being motivated by being 'family friendly'.[1]

[1] Here you tell the examiner what you will argue. You can only do this clearly after you have spent some minutes planning your essay.

Any cursory examination of a statute book will reveal a plethora of legislative reforms during the period 1997–2010. These include[2] new rights for fixed-term employees not to be treated less favourably (**Fixed-term Employees (Prevention of Less Favourable Treatment) Regulations 2002**), new protections against detriment and dismissal for whistle-blowing, which can now be found in the **Employment Rights Act 1996 ('ERA')**, reform of maternity rights, the introduction of paid paternity leave, and the extension of discrimination protection to cover the characteristics of religion or belief, sexual orientation, and age.

[2] If this was a coursework question, you could expand on the various reforms introduced.

With regards to the claim that the New Labour government was 'family friendly', it is true that it introduced a considerable amount of 'family-friendly' legislation.[3] It extended the period of maternity leave by virtue of the **Work and Families Act 2006** to its current period of fifty-two weeks. It also departed from the historic position of only granting mothers paid leave by introducing a new right for fathers to take paid paternity leave by the **Paternity and Adoption Leave Regulations 2002**. There are, however, concerns that these Regulations have not encouraged more fathers to take leave for childcare. For Caracciolo Di Torella (E. Caracciolo Di Torella, 'New Labour, new dads: the impact of family-friendly legislation on fathers' (2007) 36(3) *Industrial Law Journal* 318), the limited right to take a short period of paternity leave paid at the same rate as statutory maternity pay was unattractive to fathers and reinforced ideas that the

[3] Refers back to the question to show that you are providing an answer to it.

primary responsibility of childcare rests with mothers. This is a view also shared by James, who has been critical of how the government promoted paternity leave as a way of fathers helping to 'support the mother' (G. James, 'The Work and Families Act 2006: legislation to improve choice and flexibility?' (2006) 35(3) *Industrial Law Journal* 272). Family-friendly rights have now, of course, been changed significantly following the introduction of the **Shared Parental Leave Regulations 2014** but these were not a New Labour initiative.

Another family-friendly right introduced by New Labour is that addressed in the question—the statutory right to request flexible working. This right was extended by the Conservative/Liberal Democrat Coalition government in the **Flexible Working Regulations 2014 ('FWR')** so that any employee (not just those with children under a certain age) who has been continuously employed by an employer for a period of twenty-six weeks (**reg. 3 FWR**) may make a statutory request to work flexibly. An employer may refuse any application for certain prescribed business reasons under **s80G ERA**, including the burden of additional costs and a detrimental impact on being able to meet customer demand. The right is only a right to request flexible working, not for it to be granted.

Was this the most important reform introduced by the New Labour government? I would argue that it was not.[4] The ability of an employer to refuse a request on certain grounds has the effect of neutering how powerful and important it could be as a right. Moreover, there are arguably other reforms that could compete with the right to request flexible working as being the most important reform introduced during 1997–2010. During this period, we also saw the creation of the Equality and Human Rights Commission, the consolidation of various discrimination legislation into the **Equality Act 2010**, and the introduction of (admittedly short-lived) statutory dispute resolution procedures governing the treatment of workplace grievances and disciplinary matters. These both shaped the employment law landscape and influenced industrial relations practice. One further reform that has been considerably important for the lowest paid workers in the UK has been the introduction of the statutory minimum national wage and it is to this that I will now turn.[5]

[4] Presents your own view clearly, then goes on to provide a justification for your position.

[5] Here you discuss another important reform that could arguably be of even greater importance than the family-friendly legislation.

Historically in the UK, wages councils made up of employee and employer representatives could set minimum rates of pay for certain industries or sectors. These were gradually wound up over time with the last of the wages councils being abolished by the **Trade Union Reform and Employment Rights Act 1993**. When New Labour took power in 1997, it intended to introduce a universal national minimum wage to apply across all sectors at a set rate. **Section 1 of the National Minimum Wage Act 1998** provides that a person who qualifies for the national minimum wage must be paid at a rate which is not less than the national minimum wage, which will be a single hourly rate prescribed from time to time. This leaves an employer free to pay more than the minimum hourly rate but it cannot drop below this statutory floor. Although we might debate the rate at which the national minimum wage is set, undoubtedly it will be of benefit to the lowest paid workers. Moreover, Davidov has argued that the minimum wage has other important consequences including upholding a worker's dignity:[6] 'Respect for the dignity of the worker as a human being dictates that human labour should not be sold for less than a certain minimum' (G. Davidov, 'A purposive interpretation of the National Minimum Wage Act' (2009) 72 *Modern Law Review* 581).

[6] Shows a critical appreciation of another aspect of wage legislation.

Looking back at the legislative reforms of the New Labour period, it is clear that there were a number that fell within the ambit of being family friendly including the statutory right to request flexible working. However, was this the most important reform of the thirteen years of New Labour rule? Arguably not.[7]

[7] A concise conclusion which answers the question.

## LOOKING FOR EXTRA MARKS?

- Do not be afraid to give your opinion, as long as it is supported by authority. It does not matter whether the examiner shares your views on what you think is the most important reform of the New Labour period. What matters is that you can sustain a well-supported and convincing argument.

## QUESTION 3

You are a legal adviser for a large local authority. As part of your client relationship-building activities, once a week you visit the HR team at the local authority so that they can raise any tricky queries with you. At this week's meeting, the team raised the following issues with you.

**Advise the team on what they should do in respect of the following.**

**(a)** Ellen: she has been absent from work for some months now. Her previous attendance record has been poor with lots of short-term absences for unrelated health issues, such as colds, flus, sickness, etc. She drives a lot in her role as a housing officer and claims that sitting for long periods of time hurts her back. Her recent sick notes refer to 'back pain'. Her line manager, Rose, held a sickness absence review meeting with Ellen after her first few weeks off sick when Ellen claimed that her back was so painful that she had trouble sitting and walking and was on strong painkillers. Since then, Rose has referred Ellen to an occupational therapist who

expressed some doubt about Ellen's condition. The occupational therapist has also obtained a report from Ellen's GP who has said that there is no underlying medical condition but merely localised back pain, for which exercise should help. The GP's view is that Ellen should be capable of performing her job but that she should not sit for long periods of time. Rose has made a number of suggestions to Ellen to help her, including removing her driving duties from her, having occupational therapy provide her with an adjusted desk and chair, and varying her hours so that she can take regular breaks away from her desk. Ellen insists that she is not fit to return to work and that her back is so bad that she can barely get out of bed. Rose, who is a friend of Ellen's on Facebook, has spotted pictures of Ellen zip-lining and surfing on holiday in Spain. There are also messages that clearly show that Ellen has travelled to Spain by coach. Rose desperately needs someone to carry out the work of housing officer and is unclear how much longer she can tolerate Ellen's absence as there is no one picking up her work. Rose has called HR to ask about 'letting Ellen go'.

**(b)** Flora: she works as a cleaner and has been told that all cleaning staff will be transferred to Clean-Easy Ltd, which from next month will provide all cleaning services to the local authority. Flora has been thinking for some time of leaving her job to set up her own cleaning business and thinks this will be a good time to make the move. Her supervisor has told her that everyone must move across to Clean-Easy Ltd and the work will remain exactly the same but Flora wants to leave.

**(c)** Michelle: she has raised a grievance that a more senior colleague in her department (Gary) has behaved inappropriately towards her. The allegations include texting her on her work phone outside office hours about non-work matters, asking her out for a drink repeatedly (despite her saying no), and making sexually suggestive comments about her figure. When she tried explaining to him that his behaviour made her uncomfortable, he told her that she could not take a joke and that she should be flattered. Since raising a grievance about Gary's behaviour, he has excluded Michelle from social gatherings with the team. Gary's view is that it is best to keep Michelle at arm's length now as she is 'trouble'.

## CAUTION!

- This question covers a range of issues and it may be that an examiner would not cover such a vast range of issues in an exam. If you are unsure about any aspect or can only confidently address one or two points of the question, attempt another one. Unless you are told otherwise, each part will be allocated equal marks.
- This is an excellent opportunity for a confident student to show off a sound sense of relevance and ability to write succinctly. You will likely have only fifteen to twenty minutes at the most in an exam to deal with each part so you need to be able to spot the issues quickly, cut to the heart of the matter, and write a full yet concise answer.

## DIAGRAM ANSWER PLAN

**Identify the issues**

- Can the local authority take action against Ellen for her long-term absence? If so, should this be on grounds of capability or conduct?
- Is Flora obliged to transfer to the new contractor?
- Does Gary's treatment of Michelle amount to harassment and/or victimisation? Will the local authority be liable? What steps should it take in respect of Gary?

**Relevant law**

- Ellen: s 98 Employment Rights Act 1996, *Spencer*, *Ajaj*, *East Lindsey District Council*, *Burchell*
- Flora: TUPE Regulations 2006
- Michelle: ss 26 and 27 Equality Act 2010, *Micheldever*

**Apply the law**

- Ellen: 'pulling a sickie' falls under misconduct not capability
- Flora: can object to the transfer and her contract will be terminated
- Michelle: Gary's actions amount to harassment and victimisation

**Conclude**

- Ellen: local authority should investigate the alleged misconduct
- Flora: can object and her employment will terminate but she will not be treated as having been dismissed
- Michelle: local authority may be vicariously liable for Gary's actions unless it took steps to prevent his conduct; Gary's actions may give rise to gross misconduct

## SUGGESTED ANSWER

### Ellen

At first glance, Ellen's case appears to raise issues of capability for the role as she has been absent due to ill health for some time but there is clearly a concern that she is misleading her employer, which would amount to misconduct.[1] Rose would like to let Ellen go, i.e. dismiss her. The question is can she do this without incurring liability for the local authority and on what grounds?

[1] It can be hard to spot the dividing line between capability and conduct. Here you are showing the examiner that you have spotted the issue immediately.

Ellen has the right not to be unfairly dismissed by her employer (**s94(1) Employment Rights Act 1996 ('ERA')**). An employee will be treated as dismissed in a limited range of circumstances but these include where the contract is terminated by the employer, whether with or without notice (**s95(1)(a) ERA**). Of course, Ellen has not yet been dismissed and we do not know whether she has the necessary two years' service to allow her to claim unfair dismissal were she to be dismissed unfairly (**s108(1) ERA**). The immediate question for Rose is how she should handle Ellen's situation.

**Section 98(2)(a) ERA** provides that the capability of an employee is a potentially fair reason to dismiss. Capability includes the employee's health (**s98(3)(a) ERA**). The leading authority regarding long-term absence on grounds of ill health is ***Spencer* v *Paragon Wallpapers Ltd* [1976] IRLR 373**. That held that the key issue is whether the employer can expect to hold the job open any longer and for how much longer. Considerations that will affect this will be whether Ellen has exhausted her sick pay entitlement (we do not know what her entitlement is but having been off for some months she will be close to the end of her statutory sick pay entitlement) and the size of the organisation (the local authority will typically be a relatively large employer although it is clear that Rose is unable to cover the role with temporary cover perhaps due to economic constraints). The local authority should also consult Ellen about her circumstances (which it has done), look for suitable alternative work (***Carricks (Caterers) Ltd* v *Nolan* [1980] IRLR 259**) (Rose has offered alternative duties), and consult with Ellen's GP (which it has also done) (***East Lindsey District Council* v *Daubney* [1977] IRLR 181**). There appears little to suggest that Ellen has a disability (**s6 Equality Act 2010 ('EA')**), although this should not be discounted but in any event it appears that the local authority has taken steps to make adjustments to the role (**s20 EA**). All this suggests that the local authority has acted reasonably to date and may wish to consider taking formal action against Ellen which may ultimately lead to her dismissal on grounds of capability,[2] had the Facebook pictures not come to light.

[2]Good analysis showing that you understand the different considerations that will apply in a long-term, ill-health absence case.

Recent events, however, suggest that Ellen's behaviour falls not within the category of 'capability' but rather 'conduct'. This is also a potentially fair reason to dismiss an employee (**s98(2)(b) ERA**) but the procedure to be followed will differ. In the case of ***Metroline West Ltd* v *Ajaj* [2015] UKEAT/0185/15/RN**, the EAT held that 'pulling a sickie' could amount to serious misconduct capable of constituting a fundamental breach of contract, i.e. gross misconduct.[3] In this case, it appears that Ellen has misrepresented and exaggerated her condition to her employer which may amount to a fundamental breach of trust and confidence. In accordance with ***British Homes Stores Ltd* v *Burchell* [1980] ICR 303**, the first step will be for the local authority to investigate the alleged misconduct. If the local authority's process ends with the dismissal of Ellen, a tribunal will consider whether the local authority believed Ellen to be guilty of misconduct, whether it had reasonable grounds to sustain that belief, and whether it had carried out as much investigation into the matter as was reasonable in the circumstances of the case.

[3]Here the student does well to spot that this could be misconduct and cites a relevant case.

**Flora**

Under **reg. 3(1)(b) of the Transfer of Undertakings (Protection of Employment) Regulations 2006 ('TUPE Regulations')**, the protections of the **TUPE Regulations** apply to a service provision change, which can include a situation where activities cease to be carried out by a person on their own behalf and are carried out instead by another person (**reg. 3(1)(b)(i)**). Those activities post-transfer should be 'fundamentally the same' as the activities pre-transfer (**reg. 3(2A)**). Moreover, immediately before the service provision change there is an organised grouping of employees situated in Great Britain which has as its principal purpose the carrying out of the activities concerned and the transferor intends that the activities post-transfer will be carried out by the transferee other than in connection with a single specific event or task of short-term duration (**reg. 3(3)(a)**). Finally, the activities should not consist wholly or mainly of the supply of goods for the transferor's use (**reg. 3(3)(b)**). These conditions are met here.[4] The local authority is ceasing to carry out cleaning services on its own behalf, there is an organised group of employees working as cleaners presently, and the intention is that the contractor will provide precisely the same services in the future.

[4] Clear application of the IRAC method.

Having established that there is a TUPE transfer situation, certain consequences flow from this. One of the most important and the relevant one for Flora's situation is that a relevant transfer will not terminate the contract of employment of any person employed by the transferor and assigned to the organised grouping that is subject to the transfer.[5] Instead, 'any such contract shall have effect after the transfer as if originally made between the person so employed and the transferee' (**reg. 4(1)**). This is subject, however, to any objection made under **reg. 4(7)** (**reg. 4(1)**). **Regulation 4(7)** allows Flora to inform the local authority or the new contractor that she objects to becoming employed by the new contractor. The effect of so objecting will be that the relevant transfer will operate to terminate her contract of employment with the local authority but she 'shall not be treated, for any purpose, as having been dismissed by the transferor' (**reg. 4(8)**). This would mean that as there is no dismissal, she would not be able to bring a claim of unfair dismissal if those circumstances arose. There is no suggestion that the transfer will involve a substantial change in working conditions to Flora's material detriment, such that Flora could treat herself as having been dismissed (**reg. 4(9)**). It is simply the case that Flora does not want to transfer but has erroneously been told that she has to. The simplest thing for Flora to do is to inform the local authority that she objects to the transfer and her contract of employment will be terminated.[6]

[5] This is a neat way of getting to the most relevant right under the **TUPE Regulations** for Flora.

[6] Provides a clear answer to Flora's issue.

**Michelle**

Gary's actions towards Michelle are likely to amount to harassment[7] under **s26(1) of the Equality Act 2010 ('EA')**. Harassment occurs if a person engages in unwanted conduct related to a relevant protected characteristic (in this case, sex) and the conduct has the purpose or effect of violating Michelle's dignity or creating an intimidating, hostile, degrading, humiliating, or offensive environment for her. The fact that Gary has asked her out and has commented on her figure suggests that his conduct relates to her sex. Harassment can also include unwanted conduct of a sexual nature (**s26(2) EA**) and this could capture the comments about her figure. It is clear that Michelle considers Gary's conduct to be unwanted and that it is creating an intimidating environment for her. She has asked him to stop and been sufficiently concerned about the matter to raise a grievance. While Michelle's subjective views of the conduct are important, a tribunal will also consider objectively whether the conduct could reasonably be considered to have such an effect on Michelle (***Richmond Pharmacology Ltd* v *Dhaliwal* [2009] IRLR 336**). Making sexually suggestive comments to a colleague and pestering her to go out with him can reasonably be regarded as conduct that would give rise to an intimidating environment. It is also clear that this has not been a one-off event that may not create the requisite environment but a course of conduct over a period of time (***Henderson* v *GMB* [2015] IRLR 451**). Michelle may also have grounds for a claim under the **Protection from Harassment Act 1997** if the conduct is deemed oppressive and unacceptable (***Majrowski* v *Guy's and St Thomas' NHS Trust* [2006] UKHL 34**).

[7] You could also discuss the fact that harassment may amount to direct discrimination but for that a comparator is required. The easier and more direct claim for Michelle will be one under **s26**.

Gary's behaviour towards Michelle since she raised her grievance may constitute victimisation under the **EA**. Victimisation occurs where a person is subjected to a detriment for having done a protected act, which includes making an allegation that a person has contravened the **EA** (**s27(1) and (2) EA**). Excluding Michelle from work-related social gatherings and commenting that she is trouble are likely to constitute a detriment and, considering the reason why Gary has behaved like this, it is reasonable to assume that it was because of Michelle's protected act given his comments about her being 'trouble' and the fact that he only started to exclude her after the grievance was raised (***Micheldever Tyre Services Ltd* v *Burrell* [2014] ICR 935**).

Gary's conduct is likely to constitute misconduct and possibly gross misconduct and so the local authority is correct to investigate the matter properly (***British Home Stores Ltd* v *Burchell* [1980] ICR 303**). With regard to the local authority's liability for Gary's actions, **s109(1) EA** provides that anything done by a person in the course of their employment must be treated as also done by the employer.[8] Gary's conduct has taken place at work or, if outside work, via

[8] An important point as any claim brought by Michelle may name the local authority as a respondent.

Michelle's work phone. It does not matter whether it was done without the local authority's knowledge or approval, indeed it is difficult to imagine the local authority approving such behaviour (**s109(3) EA**). The local authority will have a defence, however, if it can show that it took all reasonable steps to prevent Gary from doing the alleged acts (**s109(4) EA**). This could include having a robust harassment policy, providing training on harassment, and making clear to colleagues that such behaviour will be treated seriously and possibly as an issue of gross misconduct.

## LOOKING FOR EXTRA MARKS?

- Tutorials can often take the form of answering short case studies/problem questions and provide you with an excellent opportunity to practise your problem question technique. Once you have prepared your tutorial reading, try writing out a full answer to any case study set in timed conditions. This has a number of benefits. It allows you to consolidate the more abstract reading you have done and can help you spot any gaps in your learning when you go through your answer in class. Many students only find this out when they come to apply their reading. Reading by itself is very passive but answering questions is far more active and will help you learn better. You will also refine your technique and get into the habit of revising early. Giving yourself a strict time limit to attempt such questions may even help you manage your study time more effectively.

# Skills for success in coursework assessments

# 15

Methods of assessment vary and examinations are only one form of assessment. The setting of a piece of coursework is one obvious alternative. When a student is set a piece of coursework, they are being asked to write a certain number of words on a topic (usually with only one question) and to submit the work by a certain date. There is, of course, more to it than just that. The requirements for coursework will vary from institution to institution and the first step is to ensure that you are familiar with, and understand, the requirements of your examiner.

You need to know what the examiners are looking for before you start but it is unlikely that they will only be looking for a straightforward descriptive and factual answer to a set question. One of the purposes of setting a piece of work over a period of time is to enable the student to show evidence of wide reading, research, and reflection on the issue being assessed.

## Researching, planning, and preparing to write

Begin by considering carefully the question set. What is the issue being examined and what are you being asked to do? Are you expected to compare different interpretations of the law? Are you being asked to reach a view on how effective the law is? Identify the key words in the question—such as critically evaluate or discuss—and be sure to do what they ask of you.

Once you are confident that you know what is being asked of you, you now need to gather relevant materials. To do well, you will need to do more than read the core or other relevant textbooks. These give you a helpful overview of the area but you will need to read beyond these core materials. Gather relevant articles and remember that there is likely to be a range of articles available, or waiting to be discovered, on the subject matter outside your set reading. These may examine aspects of the question in more detail or present an alternative view or perspective on the assignment question. This can help you form your own views, but remember whenever you use the ideas of another person you must cite that work in your references. You can find relevant material by looking at the footnotes cited in textbooks or other articles, and using the internet and legal databases. Make sure that you take careful notes of your sources when you are preparing to write.

## Critical analysis and evaluation

In coursework, you have time to reflect upon the issues raised in the assignment. A good piece of written law coursework is likely therefore to consider arguments in favour of and against a particular viewpoint. The display of a considered reflection of both sides of an argument is important, so long as that consideration can be supported by citing cases or other material. It is not enough to express a point of view on its own. It needs to be a point of view supported by the evidence presented in the assignment.

Consider the following example. You have been asked to respond to the following coursework title: 'Zero hours contracts are a novel phenomenon and are a further indication of the erosion of labour rights in the UK. Discuss.' You agree with this statement and write the following as part of your coursework: 'The emergence of zero hours contracts into the labour market in recent years signals further pro-employer bias in how the UK's labour market is structured. The flexibility afforded to employers under zero hours contracts is purely in their favour.' What might an examiner think of this? Three points jump out. First, how true is it to say that zero hours contracts 'emerged' in recent years? They have actually been in use for many years but they appear to be more commonly used recently. You could support this claim by referring to labour market statistics. Second, the student here talks of 'further pro-employer bias'. Is there evidence that the labour market is structured in favour of employers? If so, this could be addressed in a sentence or two with examples. Finally, is stating that the flexibility of zero hours contracts operates 'purely' in the employer's favour putting the matter too strongly? This will depend on your viewpoint. A more subtle answer might begin by reflecting that 'While zero hours contracts afford welcome flexibility for some workers' overall they might favour employers.'

Sometimes students can struggle with what is meant by showing 'critical analysis'. Reading academic articles can help you develop these skills as you see how academics themselves engage in critical analysis. One technique that can also help is to learn how to read critically and for a purpose. Start with a short article and try to summarise the key argument that the article makes in a sentence. Sometimes the author will help you by stating this clearly in the abstract or introduction. Then, jot down one or two points made by the author which they have given to support their claim. To begin to analyse the article, ask yourself whether you agree or disagree with what has been written. Is it convincing? If so, why? If you were not convinced, why not? Are there others who would disagree or can offer an alternative point of view? If there are conflicting views, which one do you prefer? By questioning the article as you read, you will soon get into the habit of reading critically and will hone your skills of argument.

## Relevance and sticking to the word limit

One thing that the assessor will be judging is your ability to write succinctly and to provide only relevant material. This means that you must only include information and points that are relevant to the answer. One way of ensuring that you do not stray from what is being asked of you is to ask yourself as you write 'how is this helping me answer the question?' If you find that you are spending too much time on background information, cut this from your answer.

This also relates to word limits and it is usual for coursework to have set word limits with penalties for students who exceed them. In some cases, these penalties can result in a significant amount of marks being deducted—make sure that you do not lose marks for this. Check the rules carefully to see what counts towards the word limit and build in sufficient time so that you can edit your work to ensure that your answer is not too long.

## Referencing and citation of legal authorities

People who mark coursework are aware of the possibility of plagiarism. Plagiarism is the production of someone else's work as if it were your own. This is work contained in books and articles as well as the internet. Most institutions use computer software to check whether coursework submitted contains plagiarised material. It is acceptable to use the work and ideas of other people. Indeed, such usage will enhance the marks and evidence of widespread reading will increase the quality of the coursework. What is important is that you acknowledge, either in the text of your work or in a footnote or endnote, the source of the work that you are using. Plagiarism is easy to avoid by acknowledging your sources. This can be done by using quotation marks (and noting the source) when putting in the words of others; making sure that you have adequate references to sources in your footnotes or endnotes (a reference has to be sufficient so that examiners can easily find the material themselves using the data that you have provided); having a comprehensive and detailed bibliography; or referring to the author if using someone else's ideas. Your institution will have its own recommended guidance on referencing so you need to make sure that you are aware of it and use it.

## Checklist

- Do I know precisely what is being asked of me in terms of the question, submission date, word length, and marking criteria?
- Have I read the question carefully and am I clear about what is being assessed? Keep referring back to the actual question so that you do not risk paraphrasing it.
- Have I gathered all relevant material noting carefully the details of each source? This means reading beyond textbooks to look at primary materials such as cases and statute and secondary materials such as academic articles.
- Am I clear on my own views of the material? Do I have authority to support the arguments I want to make? Am I aware of the counter-arguments and can I deal with these appropriately?
- Beginning to write—how best will I structure this essay? Do I have a clear plan?
- Have I stuck to the word limit? If I am over, what bits can I cut? Is everything I have written helpful to the answer?
- Are my references full and accurate? Have I made sure to acknowledge the ideas of others?
- Have I left myself enough time to submit the work? Remember that some institutions have strict penalties for late work and IT problems are often not treated as circumstances allowing late submission.

# Index

## A



## B



## C

## D

## E

## G



## H



## I

## R

## S

## T

## Z